NORTHBROOK PUBLIC LIBRARY
1201 CEDAR LANE
NORTHBROOK, IL 60062

AUG 3 0 2012

Northbrook Public Library

3 1123 01004 1443

D1288910

HELEN NASH'S
NEW KOSHER CUISINE

HELEN NASH'S
NEW KOSHER CUISINE
HEALTHY, SIMPLE & STYLISH

PHOTOGRAPHS BY ANN STRATTON

THE OVERLOOK PRESS
NEW YORK

This edition first published in the United States in 2012 by
The Overlook Press, Peter Mayer Publishers, Inc.
141 Wooster Street
New York, NY 10012
www.overlookpress.com

For bulk and special sales, please contact sales@overlookny.com

Copyright © 2012 Helen Nash

All rights reserved. No part of this publication may be reproduced
or transmitted in any form or by any means, electronic or mechanical,
including photocopy, recording, or any information storage and retrieval
system now known or to be invented, without permission in writing from the
publisher, except by a reviewer who wishes to quote brief passages in connection
with a review written for inclusion in a magazine, newspaper, or broadcast.

Cataloging-in-Publication Data is available from the Library of Congress

Book design by Deborah Thomas

Manufactured in China

FIRST EDITION

2 4 6 8 10 9 7 5 3 1

ISBN 978-1-59020-863-2

In memory of my husband Jack

And for my children,
Pamela, Joshua, George, and Beth
and my grandchildren,
Rebecca, Daniella, Alex, Nina, Samantha, and Jason

By the same author

Kosher Cuisine: Gourmet Recipes for the Modern Home

Helen Nash's Kosher Kitchen

CONTENTS

Introduction 9

Hors d'Oeuvres 11
Appetizers 31
Soups 53
Salads 87
Vegetables, Potatoes & Legumes 113
Pasta, Rice & Grains 133
Fish 161
Poultry: Chicken, Capon, Turkey & Duck 191
Meat 223
Luncheon Dishes 247
Desserts 277

Helpful Tips 337
Notes on Ingredients 339
Notes on Equipment 345
Notes on Technique 351
Acknowledgments 353
Index 354

INTRODUCTION

Cooking has been a passion for me, and passing on my knowledge and experience to a new kosher audience, one of my greatest joys. When my two earlier books were published—*Kosher Cuisine* and *Helen Nash's Kosher Kitchen*—that joy was mingled with regret at having to exclude so many more appetizing dishes and ideas about cuisine, nutrition, and a healthful approach to everyday meals. At the time, though, I couldn't imagine going back to the arduous process of developing, refining, testing, and retesting new recipes. But then a personal tragedy gave me a compelling desire to start working on another book.

My husband of five decades—a brilliant, visionary, and passionate man with great generosity of spirit—suffered a massive stroke, and for many years he was ill and homebound. Jack loved good food, and one of the ways I tried both to give him pleasure and keep him relatively healthy was to cook for him. As everything about our life changed, cooking creatively also became a way for me to maintain a positive attitude. And in trying to keep Jack's spirits up, I raised my own.

I discovered that even when Jack was ill, he was receptive to new tastes. So I began experimenting with novel kosher ingredients that were just coming to the market. Wasabi powder, miso, panko (Japanese breadcrumbs), balsamic and rice vinegars, and a variety of oils—truffle and sesame—hadn't been available to kosher cooks when I wrote my first two books, so Jack and I became acquainted with them together. In coming up with new dishes, their nutritional value was, of course, a decisive factor. But so was their appeal to the palate and to the eye. Those criteria informed my selection of recipes for this volume.

Until the very end, Jack looked forward to the meals I made for him, so I counted my experiments a success. Yet as his illness progressed, comfort foods—meatloaf, soups, frittatas, risottos, vegetable burgers, tuna burgers, turkey scaloppini, and most chicken dishes—were more to his liking than some of my more modern innovations. That made perfect sense to me—in cooking, as with any gift, you seek to gratify the recipient. I have included some of his favorite recipes in the pages that follow.

In developing new menus for my husband I had, to be sure, a captive audience. But I also solicited the opinion of family and friends, and their comments or criticisms helped me refine my culinary research. My dishes, I believe, became better—more subtle and delicate in some cases, more intense and savory in others—thanks, in part, to their generous feedback, for which I am deeply grateful.

Those readers familiar with my previous books know my philosophy: Eating well on a daily basis requires good planning, portion control, and nutrition. It also demands a bit of imagination—not only for the dishes or the menu, but for the needs of the cook. I am fully aware of the time constraints that are so much a part of modern life. And while I have included a number of traditional dishes that are somewhat labor-intensive, I have also concentrated on dishes that are easy to make and to serve and on ingredients that are readily available in supermarkets and local specialty stores. Wherever possible, I recommend how to prepare and freeze a dish in advance, so that you can feed a family or entertain without too much hassle at the last minute.

I cannot emphasize enough how important it is to select ingredients of the highest quality and, whenever possible, seasonal products. Indeed, if I have one rule for both cooking and eating, it is that what is best and freshest at the market—fish, vegetables, fruit, and meat—should dictate the menu. The better your ingredients, the better your results.

Keeping kosher is more, to me, than just a sensible way to live and to eat healthfully. The ancient Jewish dietary laws help to organize my life around family, Friday nights, and holidays. They remind me of the importance of community and anchor me to the other rituals of our religion. Their observance inspires me to study our texts more deeply—a search for meaning that, in turn, heightens my respect for human nature. The Torah says it all in its reverence for life.

For all these reasons and many more, I lovingly dedicate this book to the memory of my partner in life for more than half a century, Jack Nash.

Hors d'Oeuvres

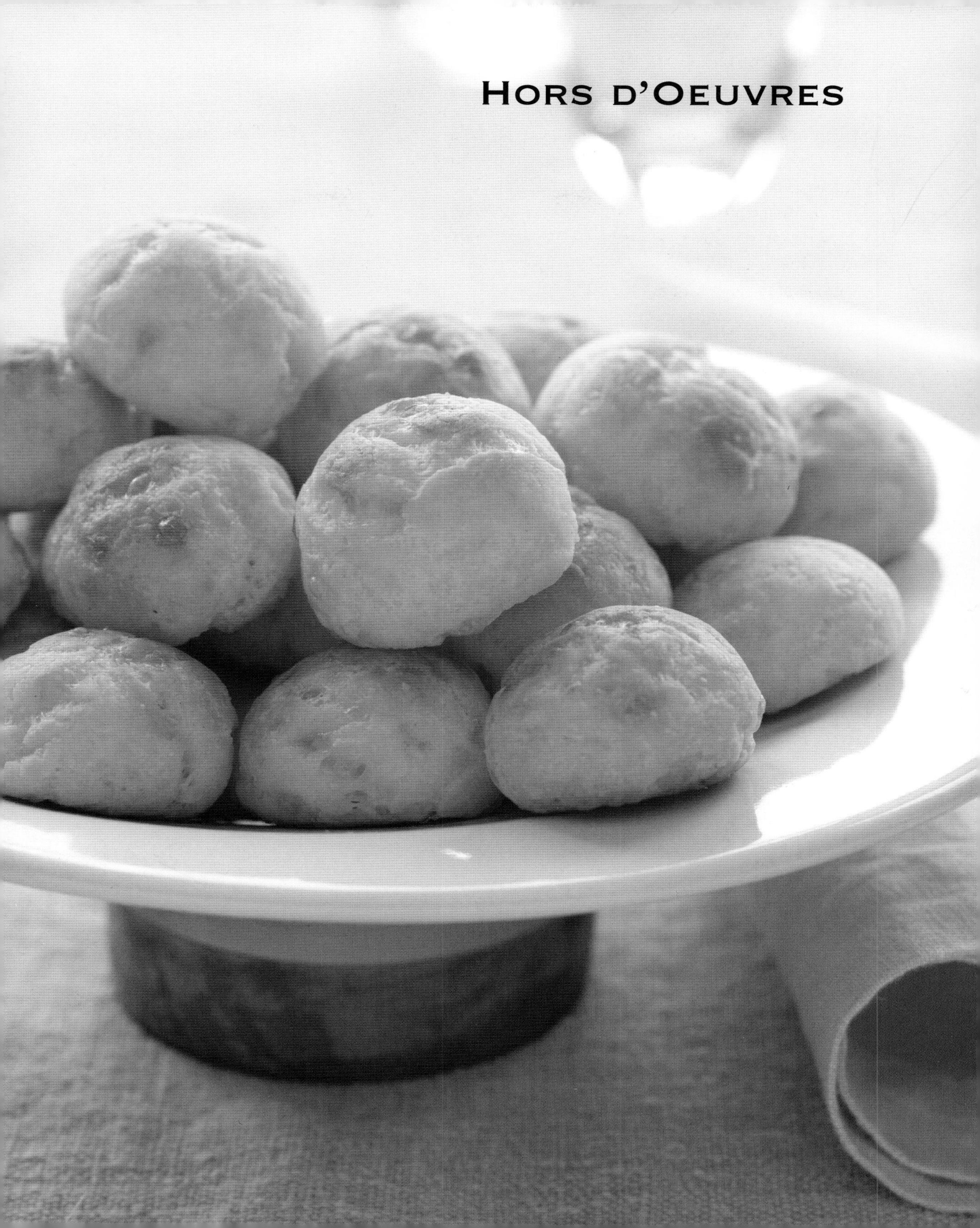

HORS D'OEUVRES

DAIRY
PARMESAN PUFFS
PARMESAN CRISPS

MEAT
CHOPPED CHICKEN LIVER
CURRIED WONTONS
PEARL TIDBITS

PAREVE
GRAVLAX WITH MUSTARD-DILL SAUCE AND POTATO BREAD
SMOKED WHITEFISH PÂTÉ
WONTON SHELLS WITH MUSHROOMS
EGGPLANT CAVIAR
POTATO LATKES
SMOKY EGGPLANT
HUMMUS

PARMESAN PUFFS

• Makes about 6 dozen hors d'oeuvres

These little puffs are quite easy to make. Because they freeze well, they are perfect to have on hand when unexpected guests arrive. They are also wonderful for large parties.

5 tablespoons (75 g) unsalted butter
¼ cup (60 ml) milk
¼ cup (60 ml) water
½ teaspoon kosher salt
½ cup (64 g) unbleached all-purpose flour
2 large eggs, at room temperature
1 cup (100 g) grated imported Parmesan cheese
Freshly ground black pepper

Place a shelf in the upper third of the oven and preheat the oven to 400°F (205°C). Grease two cookie sheets, using ½ tablespoon (7.5 g) of the butter for each sheet.

In a small enamel-lined saucepan, combine the milk, water, salt, and the remaining butter. Bring to a boil over high heat. Lower the heat to moderate, add the flour, and stir the mixture with a wooden spoon until it thickens and becomes dough-like, about 2 minutes. Transfer the mixture to a medium bowl to cool.

With a wooden spoon, stir in the eggs one at a time, combining well after each addition. Stir in the Parmesan and add pepper to taste.

Place ½ teaspoon of the mixture in the palm of your hand, shape into a smooth ball, and place on a cookie sheet. Repeat with the remaining dough, placing the balls about ½ inch (13 mm) apart.

Bake one sheet at a time until the puffs are golden, about 15 minutes.

Notes: These puffs can be made a day ahead and refrigerated in an airtight plastic container lined with wax paper, separating the layers with wax paper. To reheat, arrange on a cookie sheet and bake in a preheated 300°F (150°C) oven for 8 minutes, or until hot.

To freeze: Place the baked puffs side by side in layers in an airtight plastic container, separating the layers with wax paper. To reheat, take them straight from the freezer and arrange on a cookie sheet. Place in a preheated 350°F (175°C) oven for 10 minutes, or until hot.

PARMESAN CRISPS

• Makes about 3 dozen hors d'oeuvres

These lacy crisps can be made in any size, but I like mine dainty—about 2 inches (5 cm) in diameter. I serve them with drinks before dinner as well as with soups and salads, and they are always a favorite.

1 cup plus 2 tablespoons (about ¼ pound/113 g) grated imported Parmesan cheese

Preheat the oven to 400°F (205°C).

Place level teaspoons of cheese about 2 inches (5 cm) apart on a heavy nonstick cookie sheet. (You will need two sheets.) Bake for 4 minutes, or until the cheese has melted and the crisps are lightly golden.

Let the crisps rest for a few moments, then lift them with a thin metal spatula onto a wire rack to cool.

Notes: You can grate the Parmesan in a food processor, but be sure to cut it into small pieces first.

Parmesan crisps keep well in the refrigerator. Place them in an airtight plastic container, separating the layers with wax paper.

CHOPPED CHICKEN LIVER

- Makes about 1½ dozen hors d'oeuvres
- Makes 8 appetizer servings

This version of chopped chicken liver, which is incredibly easy to make, actually tastes like a pâté. My guests always love it.

For an hors d'oeuvre, I like to serve this dish on whole-grain crackers, toasted Potato Bread (page 22), cucumber slices, or endive petals. For an appetizer, I like to place sliced radishes and sliced cucumbers on the plate as accompaniments.

1 pound (450 g) chicken livers
⅓ cup (80 ml) vegetable oil
4 medium onions, coarsely chopped
4 large eggs, hard-boiled and quartered
2 to 3 tablespoons sherry
Kosher salt
Freshly ground black pepper

Preheat the broiler. Set the rack in the broiler pan and cover it completely with foil.

Remove from the livers any green spots, which are bitter, as well as any fatty particles. Make a shallow "basket" with a piece of heavy foil, crimping it at the corners so that the liquids don't spill out. (See Notes on Techniques, page 351.) Set the basket on the broiler rack, and arrange the livers inside. Place the broiler pan in the oven (or broiling unit), as close as possible to the heat source. Broil for about 4 minutes per side, until cooked through. Cool.

In a large skillet, heat the oil over medium-high heat. Add the onions and sauté until the onions are brown. Cool.

Place half the onions, livers, and eggs in a food processor and pulse, adding sherry through the feed tube, until the mixture is moist and almost smooth. Transfer the first batch to a container and repeat the process. Season to taste with salt and pepper.

CURRIED WONTONS

• Makes about 3 dozen hors d'oeuvres

Wonton wrappers are small, thin squares of egg noodle dough, available in supermarkets and Chinese grocery stores. I fill them with chopped beef, flavored with a touch of curry powder, for a tasty and unusual cocktail bite.

> **1 red-skinned potato, about 3 inches (7.5 cm) long**
> **2 scallions, including the green part, finely chopped**
> **3 tablespoons vegetable oil, plus 1 cup (250 ml) for frying**
> **½ pound (227 g) ground beef**
> **1 tablespoon low-sodium soy sauce**
> **½ teaspoon imported curry powder**
> **¼ teaspoon kosher salt**
> **12 ounces (340 g) thin wonton wrappers (at least 36 wrappers)**

TO MAKE THE FILLING: Steam the potato until tender. When cool enough to handle, peel off the skin. Place the potato in a medium bowl and mash it with a fork until smooth. Combine with the scallions.

Heat a wok over medium-high heat and add 3 tablespoons of the oil. When the oil is hot, add the ground meat and stir-fry until it cooks through. Combine the meat with the potato and scallion mixture. Add the soy sauce and curry powder. Season to taste with the salt. Cool.

TO FILL THE WONTONS: To prevent the wrappers from drying out, keep them covered with a damp paper towel. Have a little bowl of cold water nearby for moistening.

Working with one wrapper at a time, place the wrapper on a cutting board, with one corner pointing toward you. Place a level ¾ teaspoon of the filling on this corner. Roll the corner over twice, so the filled section comes to the center of the wrapper. Moisten the left and right corners of the rolled wrapper with water and fold them down and around so that the two corners overlap at the bottom of the filled section, forming a circle. Press the two corners together to seal. Place the filled wonton on a cookie sheet. Continue until all the filling is used, separating the layers of wontons with wax paper. Cover with a slightly damp towel and refrigerate until you are ready to deep-fry.

TO DEEP-FRY: Heat a wok over medium-high heat and add the remaining 1 cup (250 ml) oil. (To test if the oil is hot enough, drop in a small piece of a wrapper. If it sizzles, the oil is ready.) Line a platter with several layers of paper towels.

Place into the hot oil as many wontons as will float freely. Fry until they are lightly golden, turning them once or twice. Remove them with a wire skimmer and drain on the paper towels.

If not serving the wontons immediately, cover with cling wrap, and refrigerate. To reheat, arrange the wontons on a wire rack set over a cookie sheet in a preheated 300°F (150°C) oven for 5 minutes.

Notes: Wrap unused wonton wrappers in wax paper and then in aluminum foil. Place in a plastic freezer bag and freeze. Defrost in the refrigerator before using.

Curried wontons freeze well. Place them side by side in an airtight plastic container lined with wax paper, separating the layers with wax paper. To reheat, take them straight from the freezer and arrange on a wire rack set over a cookie sheet. Place in a preheated 325°F (165°C) oven for 10 to 15 minutes.

PEARL TIDBITS

• Makes about 4 dozen hors d'oeuvres

I call these light, well-seasoned mini balls "pearl," because that is what their sushi rice coating reminds me of. Prepared earlier in the day, they remain crisp even after reheating.

½ cup (80 g) raw sushi rice
¾ cup (180 ml) cold water
4 dried shiitake mushrooms
Boiling water, as needed
½ pound (227 g) finely ground breast of chicken
1-inch (2.5 cm) piece ginger, peeled and grated
2 scallions, including green parts, finely chopped
1 tablespoon low-sodium soy sauce
1 tablespoon sesame oil
¼ teaspoon wasabi powder
Kosher salt
Freshly ground black pepper
½ cup (125 ml) vegetable oil, plus 1 tablespoon for greasing your palms

Place the rice and cold water in a small enamel-lined saucepan. Bring to a boil, lower the heat, cover, and simmer for 8 minutes. Spread the rice on a plate and cool.

Meanwhile, place the dried mushrooms in a small bowl and pour boiling water over them. Cover and let stand for 15 minutes, or until soft. Pour off and discard the liquid. Squeeze the mushrooms dry. Cut off and discard the stems. Mince the caps.

In a medium bowl, combine the mushrooms, chicken, ginger, scallions, soy sauce, sesame oil, and wasabi powder. Season with salt and pepper. Lightly grease the palm of your hand and form a ball with a level ½ teaspoon of the mixture. Roll each ball in the rice until it is fully coated and the grains have firmly adhered.

Heat the oil in a wok until it is hot. (The oil is ready when a few grains of rice sizzle when dropped in.) Deep-fry the tidbits, 6 or 8 at a time, until they are cooked through and light brown, adjusting the heat as necessary. Remove with a slotted spoon and place on the paper towels. If not serving immediately, cover and refrigerate. To reheat, place the tidbits on a wire rack set over a cookie sheet in a preheated 350°F (175°C) oven for 5 minutes.

Note: To freeze, place the tidbits in an airtight container lined with wax paper; separating the layers with wax paper. To reheat, take them straight from the freezer and arrange on a wire rack set over a cookie sheet in a preheated 325°F (165°C) oven for 10 to 15 minutes.

GRAVLAX WITH MUSTARD-DILL SAUCE AND POTATO BREAD

- Makes about 2½ dozen hors d'oeuvres
- Makes 14 appetizer servings

In this Scandinavian delicacy, fresh salmon is cured with salt, sugar, pepper, and dill for 2 to 4 days. With its rich, varied colors and textures, it always seems to me a thing of beauty that is worth every bit of the effort. Have the fishmonger remove the center bone of the salmon without separating the fillets. (This is called butterflying.)

For an hors d'oeuvre, I like to serve gravlax, topped with a drop of sauce, on multi-grain crackers, toasted Potato Bread (recipe follows on page 22), cucumber slices, or endive petals. For an appetizer, I spoon some sauce on top of the gravlax and surround it on the plate with watercress, fresh greens, or cucumbers.

SALMON
3½ pounds (1.59 kg) center-cut salmon fillet
¼ cup (50 g) sugar
¼ cup (40 g) kosher salt
2 tablespoons freshly ground black pepper
1 bunch fresh dill, including stems, cut into 2-inch (5 cm) pieces

MUSTARD-DILL SAUCE
4 tablespoons honey mustard
2 tablespoons Dijon mustard
2 tablespoons rice vinegar
⅔ cup (160 ml) extra virgin olive oil
15 dill sprigs, snipped finely with scissors

TO CURE THE SALMON: Pat the salmon dry with paper towels. In a small bowl, combine the sugar, salt, and pepper and rub the mixture all over the fish.

Fold the fish in half, placing the cut dill between the layers. Place it in a glass dish large enough to hold it. Cover the dish with wax paper, then foil. Place a cutting board on top of the foil and weight it down with a heavy object, such as a pot filled with large cans. (It is important that the fish is weighted down with something heavy.) Refrigerate for 2 to 4 days. Once a day, turn the fish over and pour off the accumulated liquid. Re-cover and replace the weights each time.

TO MAKE THE SAUCE: Whisk all the ingredients in a small bowl to blend thoroughly. Refrigerate in a glass jar.

TO SERVE: Place the folded salmon on a cutting board. Unfold the fillet. Cut in half, following the line of the removed center bone. Scrape off the curing mixture.

Place a sheet of wax paper on top of a sheet of foil. With a gravlax knife or thin-bladed slicing knife, cut the fillets on the diagonal into slices of desired thinness. (I like mine as thin as possible, but others prefer it thicker.) As you cut, place the slices on the wax paper.

Serve with the sauce and potato bread, if desired.

Note: To freeze gravlax, place the cut slices on a piece of wax paper over a piece of foil. Separate the layers with wax paper. Cover with wax paper, then a piece of foil, and place in a plastic freezer bag. To defrost, leave the freezer bag at room temperature for a minute or so, and then peel off the desired number of sheets of gravlax. Let the gravlax stand at room temperature for 2 to 5 minutes, depending on thickness.

POTATO BREAD

• Makes 2 free-form loaves

I love to serve thin slices of this delicious bread with gravlax, chopped liver, herring salad, and smoked whitefish.

1 large Idaho baking potato
1 quart (1 liter) water
1½ envelopes active dry yeast (each envelope is 2¼ teaspoons/7 g)
7½ cups (960 g) unbleached all-purpose flour
1½ tablespoons salt
1½ tablespoons caraway seeds
½ tablespoon vegetable oil

Wash the potato well. Place it in a saucepan and cover with the water. Bring to a boil, then lower the heat and simmer until the potato is soft, about 15 minutes. Drain the potato, reserving the potato water. Slip off and discard the potato skin and grate the potato finely.

Pour ½ cup (125 ml) of the warm potato water into the bowl of an electric stand mixer. Add the yeast and 3 tablespoons of the flour and stir lightly with a spoon. Cover with a towel and place in a warm, draft-free place (such as a food warmer or a warm, turned-off oven) for 10 to 15 minutes, until bubbles appear. (This is called proofing the yeast to make sure it is still active.)

To this mixture add 2 cups (500 ml) of the remaining potato water, the grated potato, 7 cups (895 g) of the flour, the salt, and caraway seeds. Fit the dough hook onto the mixer and knead the mixture at low speed for about 10 minutes, adding more flour as needed to make the dough smooth and stiff.

Turn the dough out on a floured pastry board or work surface and knead with the heel of your hand, adding more flour as needed, to make a smooth, elastic dough that does not stick to your hands.

Wash and dry the mixer bowl. Grease the inside of the bowl with the oil and place the dough in it, turning it on all sides to coat. Cover the bowl with a towel and set it in a warm place for 75 to 90 minutes, until the dough doubles in bulk.

Punch the dough down and divide it into two equal pieces. Form each of them into an oblong loaf and place them side by side, but not touching, on a 12 by 17-inch (30 by 45 cm) baking sheet. Put them in a warm place for 25 minutes so they can rise for the last time.

Preheat the oven to 400°F (205°C). Using a pastry brush, brush the loaves lightly with cold water. About 2 inches (5 cm) from each end of the loaf, cut a cross with a knife.

Bake on the middle shelf of the oven for 45 minutes, or until golden brown and crusty. Cool on a wire rack.

Note: Potato bread freezes well. Wrap the loaf in wax paper, then in foil, and place it in a plastic freezer bag. It is not necessary to defrost before serving. Remove the wrappings and place the loaf directly on the shelf in a preheated 200°F (95°C) oven. Bake for about 1 hour, until warm.

SMOKED WHITEFISH PÂTÉ

• Makes 4 dozen hors d'oeuvres

This elegant pâté is light but well-seasoned, and the wasabi flavor adds subtle—and surprising—depth. I like to serve it on endive petals, whole-wheat toast triangles, or whole-grain crackers, garnished with capers.

> **1 pound (450 g) smoked whitefish**
> **2 tablespoons homemade Mayonnaise (page 112)**
> **¼ teaspoon wasabi powder**
> **2 tablespoons freshly squeezed lemon juice**
> **3 scallions, including green parts, finely chopped**
> **Freshly ground black pepper**
> **Small capers, for garnish**

Skin and bone the fish, making sure to remove all the small bones. Place in a food processor and add the mayonnaise, wasabi, lemon juice, and pepper. Pulse until the texture is smooth, scraping the sides of the work bowl from time to time. Transfer to a bowl and stir in the scallions. Season to taste. Garnish with capers.

WONTON SHELLS WITH MUSHROOMS

• Makes about 3 dozen hors d'oeuvres

These filled wontons are a perfect example of fusion food, in which Eastern and Western ingredients seamlessly blend. They are delicate and delicious.

4 tablespoons extra virgin olive oil, plus 1 tablespoon for greasing the pans
12 ounces (340 g) thin wonton wrappers
10 ounces (284 g) mixed wild mushrooms, such as porcini, shiitake, cremini,
**   or oyster mushrooms**
2 shallots, minced
2 garlic cloves, minced
Leaves from 8 thyme sprigs
1 tablespoon low-sodium soy sauce
1 tablespoon freshly squeezed lemon juice
Kosher salt
Freshly ground black pepper

Preheat the oven to 350°F (175°C). Grease three mini muffin pans, each with 12 depressions 1¾ inches (4.5 cm), with 1 tablespoon of the oil.

With a 3-inch (8 cm) round cookie cutter, cut out 36 wonton circles and gently press one into each cup. Bake for about 6 minutes, until lightly browned. Remove the shells from the pans.

Lower the oven temperature to 325°F (165°C).

Wipe the fresh mushrooms with a damp paper towel. If using shiitakes, cut off and discard the stems. Chop the mushrooms coarsely in a food processor, scraping down the sides. Heat 2 tablespoons of the oil in a nonstick skillet. Add the shallots and the garlic and sauté over low heat until soft, about 2 minutes. Add the remaining 2 tablespoons oil and the mushrooms. Raise the heat and sauté for a few minutes, until the mushrooms give off liquid and then become dry. Remove from the heat. Stir in the thyme, soy sauce, lemon juice, salt, and pepper. Season to taste.

Spoon ½ teaspoon filling into each wonton shell. Arrange on a wire rack set over a cookie sheet. Bake for 10 to 15 minutes, until heated through.

Notes: For extra mushroom flavor, I like to add ½ ounce (14 g) dried porcini mushrooms to the filling. To reconstitute them first, pour boiling water over the mushrooms, cover, and let stand for 15 minutes; squeeze the mushrooms dry and chop coarsely.

Unfilled wonton shells can be refrigerated for several weeks in an airtight container. The filling can be refrigerated for several days. To reheat filled wonton shells, arrange on a wire rack set over a cookie sheet. Place in a preheated 325°F (165°C) oven for 10 to 15 minutes.

EGGPLANT CAVIAR

- Makes about 12 servings as a dip
- Makes 6 appetizer servings

In the country of Georgia, where this dish originated, eggplants are plentiful and generally seedless. There, it is called "the poor man's caviar." I like to serve eggplant caviar as a dip, with slices of colorful bell peppers, cucumbers, and whole-grain crackers.

1 large eggplant (about 1½ pounds/680 g)
4 tablespoons extra virgin olive oil
1 medium onion, coarsely chopped
2 tablespoons double-concentrate tomato paste
1 tablespoon freshly squeezed lemon juice
Kosher salt
Freshly ground black pepper

Preheat the oven to 400°F (205°C). Line the broiler pan with heavy foil.

Place the eggplant in the pan and bake for 35 minutes, turning once, until soft to the touch. Remove from the oven to cool.

While the eggplant is baking, heat the oil in a medium skillet. Add the onion and sauté over low heat until soft and transparent. Remove from the heat.

When the eggplant is cool enough to handle, cut off the ends. Cut the eggplant in half lengthwise and scrape off some of the seeds. Spoon the flesh into a food processor, add the onions and pulse until almost smooth.

Transfer the eggplant-onion purée to the skillet, stir in the tomato paste, and cook for 1 minute over medium-low heat. Remove from the heat. Season to taste with the lemon juice, salt, and pepper.

POTATO LATKES

• Makes 6 dozen bite-size latkes

Potato latkes are one of the staples of Eastern European cooking, and there are almost as many ways to make them as there are cooks. But I think my version of this beloved dish stands out—not only because the latkes are so delicious, but also because they are so light. My secret? I bake the latkes rather than fry them.

Latkes are traditional at Hanukkah, but because they are always in demand at my home, I serve them any time.

4 tablespoons vegetable oil
1 medium onion, quartered
4 medium Idaho baking potatoes
¼ cup (32 g) unbleached all-purpose flour
1 large egg plus 1 large egg white, lightly whisked
1½ teaspoons kosher salt
¼ teaspoon freshly ground black pepper

Place an oven shelf in the lowest position and preheat the oven to 450°F (230°C). Brush three heavy nonstick cookie sheets with 1 tablespoon oil each. (The thickness of the sheets allows the bottoms of the latkes to become golden.)

Pulse the onion in a food processor until finely chopped. Transfer to a large bowl.

Remove the metal blade from the processor and put on the medium shredding attachment. Peel the potatoes and cut them lengthwise into quarters. Insert them into the food processor's feed tube and grate.

Combine the potatoes with the onion. Add the flour, egg, egg white, and the remaining 1 tablespoon oil and mix well. Season to taste with the salt and pepper.

Place 1 level tablespoon of the potato mixture slightly apart on the greased cookie sheets. Bake the latkes one sheet at a time on the lowest shelf for 11 minutes, or until the bottoms are golden brown. Turn the latkes over and bake for another 6 minutes, or until they are lightly golden.

Notes: Latkes can be baked earlier in the day and reheated. Arrange on a wire rack set over a cookie sheet in a preheated 350°F (175°C) oven until hot, about 6 minutes. The wire rack prevents them from getting soggy.

To freeze: Place latkes side by side in an airtight plastic container lined with wax paper, separating the layers with wax paper. To reheat, take them straight from the freezer and arrange on a wire rack set over a cookie sheet. Place in a preheated 400°F (205°C) oven until hot, 8 to 10 minutes.

SMOKY EGGPLANT

•Makes 8 to 10 servings as an hors d'oeuvre or dip
•Makes 4 appetizer servings

Eggplants are plentiful in the Middle East and are well represented in the cuisines of Israel and its neighbors. Though this dish isn't made over an open fire, it reminds me of babaghanoush, which is a favorite of mine as well as my children and grandchildren. I serve it with lots of raw vegetables—bell peppers, cucumbers, and zucchini—and warm pita. Perfect with drinks or as a healthful snack, it's always in season.

> **1 medium eggplant (about 1¼ pounds/570 g)**
> **3 tablespoons freshly squeezed lemon juice**
> **1 tablespoon extra virgin olive oil**
> **1 garlic clove, minced**
> **3 tablespoons tahini (sesame paste)**
> **¼ teaspoon ground cumin**
> **Kosher salt**
> **Freshly ground black pepper**

Preheat the broiler. Line the broiler pan with heavy foil and put in the eggplant.

Place the the pan in the oven (or broiling unit), as close as possible to the heat source. Broil the eggplant for about 20 minutes, until soft, turning it once. (This gives it the smoky taste.) Cool.

When the eggplant is cool enough to handle, cut off the ends. Cut it in half lengthwise and scrape off some of the seeds. Spoon the flesh into a sieve to drain.

Place the eggplant in a food processor. Add the lemon juice, oil, garlic, tahini, cumin, salt, and pepper. Pulse to a smooth consistency. Season to taste.

HUMMUS

• Makes about 10 servings as an hors d'oeuvre or dip
• Makes 6 appetizer servings

This pale lemon, creamy dish can be found all over the world, and my family and friends always love it. I usually serve it before dinner as a dip with cucumbers, radishes, bell peppers, and toasted pita triangles. But it also makes a simple and delicious appetizer. Since it refrigerates well, I try to keep it on hand as a nutritious snack for my children and grandchildren.

Because the chickpeas are canned, my version is easy to prepare. It is also less garlicky than the norm, because the garlic is baked first.

8 unpeeled garlic cloves
One 15.5-ounce (440 g) can Goya chickpeas, drained
3 tablespoons tahini (sesame paste)
¼ cup (60 ml) freshly squeezed lemon juice
1 teaspoon kosher salt
¼ teaspoon ground cumin
⅓ cup plus 2 tablespoons (110 ml) cold water

Wrap the garlic tightly in a piece of foil. Bake in a toaster oven at 350°F (175°C) for 15 minutes, or until soft. Remove and let cool until you can handle the cloves.

Squeeze the pulp from each clove into a food processor. Add the chickpeas, tahini, lemon juice, salt, and cumin. Pulse until smooth, adding water through the feed tube until the mixture is creamy and has a mayonnaise-like consistency. Season to taste.

APPETIZERS

PAREVE

CEVICHE

SALMON TARTARE

TUNA TARTARE

TUNA TARTARE WITH AVOCADO

HERRING SALAD

HARICOTS VERTS WITH MUSTARD DRESSING

BEETS WITH GINGER

BEETS WITH WALNUTS

SAUTÉED BABY ARTICHOKES

BAKED BABY ARTICHOKES

CAULIFLOWER WITH CAPERS

ROASTED BELL PEPPERS

MUSHROOM TARTS

EGGPLANT WITH TAHINI DRESSING

EGGPLANT RELISH

ORIENTAL EGGPLANT

EGGPLANT WITH MUSHROOMS

CEVICHE

• Makes 6 to 8 servings

This classic South American dish is perfect in the summer. Depending on your taste and the preference of your guests, you can make it subtle and mild or spicy. I like to use tilapia, but any white-fleshed fish is appropriate.

2 pounds (900 g) tilapia fillets
¼ cup (60 ml) freshly squeezed lime juice (about 3 limes)

LIME-CILANTRO SAUCE
2 small green serrano peppers
3 tablespoons freshly squeezed lime juice (about 2 limes)
⅓ cup (80 ml) extra virgin olive oil
A few drops of Tabasco sauce
4 scallions, including green parts, finely chopped
2 garlic cloves, finely chopped
Kosher salt
Freshly ground black pepper
½ cup (20 g) tightly packed cilantro leaves

Cut the fillets into ¼-inch-wide (6 mm) strips and transfer them to a glass container. Pour the lime juice over the fish. Cover and refrigerate overnight.

A few hours before serving, pour off the lime-juice marinade. Cut the serrano peppers in half lengthwise, and remove the core and the seeds. Chop finely (see note).

Mix the peppers, lime juice, oil, Tabasco, scallions, and garlic in a small bowl and combine with the fish. Refrigerate until ready to use.

Just before serving, season to taste with salt and pepper and toss with the cilantro.

Note: When seeding serrano peppers, I advise wearing thin plastic gloves to avoid irritating your skin or your eyes.

SALMON TARTARE

• Makes 6 servings

This elegant dish, served with daikon (a Japanese radish with a mild flavor) and kirby cucumbers, makes an interesting alternative to Gravlax with Mustard-Dill Sauce (page 21). The salmon lovers among your friends and family will be impressed!

> 1½ pounds (680 g) sashimi-quality center-cut salmon fillets, skinned
> 2 scallions, including green parts, finely chopped
> 1 tablespoon sesame oil
> 2 tablespoons low-sodium soy sauce
> 1 tablespoon seasoned rice vinegar
> ¼ cup (10 g) loosely packed cilantro leaves
> Kosher salt
> Freshly ground black pepper
> Kirby cucumbers, ends removed, seeded and thinly sliced, for serving (see note)
> Daikon radish, peeled and julienned, for serving

Carefully pick over the salmon and remove any bones. (Tweezers are good for this.) Cut the salmon into ¼-inch-wide (6 mm) strips, then into ¼-inch (6 mm) cubes. Transfer to a bowl and add the scallions, sesame oil, soy sauce, vinegar, cilantro, salt, and pepper. Season to taste.

TO SERVE: Pack the salmon mixture tightly into a ½-cup (125 ml) measure and invert onto each appetizer plate. Serve with cucumbers and daikon radish.

Note: The best way to remove cucumber seeds is to cut the cucumber in half lenghtwise and scoop out the seeds with a spoon.

TUNA TARTARE

• Makes 8 servings

I am very fond of this dish, but as a hostess I know that serving raw fish can be a bit tricky. So to avoid possible embarrassment, I suggest that you check with your guests beforehand. I like to serve tuna tartare with daikon (a mild-flavored Japanese radish), kirby cucumbers, or for a colorful contrast, dressed frisée.

2 pounds (900 g) sashimi-quality tuna
4 scallions, including green parts, finely chopped
1 tablespoon extra virgin olive oil
1 tablespoon sesame oil
2 teaspoons wasabi powder
1 tablespoon low-sodium soy sauce
Kosher salt
Freshly ground black pepper
Dressed frisée, for serving (see Oriental Dressing, page 51)
Kirby cucumbers, ends removed, seeded and thinly sliced, for serving (see note)
Daikon radish, peeled and julienned, for garnish

Cut fish into ¼-inch-wide (6 mm) strips, then into ¼-inch (6 mm) cubes. Transfer the fish to a bowl and add the scallions, olive and sesame oils, wasabi powder, soy sauce, salt, and pepper. Season to taste.

TO SERVE: Pack the tuna mixture tightly into a ½-cup (125 ml) measure and invert onto each appetizer plate. Serve with frisée, cucumbers, or daikon.

Note: The best way to remove cucumber seeds is to cut the cucumber in half lenghtwise and scoop out the seeds with a spoon.

TUNA TARTARE WITH AVOCADO

• Makes 4 servings

This is one of my favorite dishes using raw tuna. The contrast between the deep garnet color of the fish and the pale green avocado always surprises and delights me. The sauce, with its fusion of Eastern and Western tastes, is a perfect complement.

1 pound (450 g) sashimi-quality tuna
2 tablespoons Dijon mustard
4 tablespoons extra virgin olive oil
2 tablespoons low-sodium soy sauce
2 tablespoons rice vinegar
1 teaspoon vegetable powder dissolved in ¼ cup (60 ml) water
Kosher salt
Freshly ground black pepper
1 firm ripe avocado
Snipped chives, for garnish

Cut the tuna into ¼-inch-wide (6 mm) strips, then into ¼-inch (6 mm) cubes. Transfer to a bowl, cover, and refrigerate.

Place the mustard, oil, soy sauce, vinegar, dissolved vegetable powder, salt, and pepper in a blender and combine. Refrigerate.

Before serving, peel the avocado and cut it into ½-inch (13 mm) cubes. Using a fork, gently combine it with the tuna. Season to taste.

TO SERVE: Place equal amounts of sauce on four appetizer plates. Pack the tuna-avocado mixture tightly into a ½-cup (125 ml) measure and invert it onto the sauce. Garnish with chives.

HERRING SALAD

- Makes 12 servings as an hors d'oeuvre
- Makes 6 appetizer servings

This piquant dish has an unusual combination of flavors, textures, and colors. Note the contrast of the ruby red beets and the pale green apples and scallions. This is a great party dish, as you can make it a day ahead. I serve it at room temperature with whole-grain crackers.

2 medium beets
2 scallions, including green parts, cut into pieces
1 small Granny Smith apple, peeled, quartered, and cored
One 6-ounce (170 g) jar imported matjes herring in spice sauce, drained
1 tablespoon extra virgin olive oil
1 tablespoon freshly squeezed lemon juice
Kosher salt
Freshly ground black pepper
12 dill sprigs, snipped finely with scissors

Preheat the oven to 400°F (205°C); you can also use a toaster oven. Line a small baking pan with foil.

Wash the beets and, while still wet, wrap each one individually in foil. (Be sure to wrap them tightly; otherwise some of the juice may ooze out.) Place in the pan and bake for 35 to 40 minutes, until tender when pierced with the tip of a paring knife.

When cool, slip the skin off the beets. Cut the beets into quarters and place them in a food processor. Add the scallions, apple, herring, and oil. Pulse to a medium-smooth consistency. Transfer to a bowl and add half the dill. Season to taste with lemon juice, salt, and pepper. Garnish with the remaining dill.

Note: I always wear thin plastic gloves when I work with beets, as this avoids staining my fingers with beet juice, which can be hard to remove.

HARICOTS VERTS WITH MUSTARD DRESSING

- Makes 4 servings

This delicately seasoned dish is one of my family's favorites. I serve it warm and follow it with a main course of Risotto (page 141) or pasta, for example Ziti with Herbs and Mozzarella (page 136) or Spaghetti with Tuna (page 154).

MUSTARD DRESSING
2 tablespoons Dijon mustard
2 tablespoons freshly squeezed lemon juice
3 tablespoons extra virgin olive oil

1 pound (450 g) haricots verts (thin French green beans)
½ cup (20 g) loosely packed flat-leaf-parsley, finely chopped
Kosher salt
Freshly ground black pepper

Place the mustard in a large bowl and whisk in the lemon juice. Whisk in the oil, a few drops at a time. (The dressing should now be creamy.)

Trim and discard the stem end of the beans. Steam the beans about 8 minutes, until just tender. (You do not want them al dente.) While warm, toss with the dressing and parsley.

Season to taste with lemon juice, salt, and pepper.

BEETS WITH GINGER

• Makes 4 servings

This is a delicious year-round appetizer. I like to serve it at room temperature, surrounded by greens lightly dressed with oil. Traditionally, beets are boiled or steamed, but I think baking gives them a much richer flavor and a gorgeous color.

5 medium beets
1-inch (2.5 cm) piece ginger, peeled and grated
2 tablespoons extra virgin olive oil
2 tablespoons rice vinegar
Kosher salt
Freshly ground black pepper
Snipped chives, for garnish
Mâche or other greens, for serving

Preheat the oven to 400°F (205°C); you can also use a toaster oven. Line a baking pan with foil.

Wash the beets and, while still wet, wrap each one individually in foil. (Be sure to wrap them tightly; otherwise some of the juice may ooze out.) Place in the pan and bake for 35 to 40 minutes, until tender when pierced with the tip of a paring knife. Remove each beet from the oven as it becomes ready.

When cool, slip the skin off the beets. Cut them into ¼-inch (6 mm) slices, then into ¼-inch (6 mm) cubes. Add the ginger, oil, vinegar, salt, and pepper, and combine well. Season to taste.

Serve on individual plates, garnished with chives, and accompanied by mâche.

Notes: I always wear thin plastic gloves when I work with beets, as this avoids staining my fingers with beet juice, which can be hard to remove.

If you're in a hurry, you can chop the beets in a food processor, but this will give them a different texture.

BEETS WITH WALNUTS

• Makes 4 servings

Traditionally, beets are boiled or steamed, but Jean-Georges Vongerichten, one of America's most innovative "star chefs," has said that he prefers baking. After trying his method, I became a convert. Baking not only preserves the beets' gorgeous ruby red color, it also keeps more of their nutrients.

5 medium beets
4 tablespoons extra virgin olive oil
6 garlic cloves, peeled
½ cup (50 g) walnuts
1 tablespoon freshly squeezed lemon juice
Kosher salt
Freshly ground black pepper
¼ cup (10 g) loosely packed flat-leaf-parsley, finely chopped, for garnish

Preheat the oven to 400°F (205°C); you can also use a toaster oven. Line a baking pan with foil.

Wash the beets and, while still wet, wrap each one individually in foil. (Be sure to wrap them tightly; otherwise some of the juice may ooze out.) Place in the pan and bake for 35 to 40 minutes, until tender when pierced with the tip of a paring knife. Remove each beet as it becomes ready.

When cool, slip the skin off the beets. Cut them into slices or wedges and place in a medium bowl.

Heat the oil in a skillet over low heat. Add the garlic and cook about 4 minutes, until the cloves begin to soften. Add the walnuts and continue cooking about 4 minutes, stirring from time to time.

Let the garlic–nut mixture cool slightly, then pulse in a food processor until it is semi-smooth. Combine it with the beets and toss with the lemon juice, salt, and pepper. Season to taste.

Before serving, garnish with parsley.

Note: I always wear thin plastic gloves when I work with beets, as this avoids staining my fingers with beet juice, which can be hard to remove.

SAUTÉED BABY ARTICHOKES

• Makes 2 servings as an appetizer or side dish

There is something pleasant about being able to eat the whole artichoke without having to remove each leaf and dunk it in some sauce, or worry about the choke. I often serve this as a side dish with chicken or duck. It can be prepared in advance and is easily reheated.

> **6 baby artichokes**
> **2 tablespoons extra virgin olive oil**
> **2 garlic cloves, finely chopped**
> **¼ cup (10 g) loosely packed flat-leaf parsley, finely chopped**
> **Kosher salt**
> **Freshly ground black pepper**

Cut off and discard the artichoke stems. Pull off the tough outer leaves as far as they will snap, leaving only the pale green ones. Cut off the top of each artichoke, about ¼ inch (6 mm) down, then cut in half lengthwise.

Heat the oil in a skillet. Add the artichokes and sauté over medium heat for 2 minutes to brown. (Tongs make the turning easier.)

Cover the skillet, lower the heat, and cook for about 5 minutes. Add the garlic and continue cooking for another 2 minutes, or until the artichokes are fork-tender.

Stir in the parsley and season to taste with salt and pepper.

BAKED BABY ARTICHOKES

• Makes 4 servings as an appetizer or side dish

Here is a favorite variation for cooking baby artichokes. These wonderful vegetables have a short season, so take advantage!

> **2 tablespoons freshly squeezed lemon juice**
> **3 tablespoons extra virgin olive oil**
> **3 garlic cloves, minced**
> **Leaves from 12 thyme sprigs**
> **12 baby artichokes**
> **Kosher salt**
> **Freshly ground black pepper**

Preheat the oven to 425°F (220°C).

In a small bowl, combine the lemon juice, oil, garlic, and thyme.

Cut off and discard the artichoke stems. Pull the tough outer leaves as far as they will snap, leaving only the pale green leaves. Cut off the tops of the artichokes, about ¼ inch (6 mm) down, then cut the artichokes in half lengthwise.

Place the artichokes in a glass, ceramic, or enamel-lined baking pan and sprinkle with the lemon juice mixture. Bake, stirring once, for 20 minutes, or until the artichokes are fork-tender. Season to taste with lemon juice, salt, and pepper.

This dish can be baked in advance and reheated for 10 minutes at 325°F (165°C).

CAULIFLOWER WITH CAPERS

• Makes 4 appetizer servings
• Makes 6 servings as a side dish

Cauliflower is available year-round and can be prepared in countless ways. This is one of the easiest and, because of the capers, most flavorful. I usually serve it warm as an appetizer, but it also makes a fine side dish with Barbecued Split Fillet (page 233), Roasted Turkey Breast (page 218), or Turkey Burgers (page 220).

1 medium head cauliflower (about 2 pounds/900 g)
1 garlic clove
½ teaspoon kosher salt
2 tablespoons small capers
1½ tablespoons freshly squeezed lemon juice
3 tablespoons extra virgin olive oil
½ cup (20 g) tightly packed flat-leaf parsley, finely chopped
Freshly ground black pepper

Cut the stalk and leaves off the cauliflower and discard. Cut the head into small florets and place them in a steamer. Cover and steam for 3 minutes, or until just tender. Transfer to a medium bowl.

Coarsely chop the garlic on a cutting board. Sprinkle with salt and, using a knife, crush it into a paste. Place the paste in a small bowl and add the capers, lemon juice, and oil. Pour the dressing over the cauliflower and stir in the parsley.

Season to taste with salt and pepper. Serve warm.

ROASTED BELL PEPPERS

• Makes 8 servings

This is such a beautiful dish, bursting with colors. I know that skinning the peppers is a bit time-consuming, but I think it is well worth it. The sweetness of the peppers melds beautifully with the honey and balsamic vinegar. This dish can be made a few days ahead, and the taste actually improves with time.

8 bell peppers, mixed red, orange, and yellow
4 tablespoons extra virgin olive oil
2 garlic cloves, thinly sliced
3 tablespoons balsamic vinegar
2 tablespoons honey
Kosher salt
Freshly ground black pepper
½ cup (20 g) loosely packed flat-leaf parsley, finely chopped
¼ cup (35 g) pine nuts, for garnish

Preheat the broiler. Set the rack in the broiler pan and cover it with foil.

Cut the peppers in half lengthwise, then core and seed them. Make a shallow "basket" with a piece of heavy foil, crimping it at the corners so that the liquids don't spill out. (See Notes on Techniques, page 351.) Set the basket on the broiler rack, and arrange the peppers inside, skin side up. Place the broiler pan in the oven (or broiling unit), as close as possible to the heat source. Broil for about 7 minutes, until the skin is blistered and charred. Cover the peppers with foil and cool. The heat will loosen the skin.

Peel the peppers, cut each piece in half lengthwise, and place in a large bowl.

Heat the oil in a small saucepan over low heat. Add the garlic and cook until golden. Add the vinegar, honey, salt, and pepper. Pour the warm dressing over the peppers. Add the parsley and mix well. Season to taste.

Roast the pine nuts in a toaster oven on the lowest setting for a minute or two. (Watch them carefully, as they burn quickly.) Sprinkle them on the peppers.

MUSHROOM TARTS

• Makes 4 servings

This dish is one of my favorites. While it may seem complicated, it is actually quite straightforward, as it can be made ahead of time in stages and assembled before baking. I like to serve it with dressed greens.

4 frozen puff pastry squares, 3½ inches (9 cm) square (see note)
5 tablespoons extra virgin olive oil, plus more for dressing the garnish
2 medium onions, sliced
½ cup (50 g) pecans or walnuts
1 pound (450 g) shiitake mushrooms
2 garlic cloves, finely chopped
Leaves from 9 thyme sprigs
Kosher salt
Freshly ground black pepper
Mâche or frisée, for garnish

Leave the pastry squares out at room temperature for 1 minute to soften. One at a time, place the squares between layers of cling wrap and roll out to 5-inch (13 cm) squares. Place the squares on a 12 by 17-inch (30 by 45 cm) nonstick baking sheet and refrigerate until ready to bake.

Heat 2 tablespoons of the oil in a skillet. Add the onions and sauté over high heat, stirring from time to time, until the onions begin to brown, about 5 minutes. Reduce the heat to medium-low and continue to cook, stirring, until the onions are soft and light brown. Cool.

Roast the nuts in a toaster oven on the lowest setting for 5 minutes. (Watch them carefully, as they burn quickly.)

Place the onions and nuts in a food processor and pulse until smooth.

Discard the mushroom stems. Wipe the caps with a damp paper towel and cut in thin slices. Heat the remaining 3 tablespoons oil in a skillet or wok. Add the garlic and sauté over low heat. Add the mushrooms, raise the heat and sauté quickly, stirring, until the mushrooms begin to wilt.

Remove from the heat. Add most of the thyme (reserve some for garnish) and season to taste with salt and pepper. (You can prepare the recipe in advance up to this point.)

Preheat the oven to 400°F (205°C). Spread one-fourth of the onion-nut topping on each pastry square, leaving some space along the edges. Spoon the mushrooms on top. Bake in the lower third of the oven for 13 to 15 minutes. The edges of the tarts will be brown.

Place on individual plates, sprinkle with the remaining thyme, and surround with mâche or frisée dressed with extra virgin olive oil.

Note: Mini puff pastry squares are available in most kosher markets. They come frozen in 20-ounce (567 g) packages. Because they are packed with cellophane in between the layers, they separate easily, and you can work with as many squares as you like at one time. You can use them for other purposes, such as desserts.

EGGPLANT WITH TAHINI DRESSING

• Makes 4 servings

This tasty appetizer, with its unusual combination of flavors, is as easy to make as it is attractive to look at. Another reason to love it: You can do most of the cooking in advance.

1 Vidalia onion
5 tablespoons vegetable oil
4 baby eggplants

TAHINI DRESSING
1 tablespoon seasoned rice vinegar
1½ tablespoons water
1 tablespoon white miso paste
1 tablespoon sugar
1 tablespoon tahini
1½ tablespoons vegetable oil
1½ tablespoons pine nuts, for garnish

Preheat the oven to 500°F (260°C).

Slice the onion as thin as possible. (A mandoline makes this step easy.) Put the slices in a baking pan and drizzle with 2 tablespoons of the vegetable oil. Bake for 15 to 20 minutes, turning occasionally, until the onion is soft and just beginning to caramelize.

Rinse the eggplants, pat dry and cut off the stems. Cut the eggplants lengthwise into quarters. Place the quarters in a baking pan in a single layer, skin side down. Drizzle with the remaining 3 tablespoons of oil and bake about 10 minutes, until almost tender.

In a small bowl, combine the rice vinegar, water, miso, sugar, and tahini. Slowly whisk in the vegetable oil.

Roast the pine nuts in a toaster oven on the lowest setting for a minute or two. (Watch them carefully, as they burn quickly.)

TO SERVE: Spread equal amounts of the dressing on each plate. Arrange the eggplant quarters attractively on top. Top with the onions and sprinkle with the roasted pine nuts.

Note: The onions, eggplants, and the dressing can be prepared earlier in the day and refrigerated until needed. Bring the dressing to room temperature. Reheat the onions and eggplants in a 250°F (130°C) oven for about 10 minutes, until warm. Then proceed as described above.

EGGPLANT RELISH

• Makes 4 generous servings

Eggplant can be combined with such a wide range of ingredients, from such a mixture of cuisines, that I think of it as the ultimate fusion food. Note that because the bell peppers don't have to be peeled, this delicious dish is easy and quick to prepare.

> **1 medium eggplant (about 1¼ pounds/570 g)**
> **3 tablespoons sesame oil**
> **1 red bell pepper**
> **1 yellow bell pepper**
> **1 tablespoon extra virgin olive oil**
> **1 small red onion, finely chopped**
> **1-inch (2.5 cm) piece ginger, peeled and grated**
> **2 small jalapeño peppers (see note)**
> **1 tablespoon sugar**
> **1 tablespoon low-sodium soy sauce**
> **2 tablespoons rice vinegar**
> **Kosher salt**
> **Freshly ground black pepper**
> **½ cup (20 g) loosely packed cilantro leaves**

Preheat the oven to 400°F (205°C). Line the broiler pan with foil.

Trim the stem and peel the eggplant. Cut it into 1-inch (2.5 cm) cubes. Place the cubes in one layer on the broiler pan and sprinkle with 1 tablespoon of sesame oil. Bake for 15 minutes, or until almost soft.

Cut the bell peppers in half lengthwise, then core and seed them. Cut them in ½-inch (13 mm) cubes.

In a medium saucepan, heat the olive oil and the remaining 2 tablespoons of sesame oil. Add the onion, ginger and jalapeño peppers. Cover and cook over low heat about 5 minutes, until the onion is soft, Add the peppers and the eggplant. Cook uncovered over medium heat to blend well, about 3 minutes.

Stir in the sugar, soy sauce, and rice vinegar. Season to taste with salt and pepper.

Before serving, add cilantro and toss.

Note: When seeding jalapeño peppers, I advise wearing thin plastic gloves to avoid irritating your skin or your eyes.

ORIENTAL EGGPLANT

• Makes 2 generous servings

I love eggplant, and this unusual dish is one of my favorites. Its piquant flavor and interesting combination of Asian ingredients make for a lovely summer appetizer,

1 medium eggplant (about 1¼ pounds/570 g)

ORIENTAL DRESSING
1 small garlic clove
¼ teaspoon kosher salt
½-inch (13 mm) piece ginger, peeled and grated
2 tablespoons low-sodium soy sauce
1 tablespoon sesame oil
¼ teaspoon sugar
1 tablespoon rice vinegar
Freshly ground black pepper
2 kirby cucumbers, for garnish
¼ cup (10 g) loosely packed cilantro leaves, for garnish

Preheat the oven to 400°F (205°C). Line the broiler pan with heavy foil.

Place the eggplant in the pan and bake for 35 to 40 minutes, turning once, until soft. When the eggplant is cool enough to handle, cut off of the stem, peel it and cut it in half lengthwise, discarding some of the seeds. Cut the flesh into ½-inch (13 mm) strips, then into ½-inch (13 mm) cubes. Remove to a medium bowl.

TO MAKE THE DRESSING: Coarsely chop the garlic on a cutting board. Sprinkle the garlic with salt and, using a knife, crush it to a paste.

Place the garlic paste in a small bowl; add the ginger, soy sauce, sesame oil, sugar, rice vinegar, and pepper. Mix well and pour over the eggplant. Season to taste.

TO SERVE: Cut both ends off the cucumbers, as they are bitter; then peel the cucumbers, spooning out the seeds. Cut the cucumbers into thin slices. Divide the eggplant mixture onto two plates and garnish with the cucumbers and cilantro leaves.

EGGPLANT WITH MUSHROOMS

• Makes 4 servings

This is a warm appetizer that I like to serve with whole-grain crackers, toasted pita, or for those who are calorie-conscious, endive petals.

1 large eggplant, about 1½ pounds (680 g)
4 white mushrooms
3 tablespoons extra virgin olive oil
3 scallions, including the green part, thinly sliced
2 garlic cloves, finely chopped
½ teaspoon ground cumin
Kosher salt
Freshly ground black pepper
1 tablespoon freshly squeezed lemon juice
½ cup (20 g) loosely packed flat-leaf parsley, finely chopped, for garnish

Preheat the oven to 400°F (205°C). Line the broiler pan with foil.

Place the eggplant in the broiler pan. Bake for 40 minutes, turning once, until soft to the touch. Remove and cool.

While the eggplant is baking, wipe the mushrooms with a damp paper towel and chop them finely. Heat the oil in a skillet. Add the scallions, garlic, and cumin. Sauté quickly over low heat. Raise the heat, add the mushroom, and sauté for a minute.

When the eggplant is cool enough to handle, remove the stem. Cut the eggplant in half lengthwise and discard some of the seeds. Scoop out the flesh and chop finely. Add the eggplant to the mushroom mixture and combine well.

Season to taste with salt, pepper, and lemon juice. Serve warm, garnished with parsley.

SOUPS

DAIRY

MUSHROOM SOUP
GREEN PEA AND ZUCCHINI SOUP
SWEET POTATO SOUP
CELERY ROOT SOUP
PURÉED VEGETABLE SOUP

MEAT

CHICKEN SOUP WITH MATZOH BALLS
CANNELLINI BEAN AND PORCINI SOUP
ZUCCHINI AND ROASTED PEPPER SOUP
ASPARAGUS SOUP
CABBAGE AND MUSHROOM SOUP
CARROT AND TOMATO SOUP

PAREVE

CARROT-GINGER SOUP
SUMMER CORN SOUP
RED LENTIL SOUP
ROASTED TOMATO SOUP
SUMMER TOMATO SOUP
SUN-DRIED TOMATO SOUP
TOMATO AND BELL PEPPER SOUP WITH BASIL GARNISH
BEET SOUP
CELERY ROOT AND PORCINI SOUP
MUSHROOM SOUP WITH SOY MILK
BARLEY SOUP WITH MISO
CHESTNUT AND MUSHROOM SOUP
GREEN BEAN AND ALMOND SOUP
FISH SOUP WITH VEGETABLES

MUSHROOM SOUP

• Makes 8 servings

This is one of my favorite winter soups. I prefer using Polish mushrooms, which grew wild in the Polish forests, have a strong aroma and a rich taste, and beautifully complement their more delicate cultivated counterparts.

1 ounce (28 g) dried Polish mushrooms (see note)
1 cup (250 ml) boiling water
1¼ pounds (570 g) white mushrooms (see note)
3 tablespoons (45 g) unsalted butter
6 scallions, including the green parts, cut into ½-inch (13 mm) pieces
1 quart (1 liter) vegetable broth
1 cup (250 ml) milk
1 bunch fresh dill
Kosher salt
Freshly ground black pepper

Place the dried mushrooms in a small bowl and pour the boiling water over them. Cover and let stand for 20 minutes.

Remove the reconstituted mushrooms with a slotted spoon. Squeeze all the liquid back into the bowl and set the mushrooms aside. Strain the mushroom liquid through a paper-lined sieve into another small bowl. Set aside.

Wipe the fresh mushrooms with a damp paper towel and slice into quarters.

Heat the butter in a large saucepan. Sauté the scallions for a minute. Add the dried and fresh mushrooms and sauté quickly until they are well coated with butter. Add the mushroom soaking liquid, vegetable broth, milk, and most of the dill. Bring the mixture to a boil over high heat. Lower the heat and cook, covered, for 10 minutes.

Remove the dill. Cool the soup a little.

Purée the soup in a blender, in batches, to a medium-coarse consistency. Return the soup to the saucepan and reheat.

Season to taste with salt and pepper. Garnish with the remaining dill, snipped finely with scissors, and serve.

Notes: You can usually find dried Polish mushrooms at specialty food shops. It they are not available, substitute dried porcini mushrooms.

When buying fresh mushrooms, I look for ones that are firm and have no separation between the stem and the cap.

GREEN PEA AND ZUCCHINI SOUP

• Makes 6 servings

This nutritious soup is truly a dish for all seasons, as it can be served at any time of year. Because it is so easy to prepare and freezes well, I usually have a batch on hand for last-minute dinner guests.

> **1 pound (450 g) zucchini**
> **4 tablespoons extra virgin olive oil**
> **4 garlic cloves, finely chopped**
> **20 ounces (570 g) frozen sweet green peas, defrosted**
> **3¼-4 cups (780-960 ml) vegetable broth**
> **10 basil leaves, torn**
> **Kosher salt**
> **Freshly ground black pepper**
> **¼ cup (25 g) grated Parmesan cheese**

Rinse the zucchini and trim the ends. Cut into ½-inch (13 mm) cubes.

Heat the oil in a medium saucepan. Add the zucchini and garlic and sauté for a minute.

Add the peas and 3¼ cups (780 ml) broth and bring to a boil over high heat. Lower the heat and cook, covered, for 5 minutes.

Cool the soup a little. Purée half the soup coarsely in a blender. Return it to the saucepan and reheat, adding more broth as needed, until the soup reaches the desired consistency. Stir in the basil. Season to taste with salt and pepper. Sprinkle with cheese and serve.

SWEET POTATO SOUP

• Makes 4 generous servings

This soup is simple to prepare and quite delicious. Since sweet potatoes are available throughout the year, you can serve it any time, but I like it best in fall and winter, around the holidays.

2 medium sweet potatoes (about 1 pound/450 g)
1 medium onion, coarsely chopped
3½ cups (840 ml) vegetable broth
¾ cup (180 ml) milk
2 teaspoons freshly squeezed lemon juice
⅛ teaspoon ground nutmeg
Kosher salt
Freshly ground black pepper

Peel the sweet potatoes and slice them into thick pieces. Place the sweet potatoes, onion, and broth in a medium saucepan and bring to a boil over high heat. Lower the heat, cover, and cook about 25 minutes, until the potatoes are soft.

Cool a little. Purée in a blender until smooth.

Return the soup to the saucepan, and add the milk, lemon juice, nutmeg, salt, and pepper. Reheat and season to taste.

CELERY ROOT SOUP

• Makes 6 servings

Celery root is a delicious vegetable that I think is woefully underappreciated. I like to serve this soup, with its creamy texture, before a light main dish, such as fish or a frittata.

1 pound (450 g) celery root
1 Yukon gold potato (about 2 inches/5 cm long)
2 tablespoons (30 g) unsalted butter
1 onion, coarsely chopped
2 garlic cloves, coarsely chopped
4 cups (960 ml) vegetable broth
1 cup (240 ml) milk
Kosher salt
Freshly ground black pepper
1 teaspoon snipped chives, for garnish

Peel the celery root and cut it into thick slices. Peel the potato and slice it into thick slices.

Melt the butter in a medium saucepan. Add the celery root, potato, onion, and garlic, and sauté over low heat for 5 minutes.

Add the broth and bring to a boil over high heat. Lower the heat and cook, covered, for 15 minutes, or until the vegetables are soft. Add the milk.

Cool a little. Purée the soup in a blender until smooth.

Return the soup to the saucepan and heat. Season to taste with salt and pepper.

Sprinkle with chives and serve.

PURÉED VEGETABLE SOUP

• Makes 8 servings

This is a lovely green soup, thickened with potatoes and bursting with flavorful vegetables. I like to serve it garnished with watercress and grated Parmesan cheese.

3 leeks
1 pound (450 g) Yukon gold potatoes
3 tablespoons extra virgin olive oil
2 garlic cloves, sliced
4½ cups (1.12 liters) vegetable broth
1 head Boston lettuce, separated into leaves
2 cups (80 g) tightly packed watercress
1 cup (40 g) loosely packed flat-leaf parsley
Kosher salt
Freshly ground black pepper
¼ cup (25 g) grated Parmesan cheese

Cut off and discard the roots and tough, dark green leaves of the leeks. Cut the white and light green parts into thick slices. Place in a sieve and rinse thoroughly under cold running water to remove any sand.

Peel the potatoes and slice them into thick pieces.

Heat the oil in a large saucepan. Add the leeks, potatoes, and garlic and sauté over low heat for 3 minutes. Add 4 cups (1 liter) of the vegetable broth and bring to a boil over high heat. Lower the heat and cook, covered, for 15 minutes, or until the potatoes are soft.

While the potatoes are cooking, rinse and spin-dry the lettuce. Remove and discard the stems from the watercress and parsley, then rinse and spin-dry the leaves. Set aside some of the watercress for the garnish.

Add the lettuce, parsley, and watercress to the soup. Bring to a boil over high heat; lower the heat and cook, covered, for 5 minutes.

Cool the soup a little. Purée in a blender, in batches, until smooth.

Return the soup to the saucepan and reheat, adding the remaining broth as needed until the soup reaches the desired consistency. Season to taste with salt and pepper.

Before serving, sprinkle with cheese and garnish with watercress leaves.

CHICKEN SOUP WITH MATZOH BALLS

• Makes 10 servings

My favorite way of using this nutritious and aromatic broth is to pair it with matzoh balls for a traditional (and justly famous) matzoh ball soup. Matzoh balls can be made in different sizes and with different seasonings, but I like mine simple, small, and fluffy.

I always serve this dish at Passover, but my family loves it throughout the year.

CHICKEN BROTH
6 pounds (2.7 kg) stewing chicken or pullets, quartered
1 carrot, peeled and quartered
1 onion, peeled and quartered
3 flat-leaf parsley sprigs

MATZOH BALLS
Kosher salt
3 large eggs, separated, at room temperature
½ cup (75 g) plus 1 generous tablespoon matzoh meal
1 tablespoon vegetable oil
Freshly ground black pepper
2 cups (500 ml) chicken broth, from above (see note)

TO MAKE THE BROTH: Rinse the chicken well and discard excess fat. Place the chicken in a large saucepan with enough cold water to cover. Bring to a boil over high heat. Add 4 ice cubes, lower the heat, and skim the foamy residue as it rises to the surface.

Add the carrot, onion, and parsley. Simmer the soup, partially covered, for 2 hours.

With a slotted spoon, remove the chicken and vegetables from the soup. Discard the vegetables. (You can use the chicken later in a soup or salad.)

Wet a double layer of paper towels with cold water and squeeze dry. Place the wet towels in the freezer for a few minutes, then line a strainer with them. Place the strainer over a clean saucepan. Ladle the soup slowly into the towel-lined strainer. The grease will adhere to the towels and you will have crystal-clear, fat-free chicken soup. Keep the soup hot while you make the matzoh balls.

TO MAKE THE MATZOH BALLS: Bring a large pot of salted water to a boil over high heat. Lower the heat to a simmer.

Beat the egg whites with an electric hand mixer until stiff. Add the yolks and combine well. Using a rubber spatula, gradually mix in the matzoh meal, always scraping the bottom of the bowl. Mix in the oil and season with ½ teaspoon salt and black pepper to taste. Refrigerate for 10 minutes.

Cover the work surface with a sheet of wax paper. Have a small bowl of cold water nearby. Moisten your hands with water and lightly shape 1 tablespoon of the matzoh mixture into a ball, placing it on the wax paper. You should end up with about 20 mini balls.

Using a spoon, place the balls carefully in the simmering water and cook, uncovered, for 15 minutes.

TO SERVE: Fill each of the soup bowls with hot chicken broth and spoon in 2 matzoh balls.

CANNELLINI BEAN AND PORCINI SOUP

• Makes 6 generous servings

This is a hearty winter soup with a wonderful rich taste. An extra reason to love it: It also freezes very well.

1 ounce (28 g) dried porcini mushrooms
1 cup (250 ml) boiling water
2 onions, quartered
2 garlic cloves, quartered
1 large carrot, peeled
2 tablespoons extra virgin olive oil
⅓ cup (65 g) medium pearl barley
5 cups (1.25 liters) chicken broth
8 thyme sprigs
One 15.5-ounce (440 g) can Goya cannellini beans, drained
Kosher salt
Freshly ground black pepper

Place the dried mushrooms in a small bowl and pour the boiling water over them. Cover and let stand for 20 minutes.

Remove the reconstituted mushrooms with a slotted spoon. Squeeze all the liquid back into the bowl and set the mushrooms aside. Strain the mushroom liquid through a paper-lined sieve into another small bowl. Set aside. Chop the mushrooms coarsely.

Chop the onions, garlic, and carrot. You can do this in a food processor: Pulse the onions and garlic until coarse; remove to a small bowl. Cut the carrot into large pieces and pulse until coarse. (If you chop everything together, the onions will become mushy.)

Heat the oil in a medium saucepan, and sauté the onions, garlic, and carrots for 5 minutes. Add the mushrooms, mushroom soaking liquid, barley, chicken broth, and 6 of the thyme sprigs. Bring to a boil over high heat. Lower the heat and cook, covered, for 20 minutes, or until barley is soft.

Add the cannellini beans and continue cooking for another 5 minutes. Remove and discard the thyme sprigs. Season to taste with salt and pepper.

Garnish with the leaves from the 2 remaining thyme sprigs and serve.

ZUCCHINI AND ROASTED PEPPER SOUP

• Makes 6 servings

This is a light, delicious soup, and its rich color will depend on the peppers you use. I love the taste of toasted cumin and think it adds an usual flavor, but if you are not a fan, just omit it.

> **4 red, yellow, or orange bell peppers**
> **1 pound (450 g) zucchini, plus 1 extra zucchini for garnish**
> **½ teaspoon ground cumin, optional**
> **2 tablespoons extra virgin olive oil**
> **1 onion, coarsely chopped**
> **2½ cups (625 ml) chicken broth**
> **Kosher salt**
> **Freshly ground black pepper**

Preheat the broiler. Set the rack in the broiler pan and cover it with foil.

Cut the peppers in half lengthwise, then core and seed them. Make a shallow "basket" with a piece of heavy foil, crimping it at the corners so that the liquids don't spill out. (See Notes on Techniques, page 351.) Set the basket on the broiler rack, and arrange the peppers inside, skin side up. Place the broiler pan in the oven (or broiling unit), as close as possible to the heat source. Broil for about 7 minutes, until the skin is blistered and charred. Cover the peppers with foil and cool. The heat will loosen the skin.

Peel the peppers and cut them into thick slices. Rinse the zucchini and trim the ends. Cut the zucchini into thick slices.

To bring out the flavor of the cumin, wrap it in foil and roast it in a toaster oven on the highest setting for 1 minute. Unwrap and cool slightly.

Heat the oil in a medium saucepan; add the onion and sauté, covered, for 2 minutes. Add the peppers, zucchini, cumin, and 2 cups (500 ml) of the broth. Bring to a boil over high heat. Lower the heat and cook, covered, about 10 minutes, until the vegetables are soft.

Cool a little. Purée in a blender until very smooth. Add the remaining broth as needed, until the soup reaches the desired consistency. Season to taste with salt and pepper.

Trim and grate the extra zucchini, for garnish.

ASPARAGUS SOUP

• Makes 8 servings

This is a silky, creamy-tasting springtime soup, when asparagus is at its best. Though it takes a bit of time to make, the delicious taste makes the effort well worth it.

3 pounds (1.36 kg) asparagus, plus tips from 8 stalks
One 10-ounce (283 g) package frozen baby lima beans, defrosted
6½ cups (1.63 liters) chicken broth
3 tarragon sprigs
Kosher salt
Freshly ground black pepper

Hold each stalk of asparagus with both hands and snap it at the point where it breaks easily. Discard the rough bottom part. Rinse the upper parts and cut into thick pieces.

Place in a medium saucepan with lima beans, broth, and tarragon. Bring to a boil over high heat. Lower the heat and cook, covered, for 10 minutes, or until the asparagus is soft.

Cool a little. Remove the tarragon. Purée the soup in a blender, in batches, until very smooth. Strain the soup through a medium-mesh sieve, pushing the solids through with the back of a spoon to obtain as much purée as possible. Be sure to scrape the underside of the sieve. Discard the pulp left in the sieve. Return the soup to the saucepan to reheat. Season to taste with salt and pepper.

Steam the asparagus tips, Coarsely chop them for garnish.

Note: This soup freezes very well. When reheating, to bring back the creamy texture, whisk it as it begins to boil.

CABBAGE AND MUSHROOM SOUP

• Makes 10 servings

This is a thick, hearty winter soup. My family and I love it.

1 pound (450 g) cabbage (about half of a small cabbage)
½ pound (225 g) shiitake mushrooms, stems removed
½ pound (225 g) cremini mushrooms
½ pound (225 g) white mushrooms
2 onions, quartered
2 garlic cloves, quartered
2 medium carrots, peeled
½ pound (225 g) Yukon gold potatoes
4 tablespoons extra virgin olive oil
7 cups (1.75 liters) chicken broth
10 dill sprigs
Kosher salt
Freshly ground black pepper

Discard the tough outer leaves of the cabbage. Cut the cabbage into quarters. Holding onto the core, finely shred the cabbage (see note).

Wipe the mushrooms with a damp paper towel and cut them into thin slices.

Chop the garlic, onions, carrots, and potatoes. You can do this in a food processor: Pulse the onions and garlic until coarse; remove to a small bowl. Cut the carrots into large pieces and pulse until coarse; add to the onions and garlic. Quarter the potatoes and pulse until coarse. (If you chop everything together, the vegetables will become mushy.)

Heat the oil in a large saucepan. Add the onions, garlic, carrots, potatoes, and cabbage and sauté for 5 minutes. Add the mushrooms and sauté for an additional 5 minutes. Add the broth and 8 of the dill sprigs and bring to a boil over high heat. Lower the heat and cook, covered, until all the vegetables are soft, about 15 minutes. Remove and discard the dill. Season to taste with salt and pepper.

Before serving, garnish with 2 dill sprigs, snipped finely with scissors.

Note: I use a mandoline to shred the cabbage, as I find it much easier to handle than a knife.

CARROT AND TOMATO SOUP

Makes 10 servings

Thanks to the bright orange of the carrots and the deep red of the tomatoes, this soup has a Matisse-like color that adds richness to any table. It is definitely one of my favorites, and I love serving it in summer when tomatoes are most flavorful. It's equally good at room termperature or hot.

> **1½ pounds (680 g) ripe tomatoes**
> **3 tablespoons extra virgin olive oil**
> **1 medium onion, coarsely chopped**
> **3 cloves garlic, coarsely chopped**
> **1½ pounds (680 g) carrots, peeled and sliced**
> **½ cup (20 g) tightly packed fresh basil leaves**
> **5½ cups (1.38 liters) chicken broth**
> **Kosher salt**
> **Freshly ground back pepper**

Core the tomatoes and cut them in half widthwise. Squeeze them gently to remove the seeds. (Some seeds will remain.) Cut the tomatoes into pieces.

Heat the oil in a large saucepan. Add the onions and garlic and sauté for 2 minutes. Add the tomatoes, carrots, basil (set aside a few basil leaves for garnish), and 5 cups (1.25 liters) of the broth. Bring to a boil over high heat. Lower the heat and cook, covered, about 20 minutes, until the carrots are tender.

Cool a little. Purée the soup in a blender, in batches, until very smooth. Return it to the saucepan and reheat, adding the remaining broth as needed, until the soup reaches the desired consistency. Season to taste with salt and pepper.

Garnish with snipped basil and serve.

Note: This soup freezes well. When reheating, whisk it as it begins to boil to bring back the creamy texture.

CARROT-GINGER SOUP

• Makes 8 servings

The apple and the ginger give this creamy soup, which is made without any cream at all, a bit of a bite. Because the ingredients are always available, you can serve it in all seasons and at any temperature—hot, cold, or room temperature. I must confess, though, that I love it best when the weather is warm.

2 tablespoons extra virgin olive oil
1 medium onion, sliced
2 garlic cloves, quartered
1¾ pounds (800 g) carrots, peeled and sliced, plus 1 extra carrot for garnish
1 small Granny Smith apple, peeled and sliced
1-inch (2.5 cm) piece ginger, peeled and sliced
5½ cups (1.38 liters) vegetable broth
1 tablespoon freshly squeezed lemon juice
Kosher salt
Freshly ground back pepper

Heat the oil in a medium saucepan. Add the onion, garlic, carrots, apple, and ginger and sauté for 3 minutes. Add the broth and bring to a boil over high heat. Lower the heat and cook, covered, about 30 minutes, until the carrots are tender.

Cool a little. Purée the soup in a blender, in batches, until smooth. Return it to the saucepan.

Season to taste with lemon juice, salt, and pepper.

TO PREPARE THE GARNISH: Steam the remaining carrot until just tender, and grate. Before serving, sprinkle each bowl with the grated carrot.

SUMMER CORN SOUP

• Makes 10 servings

I love to make this soup in the summer when fresh corn is available. It is wonderful either hot or at room temperature.

2 pounds (900 g) ripe tomatoes
1 jalapeño pepper
2 tablespoons extra virgin olive oil
1 onion, coarsely chopped
3 garlic cloves, coarsely chopped
1 quart (1 liter) vegetable broth
Kernels cut from 5 to 6 ears of cooked corn (about 2½-3 cups/355-425 g)
Kosher salt
Freshly ground black pepper
1 tablespoon freshly squeezed lime juice
Cilantro, for garnish

Core the tomatoes, then cut them in half widthwise and squeeze gently to remove the seeds. (Some seeds will remain.) Cut the tomatoes into pieces.

Cut the jalapeño pepper in half lengthwise. Remove the core and the seeds and cut the pepper into pieces (see note).

Heat the oil in a medium saucepan. Add the onion, garlic, and jalapeño pepper. Sauté over low heat for about 5 minutes, until the onion is soft. Add the tomatoes, broth, and corn. Bring to a boil over high heat. Lower the heat and cook, covered, for 15 minutes.

Cool a little. Purée the soup in a blender, in batches, until very smooth. Strain through a medium-mesh sieve, pushing the solids through with the back of a spoon to obtain as much purée as possible. Be sure to scrape the underside of the sieve. Discard the pulp left in the sieve.

Return the soup to the saucepan and season to taste with salt, pepper, and lime juice.

Garnish with cilantro leaves.

Notes: When seeding jalapeño peppers, I advise wearing thin plastic gloves to avoid irritating your skin or your eyes.

This soup freezes very well. When reheating, whisk it as it begins to boil to bring back the creamy texture.

RED LENTIL SOUP

• Makes 8 generous servings

Here is a nutritious, hearty soup, full of texture, to warm your heart on the bleakest days of winter.

2 tablespoons extra virgin olive oil
2 medium onions, finely chopped
2 garlic cloves, finely chopped
1 teaspoon ground cumin
2 quarts (2 liters) vegetable broth
1¾ cups (700 g) red lentils
⅓ cup (45 g) medium-grind bulgur
2 tablespoons double-concentrate tomato paste
1 bay leaf
Kosher salt
Freshly ground black pepper
⅛ teaspoon paprika
⅛ teaspoon cayenne

Heat the oil in a large saucepan. Add the onions and garlic, and cook, covered, over low heat for 5 minutes. Add the cumin and stir. Add the broth, lentils, bulgur, tomato paste, and bay leaf. Bring to a boil over high heat. Lower the heat and cook, covered, for about 10 minutes, until the lentils are tender. Remove and discard the bay leaf.

Cool a little. Put 2 cups (500 ml) of soup aside and purée the rest in a blender. Combine the puréed and unpuréed soup and reheat. Season to taste with salt, pepper, paprika, and cayenne.

Note: This soup freezes very well, so you can always have some on hand.

ROASTED TOMATO SOUP

• Makes 6 servings

This is an ideal summer soup, when tomatoes are most flavorful. I serve it hot or at room temperature.

1 head garlic
2 pounds (900 g) ripe plum tomatoes
2 pounds (900 g) ripe regular tomatoes
3 tablespoons extra virgin olive oil
Kosher salt
Freshly ground black pepper
Chives, finely snipped, for garnish

Preheat the oven to 400°F (205°C).

Separate the garlic cloves from the head and peel. Place the garlic in a glass, ceramic, or enamel-lined baking pan that can hold the tomatoes in a single layer. Place the tomatoes on top of the garlic. Drizzle with the oil.

Roast for 1 hour, turning the tomatoes once. They will look charred.

Pass the tomatoes, garlic, and accumulated juices through the medium blade of a food mill.

Season to taste with salt and pepper.

Garnish with snipped chives.

SUMMER TOMATO SOUP

• Makes 4 generous servings

This is a simple summer soup that can be served hot or at room temperature. The number of portions will depend on the juiciness of the tomatoes.

2 pounds (900 g) ripe tomatoes
3 garlic cloves
3 tablespoons extra virgin olive oil
7 thyme sprigs
Kosher salt
Freshly ground black pepper
⅛ teaspoon sugar (optional)

Core the tomatoes and cut them into large pieces. Peel and quarter the garlic cloves.

Place the tomatoes, garlic, oil, and 5 of the thyme sprigs in a saucepan. Bring to a boil over high heat. Lower the heat and cook, covered, about 10 minutes, until the tomatoes are very soft.

Remove the thyme sprigs and pass the soup through the medium blade of a food mill.

Season to taste with salt, pepper, and sugar.

Garnish with leaves from the 2 remaining thyme sprigs.

SUN-DRIED TOMATO SOUP

• Makes 10 servings

This soup has a silky-smooth texture and, because of the combination of sun-dried and fresh tomatoes, a wonderfully rich taste. The basil adds real zest. This is another of my favorite tomato soups, and I make it as often as I can.

4 pounds (1.80 kg) ripe tomatoes
3 tablespoons extra virgin olive oil
2 onions, coarsely chopped
3 garlic cloves, coarsely chopped
1 quart (1 liter) vegetable broth
5 sun-dried tomatoes, packed in oil (about 1 ounce/28 g)
1 pound (450 g) Yukon gold potatoes, peeled and sliced
½ cup (20 g) loosely packed fresh basil leaves
½ teaspoon sugar
Kosher salt
Freshly ground black pepper

Bring a large pot of water to a boil. Drop the tomatoes into the boiling water; bring the water back to a boil and drain. Core the tomatoes and slip off the skin. Cut the tomatoes in half widthwise and squeeze gently to remove the seeds. (Some seeds will remain.)

Heat the oil in a large saucepan. Add the onions and garlic and sauté for 2 minutes. Add 3½ cups (840 ml) of the broth, the tomato halves, sun-dried tomatoes, potatoes, basil (set aside a few basil leaves for garnish), and sugar. Bring to a boil over high heat. Lower the heat and cook, covered, for 20 minutes, or until the potatoes are soft.

Cool a little. Purée in a blender, in batches, until very smooth.

Return the soup to the saucepan and reheat, adding the remaining broth as needed, until the soup reaches the desired consistency. Season to taste with salt and pepper.

Garnish with snipped basil leaves and serve.

Note: This soup freezes very well. When reheating, whisk it as it begins to boil to bring back the creamy texture.

TOMATO AND BELL PEPPER SOUP WITH BASIL GARNISH

• Makes 12 servings

This soup has a beautiful orange color and a slightly spicy taste, and it is equally good served hot or at room temperature. To make it less piquant, substitute jalapeño pepper for the red chile. I love the basil garnish, but you can omit this if time is short. Because everything can be prepared in advance, this dish is ideal when you are expecting many guests.

SOUP
3 red bell peppers
1 small red chile or jalapeño pepper (see note)
4 pounds (1.80 kg) ripe tomatoes
4 tablespoons extra virgin olive oil
2 garlic cloves, coarsely chopped
3 cups (750 ml) vegetable broth
Kosher salt
Freshly ground black pepper

GARNISH
4 cups (160 g) loosely packed fresh basil leaves
3 tablespoons extra virgin olive oil
Kosher salt
Freshly ground black pepper

TO MAKE THE SOUP: Cut the bell peppers in half lengthwise, then core and seed them. Cut them into pieces. Cut the chile in half lengthwise and seed it. Cut into pieces. Core the tomatoes, cut them in half widthwise and gently squeeze out the seeds. (Some seeds will remain.) Cut the tomatoes into pieces.

Heat the oil in a saucepan. Add the garlic and chili or jalapeño pepper and sauté for 2 minutes over low heat. Add the bell peppers, tomatoes, and broth and bring to a boil over high heat. Lower the heat, cover, and cook for 20 minutes. Cool the soup a little. Purée the soup in a blender, in batches, for several minutes until silky smooth. (All traces of the skin from the peppers and tomatoes should be gone.) Season to taste with salt and pepper.

TO MAKE THE GARNISH: Place the basil leaves in a food processor. Add oil and pulse until smooth. Season to taste with salt and pepper.

Before serving, reheat the soup and ladle it into bowls. Garnish with 1 teaspoon of the basil purée.

Notes: When seeding chiles or jalapeño peppers, I advise wearing thin plastic gloves to avoid irritating your skin or your eyes.

This soup freezes well. When reheating, whisk it as it begins to boil to bring back the creamy texture

BEET SOUP

• Makes 6 servings

With their magnificent color, delicious flavor, and vitamin richness, beets are one of my favorite vegetables. In the summer I serve this soup at room temperature; in the winter I like it hot.

1¼ pounds (570 g) beets, plus 1 small beet for garnish
2 tablespoons extra virgin olive oil
1 small red onion, sliced
2 garlic cloves, sliced
1 McIntosh apple, peeled and sliced
4½ cups (1.08 liters) vegetable broth
2 tablespoons apple cider vinegar
1 tablespoon dark brown sugar
Kosher salt
Freshly ground black pepper

Peel and slice the beets (see note).

Heat the oil in a medium saucepan. Add the onion, garlic, and apple and sauté for 5 minutes. Add the beets and broth. Bring to a boil over high heat. Lower the heat and cook, covered, for about 30 minutes, until the beets are tender. Cool a little.

While the soup is cooking, wrap the reserved beet tightly in foil. Bake in a toaster oven at 400°F (205°C) for 30 minutes, or until just tender when pierced with the tip of a paring knife. Cool, slip off the skin, and grate.

Purée the soup in a blender until very smooth. Season to taste with the vinegar, sugar, salt, and pepper.

To serve, garnish with the grated beet.

Note: I always wear thin plastic gloves when I work with beets, as this avoids staining my fingers with beet juice, which can be hard to remove.

CELERY ROOT AND PORCINI SOUP

• Makes 10 generous servings

This wholesome soup is a blend of two distinct (and delicious) tastes—mushrooms and celery root. A touch of spice makes it even nicer.

1 ounce (28 g) dried porcini mushrooms
1¾ cups (420 ml) boiling water
1½ pounds (680 g) celery root
3 stalks celery
4 tablespoons extra virgin olive oil
2 onions, sliced
2 garlic cloves, sliced
1 carrot, sliced
⅛ teaspoon crushed red pepper
6½ cups (1.56 liters) vegetable broth
Kosher salt
Freshly ground black pepper

Place the dried mushrooms in a small bowl and pour the boiling water over them. Cover and let stand for 20 minutes.

Remove the reconstituted mushrooms with a slotted spoon. Squeeze all the liquid back into the bowl and set the mushrooms aside. Strain the mushroom liquid through a paper-lined sieve into another small bowl. Set aside.

Peel the celery root and celery with a vegetable peeler and cut them into thick slices.

In a large saucepan, heat the oil. Add the onions, garlic, carrot, celery, celery root, and crushed pepper. Sauté for 5 minutes, stirring occasionally. Add the mushrooms, mushroom liquid, and 6 cups (1.50 liters) of the broth. Bring to a boil over high heat; lower the heat and cook, covered, for about 30 minutes, until the vegetables are tender.

Cool a little. Purée in a blender, in batches, until smooth. Return the soup to the saucepan and reheat, adding the remaining broth as needed, until the soup reaches the desired consistency. Season to taste with salt and pepper.

MUSHROOM SOUP WITH SOY MILK

• Makes 6 servings

This is an unusual soup inspired by the cuisine of a region of Eastern European where mushrooms grow wild in the forests and are particularly aromatic and plentiful. The texture is wonderfully creamy, but no cream or milk is used in preparing it.

1 ounce (28 g) dried Polish mushrooms (see note)
1 cup (250 ml) boiling water
½ pound (225 g) white mushrooms
¼ pound (113 g) cremini mushrooms
¼ pound (113 g) shiitake mushrooms, stems removed
3 leeks
3 tablespoons extra virgin olive oil
2 garlic cloves, sliced
2 cups (500 ml) vegetable broth
4 tablespoons dry white wine
½ cup (125 ml) soy milk
Kosher salt
Freshly ground black pepper
Finely snipped dill, for garnish

Place the dried mushrooms in a small bowl and pour the boiling water over them. Cover and let stand for 20 minutes.

Remove the reconstituted mushrooms with a slotted spoon. Squeeze all the liquid back into the bowl and set the mushrooms aside. Strain the mushroom liquid through a paper-lined sieve into another small bowl. Set aside.

Wipe the white, cremini, and shiitake mushrooms with a damp paper towel and quarter them. Cut off and discard the roots and tough, dark green leaves of the leeks. Cut the white and light green parts into thick slices. Place in a sieve and rinse thoroughly under cold running water to remove any sand.

Heat the oil in a medium saucepan. Add the leeks and garlic. Cover and simmer for about 5 minutes, until the leeks are just tender. Add the mushrooms, mushroom liquid, broth, and wine. Bring to a boil over high heat. Lower the heat and cook, covered, for 15 minutes.

Cool a little. Purée the soup coarsely in a blender. Return the soup to the saucepan, add the soy milk, and heat. Season to taste with salt and pepper.

Before serving, garnish with the snipped dill.

Note: You can usually find dried Polish mushrooms in specialty food shops. It they are not available, substitute dried porcini mushrooms.

BARLEY SOUP WITH MISO

• Makes 12 servings

This is a delicious variation on the traditional mushroom-barley soup that most of us know (and love) from childhood. The addition of miso adds a delicate Asian flavor; the bright green dill, a nice jolt of color.

> 2 medium onions
> 3 garlic cloves
> 4 celery stalks, peeled
> 4 medium carrots, peeled
> 1 pound (450 g) white mushrooms
> 3 tablespoons extra virgin olive oil
> ½ cup (100 g) medium pearl barley
> 8 cups (2 liters) vegetable broth
> 1 bunch fresh dill
> 2 tablespoons barley miso paste (see note)
> Kosher salt
> Freshly ground black pepper

It is easy to chop the vegetables in a food processor. Quarter the onions and garlic, and pulse in the food processor until coarse; remove to a bowl. Cut the celery and carrots into large pieces. Pulse them separately until coarse, and add to the onions and garlic. Wipe the mushrooms with a damp paper towel and cut them in quarters. Pulse until coarse, and set aside. (If you chop everything together, the vegetables will become mushy.)

Heat the oil in a large saucepan. Sauté the onions, garlic, celery, and carrots for 1 minute. Add the barley and broth and bring to a boil over high heat. Lower the heat and cook, covered, for 15 minutes.

Add the mushrooms to the soup along with half of the dill. Cook for another 15 minutes, or until the barley is tender. Remove and discard the dill. Stir in the miso and season to taste with salt and pepper.

Snip the remaining dill for garnish.

Note: You can buy barley miso in most heath-food stores.

CHESTNUT AND MUSHROOM SOUP

• Makes 10 generous servings

I recommend making this festive soup in the late fall, especially around the Thanksgiving holiday, when peeled roasted chestnuts are readily available.

1 ounce (28 g) dried porcini mushrooms
1 cup (250 ml) boiling water
1 pound (450 g) white mushrooms
4 tablespoons extra virgin olive oil
1 onion, coarsely chopped
3 garlic cloves, coarsely chopped
One 14.8-ounce (420 g) jar peeled roasted chestnuts
6 cups (1.50 liters) vegetable broth
Kosher salt
Freshly ground black pepper
Snipped chives, for garnish

Place the dried mushrooms in a small bowl and pour the boiling water over them. Cover and let stand for 20 minutes.

Remove the reconstituted mushrooms with a slotted spoon. Squeeze all the liquid back into the bowl and set the mushrooms aside. Strain the mushroom liquid through a paper-lined sieve into another small bowl. Set aside.

Wipe the white mushrooms with a damp paper towel and quarter them.

Heat the oil in a medium saucepan. Add the onion and garlic and sauté, covered, over low heat for 3 minutes. Add all the mushrooms and chestnuts and sauté for another 3 minutes. Add the mushroom liquid and vegetable broth. Bring to a boil over high heat. Lower the heat and cook, covered, for 30 minutes. Cool a little.

Purée in a blender, in batches, until smooth. Return the soup to the saucepan and season to taste with salt and pepper.

Before serving, garnish with chives.

GREEN BEAN AND ALMOND SOUP

• Makes 8 generous servings

Green beans, almonds, and truffle oil are an unusual combination of ingredients, and they give this soup a wonderful texture and a delicious, almost exotic, taste. The truffle oil is optional, but I encourage you to give it a try. Though I often make this soup for special-occasion dinners, it is so easy to prepare you can really serve it anytime.

2 onions, quartered
1 garlic clove, quartered
2 carrots, peeled
2 celery stalks, peeled
1 pound (450 g) green beans
4 tablespoons extra virgin olive oil
6 cups (1.50 liters) vegetable broth
½ cup (75 g) blanched almonds, finely ground (see note)
Kosher salt
Freshly ground black pepper
Truffle oil

It is easy to chop the onions, garlic, carrots, and celery in a food processor. Pulse the onions and garlic until coarse; remove to a small bowl. Cut the carrots into large pieces and pulse until coarse; add them to the onions and garlic. Cut the celery into large pieces and pulse until coarse; add them to the other vegetables. (If you chop everything together, the vegetables will become mushy.) Cut the green beans in half.

Heat the olive oil in a medium saucepan. Add the onions, garlic, carrots, and celery and sauté over low heat, stirring occasionally, until they begin to turn golden. Add the green beans and stir for about 5 minutes. Add 5½ cups (1.38 liters) of the broth and bring to a boil over high heat. Lower the heat and simmer, covered, about 30 minutes, until the vegetables are soft. Stir in the almonds.

Cool a little. Purée the soup in a blender, in batches, until smooth. Return it to the saucepan and heat, adding the remaining broth as needed, until the soup reaches the desired consistency. Season to taste with salt and pepper.

Before serving, pour a few drops of truffle oil into each bowl.

Note: I use a Mouli grater to grind such a small amount of almonds.

FISH SOUP WITH VEGETABLES

• Makes 12 servings

This is a lovely, nutritious one-pot winter dish, perfect when you are expecting many guests. While at first glance the recipe may seem a bit intimidating, it is not complicated or overly time-consuming—and you can make it in two stages.

FISH STOCK
Frames (heads and bones) and skin from 5 pounds (2.27 kg) various kinds of exclusively white fish, such as scrod, cod, or flounder
3 leeks
5 cups (1.25 liters) cold water
1 cup (250 ml) dry white wine
1 carrot, peeled and cut in large pieces
1 onion, quartered
1 garlic clove
1 fennel bulb, quartered
2 bay leaves
6 flat-leaf parsley sprigs
7 black peppercorns

SOUP
4 pounds (1.80 kg) skinless halibut fillet
Kosher salt
3 leeks
6 plum tomatoes
1½ pounds (680 g) Yukon gold potatoes
Strained fish stock, from above
4 garlic cloves, minced
½ teaspoon saffron threads
Freshly ground black pepper
1 cup (40 g) loosely packed flat-leaf parsley, finely chopped, for garnish

TO MAKE THE FISH STOCK: Thoroughly rinse the fish frames (heads and bones) and skin and place in a large stockpot.

Cut off and discard the roots and tough, dark green leaves of the leeks. Cut the white and light green parts into small cubes. Place in a sieve and rinse thoroughly under cold running water to remove any sand. Add the leeks to the fish frames.

Add the water, wine, carrot, onion, garlic, and fennel to the fish frames. Bring to a boil over high heat. Skim the foam as it rises to the surface.

Add the bay leaves, parsley, and peppercorns. Lower the heat and simmer, partially covered, for 45 minutes. Cool.

When the stock has cooled, double a piece of cheesecloth, wet it with cold water, wring it dry, and place it in a sieve set over a large bowl. Strain the stock through the cheesecloth. When done, twist the cheesecloth to extract all the liquid and flavor from the fish and vegetables. Discard the cheesecloth and its contents.

Rinse the stockpot and return the strained stock to it. Boil briskly, uncovered, until the stock is reduced by one-third. The stock will be very strong. (The recipe can be made in advance up to this point. The stock can be refrigerated for several days or frozen.)

TO MAKE THE SOUP: Cut the halibut into 1½-inch (4 cm) cubes. Sprinkle them with 1 table-spoon salt and refrigerate.

Cut off and discard the roots and tough, dark green leaves of the leeks. Cut the white and light green parts into ½-inch (13 mm) cubes. Place in a sieve and rinse thoroughly under cold running water to remove any sand.

Bring a pot of water to a boil. Drop the tomatoes into the boiling water, bring the water back to a boil, and drain. Core the tomatoes and slip off the skin. Cut the tomatoes in half widthwise and squeeze gently to remove the seeds. (Some seeds will remain.) Cut into ½-inch (13 mm) cubes.

Peel the potatoes and cut them into 1½-inch (4 cm) cubes.

Bring the strained stock to a boil. Add the leeks, tomatoes, potatoes, garlic, and saffron. Simmer, covered, until the potatoes are tender, about 10 minutes. (You can prepare the recipe in advance up to this point.)

Before serving, return the fish to room temperature. Bring the soup to a boil, add the fish, and stir. Return to a boil and remove from the heat. At this point, the inside of the fish will have just begun to turn opaque; it will continue cooking in the hot soup.

Season to taste with salt and pepper.

TO SERVE: Ladle into individual bowls and garnish with parsley.

SALADS

DAIRY
CANNELLINI BEAN SALAD
CHICKPEA AND FETA SALAD
MEDITERRANEAN COUSCOUS AND LENTIL SALAD

MEAT
CHICKEN SALAD WITH THYME
CHICKEN SALAD WITH RADICCHIO AND PINE NUTS
CHICKEN, BLACK BEAN, AND CORN SALAD

PAREVE
CHICKPEA AND BULGUR SALAD
ANNA'S COLESLAW
SAVOY CABBAGE SALAD
NAPA CABBAGE SALAD
ASIAN CABBAGE SALAD
CARROT SALAD
RAW BEET SALAD
BLACK BEAN SALAD
BLACK BEAN AND QUINOA SALAD
BARLEY SALAD
LENTIL SALAD
RICE SALAD

SALAD DRESSINGS:
BALSAMIC VINAIGRETTE
SESAME-GINGER DRESSING
MAYONNAISE

CANNELLINI BEAN SALAD

- Makes 4 appetizer servings
- Makes 2 luncheon servings

This is a wholesome, tasty winter salad that I like to serve warm over a bed of mixed greens. Because it uses canned cannellini beans, it is also remarkably easy to make. The *soffritto*—an Italian term referring to the garlic, onion, and rosemary sautéed in olive oil— adds a wonderful depth to the flavor.

3 tablespoons extra virgin olive oil, plus more for dressing the garnish
3 garlic cloves, finely chopped
1 small red onion, finely chopped
Leaves from 10 rosemary sprigs, chopped
One 15.5-can (440 g) Goya cannellini beans, drained
3 tablespoons seasoned rice vinegar
Kosher salt
Freshly ground black pepper
Mixed greens
Extra virgin olive oil
Cherry tomatoes
Shavings of Parmesan cheese, for garnish

Heat the oil in a medium saucepan. Add the garlic, onion, and rosemary. Cook over low heat, covered, for 5 minutes, or until the onions are soft. Add the beans and vinegar and mix thoroughly. Remove from the heat and season to taste with salt and pepper.

Place the warm beans on a bed of greens and cherry tomatoes dressed with extra virgin olive oil, salt, and pepper. Sprinkle with Parmesan.

CHICKPEA AND FETA SALAD

- Makes 8 appetizer servings
- Makes 6 luncheon servings

With its mix of red, green, and white ingredients, this makes a colorful luncheon dish or appetizer. I love to make it in the summer when fresh herbs are plentiful.

1 pound (450 g) dried chickpeas
2 kirby cucumbers
2 small red chiles
1 medium red onion, finely chopped
1 cup (40 g) loosely packed fresh mint leaves, finely chopped
1 cup (40 g) loosely packed cilantro leaves
Mâche or arugula
½ pound (227 g) feta, cut into small cubes (see note)

LEMON–OLIVE OIL DRESSING
5 to 6 tablespoons (75 to 90 ml) freshly squeezed lemon juice
Grated zest of one lemon
4 tablespoons extra virgin olive oil, plus more for dressing the garnish
1 tablespoon honey
Kosher salt
Freshly ground black pepper

Place the chickpeas in a bowl, cover with cold water, and soak overnight.

Drain the chickpeas and place them in a large saucepan with enough water to cover. Bring to a boil over high heat. Lower the heat and cook, partially covered, for 35 minutes, or until they are soft. Drain in a sieve and place in a large bowl.

Trim the ends of the cucumbers. Cut the cucumbers in half lengthwise and remove the seeds. Cut the cucumbers into ½-inch (13 mm) cubes. Combine them with the chickpeas.

Cut the chiles in half lengthwise, then core, seed, and finely chop (see note). Combine them with the chickpeas and cucumbers, and add the onion, mint, and cilantro.

TO MAKE THE DRESSING: Mix the lemon juice and zest, oil, and honey. Toss with the salad and season to taste with salt and pepper. Place the dressed salad on a bed of mâche sprinkled with extra virgin olive oil. Top with the feta and serve.

Notes: There are many varieties of feta, but I prefer the milder variety.

When seeding chili peppers, I advise wearing thin plastic gloves to avoid irritating your skin or your eyes.

MEDITERRANEAN COUSCOUS AND LENTIL SALAD

• Makes 8 appetizer servings
• Makes 6 luncheon servings

Because lentils don't require presoaking, this salad is easy to prepare and is certainly one of my favorites, especially in the summer. It looks pretty plated on a bed of lettuce, topped with cubed feta and cherry tomatoes.

1 cup (400 g) French green lentils
2½ cups (625 ml) water
3 tablespoons extra virgin olive oil, plus more for dressing the lettuce
Kosher salt
2 garlic cloves
4 scallions, including green parts, thinly sliced
1 cup (175 g) couscous, preferably whole wheat
2 tablespoons freshly squeezed lemon juice
Freshly ground black pepper
Bibb or Boston lettuce
Cherry tomatoes, halved
¾ pound (340 g) feta, cut into small cubes (see note)

Place the lentils and 1½ cups (375 ml) water in a small saucepan. Bring to a boil. Lower the heat, and cook, covered, for about 25 minutes, until the lentils are tender. (If some water still remains, drain the lentils in a sieve.) Transfer the lentils to a bowl and toss with 1 tablespoon of the oil and 1 teaspoon salt.

Coarsely chop the garlic cloves on a cutting board. Sprinkle them with kosher salt and, using a knife, crush them into a paste. Add the garlic paste to the lentils along with the scallions.

Bring another cup (250 ml) of water to a boil in the saucepan. Sprinkle the couscous over the water, lower the heat, and cook for 2 minutes. Remove from heat and let the couscous stand for another 2 minutes. Add the remaining 2 tablespoons oil and 1 teaspoon of salt and fluff the grains with a fork.

Add the couscous to the lentils. Season to taste with lemon juice, salt, and pepper.

Place the salad on a bed of lettuce sprinkled with extra virgin olive oil. Surround the salad with cherry tomatoes. Top with the feta and serve.

Note: There are many varieties of feta, but I prefer the milder variety.

CHICKEN SALAD WITH THYME

• Makes 2 servings

I like to serve this simple but elegant salad on top of dressed greens, accompanied by any raw vegetables I happen to have on hand. This dish also goes well with steamed haricots verts.

2 boneless, skinless chicken breasts (about 6 ounces/170 g each)
1 garlic clove
Kosher salt
2 tablespoons freshly squeezed lemon juice
½ teaspoon grated lemon zest
1 tablespoon extra virgin olive oil, plus more for dressing the garnish
Leaves from 10 thyme sprigs
½ teaspoon coarsely ground black pepper
Extra virgin olive oil, for serving
Mixed, dressed greens, for serving
Sliced cucumbers, olives, cherry tomatoes, red peppers, or red onions, for garnish

Pat the chicken breasts dry with paper towels. Place them in a glass or nonreactive dish.

Coarsely chop the garlic on a cutting board. Sprinkle it with ¼ teaspoon salt and, using a knife, crush it into a paste.

In a small bowl, combine the garlic paste, lemon juice and zest, oil, and thyme leaves. Season to taste with salt and pepper. Pour the marinade over the chicken, cover, and refrigerate for 3 to 4 hours, turning once.

Preheat the broiler. Set the rack in the broiler pan and cover it completely with heavy foil. Meanwhile, bring the marinated chicken breasts to room temperature.

Make a shallow "basket" with a piece of heavy foil, crimping it at the corners so that that the juices don't spill out. Set the basket on the broiler rack, arrange the chicken in it, and place the pan in the oven (or broiling unit) as close as possible to the heat source. (See Notes on Techniques, page 351.) Broil the chicken for 5 minutes. Turn and broil for another 2 to 3 minutes. The chicken should be slightly pink on the inside. Wrap in the lining foil and let rest for a minute.

TO SERVE: Remove the chicken from the foil and cut it on the diagonal into medium slices. Place on a bed of greens, dressed with olive oil, salt, and pepper. Serve with cucumbers, olives, cherry tomatoes, red peppers, or thinly sliced red onions.

CHICKEN SALAD WITH RADICCHIO AND PINE NUTS

• Makes 6 servings

This is a colorful and delicious salad with an interesting mixture of textures and tastes. The currants and pine nuts add an unusual Mediterranean piquancy.

1 small red onion, very thinly sliced
6 boneless, skinless chicken breasts (about 6 ounces/170 g each)
2 tablespoons extra virgin olive oil, for greasing the chicken
Kosher salt
Freshly ground black pepper
1 head radicchio, shredded
1 to 2 bunches arugula, leaves torn if they are large
½ cup (20 g) loosely packed flat-leaf parsley, finely chopped

SWEET AND SOUR DRESSING
⅓ cup (80 ml) extra virgin olive oil
½ cup (70 g) pine nuts
½ cup (115 g) raisins or currants
2 tablespoons Marsala wine
2 tablespoons balsamic vinegar

Place the onion slices in a small bowl and cover with cold water. Let stand for 30 minutes. Drain and pat dry. Place in a large serving bowl.

Pat the chicken dry with paper towels and grease with oil. Season lightly with salt and pepper.

Place each chicken breast in the center of a piece of cling wrap and wrap it so that it is completely covered. Place the packages in a steamer, cover, and steam over high heat for about 9 minutes. (The inside of the chicken should still be pale pink.) Turn off the heat and let stand for 1 minute.

Remove the chicken and cool, still wrapped.

When cool, unwrap the chicken and cut it on the diagonal into thin strips. Place in the bowl with the onions.

TO MAKE THE DRESSING: Heat the oil in a saucepan. Add the pine nuts and raisins and sauté over low heat until the pine nuts are lightly golden. Remove from the heat and add the Marsala and vinegar.

Add the radicchio, arugula, and parsley to the chicken and onions and toss with the dressing. Season to taste with salt and pepper.

CHICKEN, BLACK BEAN, AND CORN SALAD

• Makes 8 servings

This colorful salad with fresh corn and tomatoes makes a lovely summer luncheon dish. I like to serve it with Bibb or romaine lettuce.

> **6 boneless, skinless chicken breasts (about 6 ounces/170 g each)**
> **4 tablespoons extra virgin olive oil, plus more for dressing the lettuce**
> **Kosher salt**
> **Freshly ground black pepper**
> **One 15.5-ounce (440 g) can Goya black beans, drained**
> **Kernels cut from 3 ears cooked corn**
> **1 small red onion, finely chopped**
> **12 cherry tomatoes, halved**
> **5 garlic cloves, minced**
> **1 teaspoon ground cumin**
> **3 tablespoons balsamic vinegar**
> **½ cup (20 g) tightly packed flat-leaf parsley, finely chopped**
> **¼ teaspoon wasabi powder**
> **4 tablespoons freshly squeezed lemon juice**
> **Bibb lettuce leaves or shredded romaine lettuce**

Pat the chicken dry with paper towels and grease with 2 tablespoons of the oil. Season lightly with salt and pepper.

Place each chicken breast in the center of a piece of cling wrap and wrap it so that it is completely covered. Place the packages in a steamer, cover, and steam over high heat for about 9 minutes. (The inside of the chicken should still be pale pink.) Turn off the heat and let stand for 1 minute.

Remove the chicken and cool, still wrapped.

When cool, unwrap the chicken and cut it on the diagonal into thin strips. Place the chicken into a large bowl and add the beans, corn, onion, and tomatoes.

Heat the remaining oil in a small skillet over medium heat. Add the garlic and sauté until it just begins to color. Add the cumin and stir until it becomes fragrant. Remove from the heat and add to the chicken. Add the vinegar, parsley, and wasabi and mix well. Season to taste with lemon juice, salt, and pepper.

Serve with greens dressed with olive oil, salt, and pepper.

CHICKPEA AND BULGUR SALAD

• Makes 6 to 8 servings

This nutritious and tasty salad requires no cooking and goes with any kind of poultry or meat.

1 cup (135 g) coarse-grind bulgur
1 cup (250 ml) boiling water
2 garlic cloves
Kosher salt
2 scallions
3 kirby cucumbers
One 15.5-ounce (440 g) can Goya chickpeas, drained
3 tablespoons extra virgin olive oil
1 cup (40 g) loosely packed flat leaf parsley, finely chopped
3 tablespoons freshly squeezed lemon juice
1 teaspoon paprika
Freshly ground black pepper

Place the bulgur in a medium bowl and add the boiling water. Cover and let stand for 25 minutes, or until the bulgur is tender and the water has been absorbed. (If some water still remains, drain the bulgur in a sieve and return it to the bowl.)

Coarsely chop the garlic cloves on a cutting board. Sprinkle them with kosher salt and, using a knife, crush them into a paste. Add the garlic paste to the bulgur.

Cut the scallions, including the green part, into thin slices. Trim the ends of the cucumbers. Slice them in half lengthwise, remove the seeds, and cut the cucumbers into small cubes. Combine the scallions and cucumbers with the bulgur. Add the chickpeas, oil, and parsley and mix well.

Season to taste with the lemon juice, paprika, salt, and pepper.

ANNA'S COLESLAW

• Makes 12 servings

I love coleslaw, and this is, hands down, my favorite recipe. Delicious, nutritious, and easy, it is made in the Eastern European style without mayonnaise.

> 1 small head cabbage (about 1½ pounds/680 g)
> 1 carrot
> 3 tablespoons vegetable oil
> 3 tablespoons freshly squeezed lemon juice
> 1½ tablespoons sugar
> 1 teaspoon kosher salt
> Freshly ground black pepper

Discard the tough outer leaves of the cabbage. Cut the cabbage in half, then into quarters. Holding onto the core, finely shred the cabbage (see note) into a large bowl. Peel and grate the carrot, and combine with the cabbage.

In a small bowl, mix the oil, lemon juice, sugar, salt, and black pepper. Pour the dressing over the cabbage and carrot and toss. Season to taste.

Note: I use a mandoline to shred the cabbage, as I find it much easier to handle than a knife.

SAVOY CABBAGE SALAD

• Makes 6 servings

This is a nice change from the coleslaw that most of us are familiar with. The touch of Oriental flavor, along with the capers, give it an unusual taste and texture.

> 1 small head savoy cabbage (about 1 pound/450 g)
> 3 tablespoons seasoned rice vinegar
> 4 tablespoons vegetable oil
> 3 tablespoons drained small capers
> ½ cup (20 g) loosely packed flat-leaf parsley, coarsely chopped
> Kosher salt
> Freshly ground black pepper

Discard the tough outer leaves of the cabbage. Cut the cabbage in half, then into quarters. Holding onto the core, finely shred the cabbage (see note) into a large bowl. Add the vinegar, oil, capers, and parsley and mix well. Season to taste with salt and pepper.

Note: I use a mandoline to shred the cabbage, as I find it is much easier to handle than a knife.

NAPA CABBAGE SALAD

• Makes 6 servings

Napa cabbage is a Chinese cabbage, sweeter and softer than most of the varieties sold here.

1 head napa cabbage (about 1½ pounds /680 g)

RICE-VINEGAR DRESSING
2 garlic cloves
½ teaspoon kosher salt
2 teaspoons Dijon mustard
2 tablespoons seasoned rice vinegar
2 tablespoons low-sodium soy sauce
3 tablespoons vegetable oil
½ teaspoon freshly ground black pepper

Discard the tough outer leaves of the cabbage. Cut the cabbage in half, then into quarters. Holding onto the core, cut the cabbage into strips about ¼-inch (6 mm) wide. Place the cabbage in a large bowl.

TO MAKE THE DRESSING: Coarsely chop the garlic cloves on a cutting board. Sprinkle with kosher salt and, using a knife, crush them into a paste. Put the paste into a bowl and whisk in the mustard, vinegar, soy sauce, oil, and pepper.

Several hours before serving, pour the dressing over the cabbage and toss. The cabbage will absorb the dressing and slightly soften.

Season to taste.

ASIAN CABBAGE SALAD

• Makes 10 servings

Colorful, nutritious, and tasty, this is a perfect complement to any grilled main course—meat, chicken, or fish. Since the salad stays crisp and delicious for a day or so, it's also great for leftovers.

1 small head savoy cabbage (about 1 pound/450 g)
1 head red cabbage (about 1 pound/450 g)
1 teaspoon freshly ground black pepper
1 carrot
3 scallions
1 yellow bell pepper
½ cup (20 g) loosely packed cilantro leaves
1 teaspoon kosher salt

DRESSING
3 tablespoons freshly squeezed lime juice
2 tablespoons low-sodium soy sauce
1 tablespoon sesame oil
2 tablespoons extra virgin olive oil
1 tablespoon honey
1-inch (2.5 centimeter) piece ginger, peeled and grated
¼ teaspoon crushed red pepper

Discard the tough outer leaves of the cabbages. Cut the cabbages in half, then into quarters. Holding onto the core, finely shred the cabbages (see note) into a large bowl. Add salt and pepper. Peel and grate the carrot. Cut the scallions, including the green part, into thin slices. Cut the bell pepper in half lengthwise, then core and seed it. Cut it into thin slices. Add the carrot, scallions, bell pepper, and cilantro to the shredded cabbage.

Mix the dressing ingredients in a small bowl and toss with the cabbage and vegetables. Season to taste.

Note: I use a mandoline to shred the cabbages, as I find it much easier to handle than a knife.

CARROT SALAD

• Makes 8 generous servings

Sunflower seeds and chives make this carrot salad a little different. I usually serve it as a side dish, but its bright color makes it very attractive on a buffet table alongside other salads. It goes well with almost any kind of poultry or meat.

8 medium carrots (about 2½ pounds/1.25 kg)
4 tablespoons snipped chives
1 cup (145 g) roasted sunflower seeds (see note)
⅓ cup (80 ml) freshly squeezed lemon juice
1 tablespoon sugar
1 teaspoon kosher salt
½ teaspoon freshly ground black pepper
4 tablespoons extra virgin olive oil

Peel the carrots and grate them in a food processor fitted with the medium grating attachment. Remove them to a large bowl and add the chives and sunflower seeds. Whisk together the lemon juice, sugar, salt, pepper, and oil. Pour the dressing over the carrots and mix well. Let rest for a few minutes, then adjust the seasoning.

Note: You can usually buy sunflower seeds already roasted. If not, buy the seeds raw and bake them in a toaster oven on the lowest setting for about 5 minutes, until golden brown and just crisp, turning once.

RAW BEET SALAD

• Makes 4 to 5 servings

Beets seem to me a neglected vegetable, but they are so tasty and so healthful that I try to serve them to my family and friends as often as I can. This salad is made with raw beets, and it tastes even better the second day. Because of its rich color, it makes an attractive dish on a buffet table.

> **4 medium beets, peeled (see note)**
> **2 tablespoons balsamic vinegar**
> **2 tablespoons extra virgin olive oil**
> **1 tablespoon Dijon mustard**
> **¾ cup (30 g) loosely packed flat-leaf parsley, finely chopped**
> **Kosher salt**
> **Freshly ground black pepper**

Quarter the beets and place them in a food processor. Pulse until semifine. Transfer to a bowl and stir in the vinegar, oil, mustard, parsley, salt, and pepper. Season to taste.

Note: I always wear thin plastic gloves when I work with beets, as this avoids staining my fingers with beet juice, which can be hard to remove.

BLACK BEAN SALAD

- Makes 8 appetizer servings
- Makes 6 luncheon servings

Since black beans are so rich in antioxidants and fiber, as well as flavor, I tend to serve them frequently—in soups, side dishes, and, as here, in salads. This is one of my favorites. The avocado, cilantro, and jalapeño pepper give it a Southwestern twist, which is festive at any time of year.

½ pound (227 g) dried black beans
3 tablespoons extra virgin olive oil
2 plum tomatoes
1 jalapeño pepper (see note)
2 garlic cloves
Kosher salt
1 small red onion, finely chopped
2 firm ripe avocados
½ cup (20 g) loosely packed cilantro leaves
3 tablespoons freshly squeezed lemon juice
Freshly ground black pepper

Soak the beans overnight in a bowl with enough cold water to cover.

Drain the beans and place in a medium saucepan with enough cold water to cover. Bring to a boil, lower the heat, and simmer, partially covered, for 30 to 40 minutes, until the beans are very tender. Drain and transfer to a medium bowl. Toss with oil and cool.

Bring a pot of water to a boil. Drop the tomatoes into the boiling water; bring the water back to a boil and drain. Core the tomatoes and slip off the skin. Cut the tomatoes in half widthwise and squeeze gently to remove the seeds. (Some seeds will remain.) Chop the tomatoes coarsely and add to the beans.

Cut the jalapeño pepper in half lengthwise, then remove and discard the seeds. Mince and add to the beans and tomatoes.

Coarsely chop the garlic cloves on a cutting board. Sprinkle them with ¼ teaspoon kosher salt and, using a knife, crush them into a paste. Add them to the beans, tomatoes, and jalapeño pepper along with the chopped onion.

Cut the avocados in half, discard the pits, and peel. Cut the avocados into cubes. Add to the salad along with the cilantro. Season to taste with the lemon juice, salt, and pepper.

Note: When seeding jalapeño peppers, I advise wearing thin plastic gloves to avoid irritating your skin or your eyes.

BLACK BEAN AND QUINOA SALAD

• Makes 4 to 6 servings

This tasty dish goes well with any kind of meat, poultry, or fish. I especially like it with Chicken Shish Kebabs (page 202).

½ **cup (114 g) dried black beans**
½ **cup plus 2 tablespoons (155 ml) water**
Kosher salt
½ **cup (85 g) quinoa**
1 jalapeño pepper
1 red bell pepper
½ **cup (80 g) frozen corn, defrosted**
½ **cup (20 g) loosely packed cilantro leaves**
3 tablespoons extra virgin olive oil
3 tablespoons freshly squeezed lime juice
Freshly ground black pepper

Soak the beans overnight in a bowl with enough cold water to cover.

Drain the beans and place in a medium saucepan with enough cold water to cover. Bring to a boil, lower the heat and simmer, partially covered, for 30 to 40 minutes, until the beans are tender. Drain, transfer to a medium bowl, and cool.

In a small saucepan, bring the measured amount of water and ¼ teaspoon salt to a boil over high heat. Sprinkle in the quinoa, lower the heat, cover, and cook gently for about 15 minutes, until all the water is absorbed and the grains are tender. Stir with a fork to fluff the grains. Add the quinoa to the beans.

Cut the jalapeño pepper in half lengthwise, then core and seed it (see note). Mince the pepper and add to the bean-quinoa mixture.

Cut the bell pepper in half lengthwise, then core and seed it. Cut into small cubes. Add to the salad along with the corn and cilantro. Stir in the oil and lime juice, and season to taste with salt and pepper.

Note: When seeding jalapeño peppers, I advise wearing thin plastic gloves to avoid irritating your skin or your eyes.

BARLEY SALAD

• Makes 6 appetizer servings
• Makes 8 side-dish servings

This is a versatile salad that you can serve in a number of ways—as an appetizer over dressed mâche or baby arugula, as a side dish with other vegetables, or as a buffet selection with meat or grilled fish.

1 cup (200 g) medium pearl barley
1½ cups (360 ml) vegetable broth
3 tablespoons extra virgin olive oil
1 yellow or red bell pepper
3 scallions
3 radishes
3 tablespoons seasoned rice vinegar
Kosher salt
Freshly ground black pepper

Place the barley in a medium skillet over medium heat and brown lightly, shaking the pan frequently. It will take about 5 minutes.

Transfer the barley to a small saucepan. Add the broth and bring to a boil. Lower the heat and cook, covered, about 25 minutes, stirring from time to time, until the barley is cooked and the broth is absorbed. (If the liquid is absorbed and the barley is not soft enough, add a few tablespoons of boiling water and continue cooking.) Add the oil. Transfer to a medium bowl and cool.

Cut the bell pepper in half lengthwise, then core and seed it. Cut into small cubes. Add it to the barley.

Cut the scallions, including the green part, into thin slices. Cut the radishes into thin slices. Add both to the barley. Season to taste with the vinegar, salt, and pepper.

LENTIL SALAD

- Makes 4 appetizer servings
- Makes 6 side-dish servings

I love this salad because it is so tasty and attractive. And since the lentils don't require pre-soaking, it is also extremely easy to prepare. I serve it as an appetizer on a bed of dressed greens. As a side dish, I think it goes especially well with turkey or chicken.

½ pound (227 g) brown or green lentils
2 medium carrots
3 scallions
4 tablespoons extra virgin olive oil
2 teaspoons Dijon mustard
3 tablespoons freshly squeezed lemon juice
½ cup (20 g) tightly packed flat-leaf parsley, finely chopped
Kosher salt
Freshly ground black pepper

Place the lentils in a heavy saucepan. Add just enough cold water to cover and bring to a boil. Lower the heat and simmer, covered, for about 10 minutes, until the lentils are soft. (If any water remains, drain the lentils in a sieve.)

Peel the carrots. Using a box grater or the medium attachment of a food processor, grate them coarsely. Finely chop the scallions, including the green part.

Mix the oil, mustard, and lemon juice in a large bowl. Add the hot lentils, toss well, and let cool.

Add the scallions, carrots, parsley, salt, and pepper and mix well. Season to taste. Serve at room temperature.

RICE SALAD

• Makes 6 appetizer servings
• Makes 4 generous luncheon servings

This is a Japanese-style salad that can be a meal in itself. I like to serve it with arugula or watercress, drizzled with some of the Miso Dressing. For another Asian-inspired dressing, see Sesame-Ginger Vinaigrette (page 111).

1 cup (190 g) raw brown rice (see note)
1¼ cups (300 ml) water
½ teaspoon kosher salt
One 14-ounce (400 g) package extra firm tofu
2 scallions
1 yellow or orange bell pepper
8 shiitake mushrooms, stems removed
3 tablespoons vegetable oil
Arugula or watercress, for serving

MISO DRESSING
2 tablespoons barley miso (see note)
2 tablespoons sake
Generous 1½ teaspoons honey
1 tablespoon seasoned rice vinegar
Kosher salt
Freshly ground black pepper

Bring the rice, water, and salt to the boil in a small saucepan. Lower the heat and cook, covered, for 30 minutes, or until the rice is soft. Fluff with a fork. Transfer to a large bowl and cool.

Drain the tofu, pat it dry, and cut into 1-inch (2.5 cm) cubes.

Cut the scallions, including the green part, into thin slices. Cut the bell pepper in half; then core and seed it, and cut into thin slices. Wipe the mushroom caps with a damp paper towel and cut into thin slices.

Heat the wok over medium-high heat. Add 1 tablespoon of the oil and heat for less than a minute. Add the tofu and scallions and stir-fry about 1 minute. Combine with the rice.

Add the remaining 2 tablespoons oil to the wok and heat. Stir-fry the pepper and mushrooms quickly, about 1 minute. Add to the rice.

TO MAKE THE DRESSING: Combine all the ingredients in a small bowl. Toss the rice with about three-quarters of the dressing. Season to taste. Drizzle the remaining dressing over the greens.

Notes: While you can use regular brown rice to make this dish, I prefer premium Japanese medium-grain brown rice, as it is much creamier than other varieties. It is available in most specialty food stores.

Barley miso is available in most health-food stores.

SALAD DRESSINGS

Greens such as mâche, watercress, frisée, arugula, Bibb, Boston, and romaine lettuces are such a mainstay of daily life that I find it useful to have a variety of dressings on hand.

BALSAMIC VINAIGRETTE

• Makes ⅔ cup (160 ml)

Good vinaigrette is one of the secrets of a good salad. If you combine the ingredients in a blender, the oil doesn't separate from the other ingredients. Keep this dressing refrigerated, but be sure to bring it to room temperature before serving.

4 tablespoons balsamic vinegar
½ teaspoon honey
2 teaspoons Dijon mustard
2 tablespoons freshly squeezed lemon juice
½ cup (125 ml) extra virgin olive oil
½ teaspoon kosher salt
1 teaspoon freshly ground black pepper

Place all the ingredients into a blender and pulse until combined. Season to taste.

SESAME-GINGER DRESSING

• Makes ¾ cup (180 ml)

This dressing is quite flavorful and very light.

1-inch (2.5 cm) piece ginger, peeled and grated
2 tablespoons sesame oil
4 tablespoons seasoned rice vinegar
⅓ cup (80 ml) low-sodium soy sauce
1 tablespoon honey

Combine all the ingredients. This dressing keeps well, refrigerated.

MAYONNAISE

• Makes 1¼ cups (300 ml)

This lightly seasoned mayonnaise makes a good base for other dressings. You can add more mustard or flavor it with garlic, anchovies, capers, or herbs. It keeps for weeks refrigerated in a tightly closed container. I do not think you will ever buy commercial mayonnaise again.

½ cup (125 ml) extra virgin olive oil
½ cup (125 ml) vegetable oil
1 large egg, at room temperature
¼ teaspoon powdered mustard
½ teaspoon kosher salt
1 tablespoon rice vinegar

Combine the olive and vegetable oils in a glass measuring cup. (The spout of the cup makes it easier to control the pouring.)

Place the egg, mustard, and salt in a blender. Remove the plastic knob from the cover of the blender. Turn on the blender and after several seconds, add the vinegar.

Pour in the oil in a very slow stream. As the mixture begins to thicken, add the oil more quickly. One word of advice: Keep the blender running from the beginning of the process to the end, when all the oil has been added. When finished, transfer the mayonnaise to an airtight container and refrigerate.

VEGETABLES, POTATOES & LEGUMES

VEGETABLES, POTATOES & LEGUMES

PAREVE

Spiced Carrots

Roasted Brussels Sprouts

Broccoli with Panko

Chopped Broccoli

Red Cabbage with Capers

Roasted Cauliflower

Stir-Fried Spinach

Vegetable Medley, Asian Style

Simple Ratatouille

Shredded Sweet Potatoes with Cumin and Scallions

Acorn Squash, Sweet and Sour

Roasted Butternut Squash

Sweet Potato Fries

Parsnip and Potato Purée

Grated Potato Pancake

Thin Potato Tart

Potatoes with Garlic and Tarragon

White Bean and Potato Purée

Balsamic Lentils

SPICED CARROTS

• Makes 4 servings

I think carrots are a neglected vegetable and yet a wonderful source of nutrients. This dish has a sweet-and-sour taste and a beautiful color.

One 1-pound (450 g) package baby carrots
⅛ teaspoon ground cumin
¼ teaspoon paprika
1 tablespoon extra virgin olive oil
1 tablespoon freshly squeezed lemon juice
1 tablespoon honey
Kosher salt
Freshly ground black pepper
¼ cup (10 g) loosely packed flat-leaf parsley, finely chopped

Steam the carrots until almost soft, 4 to 5 minutes.

To release the flavors of the spices, cook cumin and paprika in the oil in a medium saucepan, over low heat, for 1 minute. Add the carrots, lemon juice, honey, salt, and pepper and cook for 5 minutes.

Toss with parsley. Season to taste.

ROASTED BRUSSELS SPROUTS

• Makes 6 servings

This is an easy but elegant way of preparing a family favorite.

18 to 24 Brussels sprouts
3 tablespoons extra virgin olive oil
Kosher salt
Freshly ground black pepper
2 tablespoons water

Preheat the oven to 400°F (205°C). Line a baking pan with foil.

Remove and discard the outer leaves of the Brussels sprouts. Trim the ends and cut the sprouts in half lengthwise. Place in the baking pan. Drizzle with the oil and season lightly with salt and pepper. Sprinkle with the water. Bake for 20 minutes. The sprouts should be tender.

BROCCOLI WITH PANKO

• Makes 4 servings

Panko are flaky Japanese breadcrumbs. They are lighter and crunchier than ordinary bread-crumbs, and when they are toasted they transform an ordinary vegetable into something quite special.

> **1 small bunch broccoli, about 3 stalks**
> **3 tablespoons extra virgin olive oil**
> **3 garlic cloves, finely chopped**
> **½ cup (28 g) panko**
> **Kosher salt**
> **Freshly ground black pepper**

Separate the broccoli into florets and set the stems aside for another use. Steam the florets until they are bright green but still crisp to the bite.

Heat the oil in a wok. Add the garlic and sauté over low heat for a few seconds. Add the panko and stir until golden. Add the broccoli and combine well. Season to taste with salt and pepper.

CHOPPED BROCCOLI

• Makes 6 servings

This is an interesting preparation of a rather uninteresting (but quite nutritious) vegetable. The steaming gives the broccoli a beautiful emerald green color.

1 bunch broccoli (about 2 pounds/900 g)
2 tablespoons extra virgin olive oil
Kosher salt
Freshly ground black pepper

Cut the tops off the broccoli and separate them into florets. Peel the stems and cut into small pieces.

Steam the florets and stems for 2 to 3 minutes, until just tender but still quite crisp.

Put the stems in a food processor and pulse until coarsely chopped. Transfer to a medium bowl. Pulse the florets in the food processor until coarsely chopped. Add to the stems.

Heat the oil in a wok or deep skillet. Add the broccoli and, over medium-high heat, quickly stir-fry.

Season to taste with salt and pepper.

RED CABBAGE WITH CAPERS

• Makes 6 servings

This colorful and tasty vegetable is available all year-round. I serve it as a side dish with poultry or meat.

1 small head red cabbage (about 1½ pounds/680 g)
3 tablespoons extra virgin olive oil
2 shallots, thinly sliced
1 tablespoon small capers
2 teaspoons freshly squeezed lemon juice
Kosher salt
Freshly ground black pepper

Discard the tough outer leaves of the cabbage. Cut the cabbage in half, then into quarters. Holding onto the core, finely shred the cabbage (see note).

Heat the oil in a wok or skillet. Add the cabbage and shallots, and cook, covered, over medium heat, until the cabbage is still crisp. Remove from the heat and add the capers. Season to taste with the lemon juice and salt and pepper.

Note: I use a mandoline to shred the cabbage, as I find it much easier to handle than a knife.

ROASTED CAULIFLOWER

• Makes 4 servings

Roasting is an easy and delicious way to transform this reliable standby into a delicious dish.

1 medium head cauliflower (about 2 pounds/900 g)
2 garlic cloves, minced
2 tablespoons extra virgin olive oil
Kosher salt
Freshly ground black pepper

Preheat the oven 400°F (205°C). Line a baking pan with foil.

Cut the stalk and leaves off the cauliflower and discard. Cut the head into small florets. Place the garlic in the baking pan. Arrange the florets on top; drizzle with the oil and season to taste with salt and pepper. Bake for 20 minutes, or until tender.

STIR-FRIED SPINACH

• Makes 6 servings

This is a delicious recipe that captures the very essence of spinach. Now that prewashed spinach is available in almost every supermarket, you can prepare this dish in minutes.

20-ounces (570 g) prewashed spinach
1½ tablespoons pine nuts
2 tablespoons extra virgin olive oil
Kosher salt
Freshly ground black pepper

Break the stems off the spinach leaves and discard.

Roast the pine nuts in a toaster oven on the lowest setting for a minute or two, until they are golden. (Watch them carefully, as they burn quickly.)

Heat a wok over high heat until hot. Add the oil. Add the spinach and stir quickly until it is just wilted, no more than a minute. Season with salt and pepper. With a slotted spoon, transfer the spinach to a serving dish. Sprinkle the pine nuts on top.

VEGETABLE MEDLEY, ASIAN STYLE

• Makes 4-6 servings

This Chinese-inspired dish is best when it is prepared right before serving. But even made an hour or so in advance, it is still delicious.

6 dried shiitake mushrooms (see note)
Boiling water, as needed
½ pound (227 g) bean sprouts
3 scallions
1 small head napa cabbage (about 1 pound/450 g)
3 tablespoons vegetable oil
2 tablespoons low-sodium soy sauce
1 tablespoon sesame oil
Kosher salt
Freshly ground white pepper

Place the dried mushrooms in a small bowl and pour boiling water over them. Cover and let stand for 20 minutes, or until soft.

Discard the liquid and squeeze the mushrooms dry. Cut off and discard the stems. Cut the caps into ½-inch (13 mm) strips.

Remove the tiny brown tips from the bean sprouts. Cut the scallions, including the green part, into ¼-inch-wide (6 mm) slices.

Discard the tough outer leaves of the cabbage. Cut the cabbage into strips about ½ inch (13 mm) wide.

Heat a wok over high heat until hot. Add 1 tablespoon of the vegetable oil and heat. Stir-fry the mushrooms quickly. Add the scallions and continue stir-frying until the scallions are wilted. Transfer the vegetables to a bowl.

Add the remaining 2 tablespoons vegetable oil to the wok and heat. Stir-fry the cabbage and bean sprouts until the cabbage is just beginning to wilt. Combine the mushrooms with the cabbage and sprouts over medium-high heat. Season to taste with the soy sauce, sesame oil, salt, and pepper.

Note: If dried shiitake mushrooms are not available, use fresh ones.

SIMPLE RATATOUILLE

- Makes 6 servings as a side dish
- Makes 4 servings as a luncheon dish

Most ratatouille recipes are time-intensive and call for a long list of seasonal ingredients. This version is easy to prepare and can be made at any time of year. I like to serve it topped with mozzarella.

2 medium zucchini
2 medium yellow squash
1 medium eggplant (about 1¼ pounds/570 g)
4 tablespoons extra virgin olive oil
1 onion, finely chopped
4 garlic cloves, finely chopped
One 14-ounce (400 g) can imported peeled tomatoes
Leaves from 4 rosemary sprigs, coarsely chopped
Kosher salt
Freshly ground black pepper
Mozzarella, grated or cubed, for garnish

Rinse and pat dry the zucchini. Trim the ends and cut in half lengthwise. Cut into 1-inch (2.5 cm) cubes.

Rinse and pat dry the squash. Trim the ends and cut the squash into 1-inch (2.5 cm) cubes.

Peel the eggplant and cut into 1-inch (2.5 cm) cubes.

Heat the oil in a saucepan. Add the onion and garlic and sauté, covered, over low heat until the onion is soft.

Add the zucchini, squash, and eggplant. Increase the heat, and stir until the vegetables are coated with oil. Add the tomatoes; bring to a boil and cover. Lower the heat and, stirring from time to time, cook for about 10 minutes, until the vegetables are soft.

Add the rosemary leaves and season to taste with salt and pepper. Top with mozzarella before serving.

SHREDDED SWEET POTATOES
WITH CUMIN AND SCALLIONS

• Makes 4 to 6 servings

Sweet potatoes have been growing in this country since long before Columbus, so I can honestly say they are more American than apple pie. This is an easy and delicious way of serving them—one that preserves their excellent nutritional qualities and, I think, enhances their flavor.

2 medium sweet potatoes (about 2 pounds/900 g)
2 tablespoons vegetable oil
½ teaspoon ground cumin
2 scallions, including the green part, finely chopped
1 teaspoon freshly squeezed lemon juice
Kosher salt
Freshly ground black pepper

Peel the potatoes and quarter them so they will fit through the feed tube of a food processor. Shred them coarsely using the medium attachment.

Heat the oil in a wok or skillet over medium-high heat. Lower the heat to medium, add the cumin and scallions, and sauté for a few seconds.

Add the potatoes and sauté until almost tender, about 3 minutes. Season to taste with the lemon juice, salt, and pepper.

ACORN SQUASH, SWEET-AND-SOUR

• Makes 6 servings

This is a pretty winter dish that goes very well with any kind of poultry or fish. I often serve it with Glazed Arctic Char (page 167).

> **1 small acorn squash (about 1½ pounds/680 g)**
> **2½ tablespoons extra virgin olive oil**
> **1 tablespoon balsamic vinegar**
> **1½ tablespoons dark brown sugar**

Preheat the oven to 400°F (205°C). Line a baking pan with foil and brush the foil with 1 tablespoon of the oil.

Rinse and pat dry the squash. Trim the ends and discard. Cut the squash in half lengthwise. Scoop out all the seeds and fibrous strings. Cut into ½-inch (13 mm) wedges.

Arrange the wedges in the pan. Brush the squash with the remaining oil, then the vinegar; sprinkle with the sugar.

Bake for 15 minutes, or until the wedges are tender and the sugar has lightly caramelized. Serve warm.

ROASTED BUTTERNUT SQUASH

• Makes 6 servings

This is one of my favorite winter vegetables, and it makes a delicious mosaic of colors when I serve it with other roasted vegetables such as cauliflower, Brussels sprouts, baby carrots, or potatoes.

> **1 medium butternut squash (about 2 pounds/900 g)**
> **2 tablespoons extra virgin olive oil**
> **Kosher salt**
> **Freshly ground black pepper**

Preheat the oven to 450°F (230°C). Line a baking pan with foil.

Trim both ends of the squash. Peel with a vegetable peeler until you see a deep orange color. Cut the squash in half and scoop out the seeds. Cut the squash into 1-inch (2.5 cm) cubes. Arrange the cubes in the pan in a single layer. Sprinkle with the oil and season to taste with salt and pepper.

Bake for 15 minutes, or until tender.

SWEET POTATO FRIES

• Makes 4 servings

Who doesn't love "fries," especially when they are as colorful and nutritious as these? Since they are so tasty, you will probably not be aware they are baked!

**2 tablespoons extra virgin olive oil,
   plus 1 teaspoon for greasing the baking sheet
2 medium sweet potatoes (about 2 pounds/900 g)
Kosher salt
Freshly ground black pepper**

Preheat the oven to 500°F (260°C). Grease a baking sheet with 1 teaspoon of the oil.

Peel the potatoes and slice into rounds about ¼-inch-thick (6 mm). Cut the rounds into ¼-inch (6 mm) strips. Spread the fries on a greased baking sheet and drizzle over the remaining oil. Bake for 10 minutes, or until soft.

Season to taste with salt and pepper.

PARSNIP AND POTATO PURÉE

• Makes 4 servings

I think of this dish as mashed potatoes with half the calories and twice the nutrition and flavor. It is a year-round favorite that goes with everything.

**2 garlic cloves
1 medium parsnip (about ¾ pound/340 g)
1 large Idaho baking potato (about ¾ pound/340 g)
1 medium carrot
1 tablespoon extra virgin olive oil
⅓ cup (80 ml) soy milk
Kosher salt
Freshly ground black pepper**

Peel the garlic and cut in half. Peel the parsnip, potato, and carrot and slice into thick pieces.

Steam all the vegetables for 10 minutes, or until tender.

Place the vegetables in a food processor and, adding the oil and soy milk through the feed tube, pulse until smooth. Season to taste with salt and pepper.

If not serving immediately, keep warm in a double boiler or a 250°F (120°C) oven.

GRATED POTATO PANCAKE

• Makes 12 servings

This large pancake is wonderful when you are expecting a lot of guests. It is fun to serve (you just cut it into cake-like wedges) and it always tastes delicious, not at all greasy. Another plus: You can prepare it ahead of time and reheat before serving.

4 large Idaho baking potatoes
Kosher salt
Freshly ground black pepper
4 tablespoons vegetable oil

Peel and quarter the potatoes. If you are not grating them immediately, place them in a bowl of cold water to prevent discoloration.

Using the medium grating attachment of a food processor, grate the potatoes coarsely. Place in a dish towel and wring dry to remove the liquid. Transfer to a bowl. Season well with salt and pepper.

Heat 2 tablespoons of the oil in a 12-inch (30 cm) nonstick skillet. Add the potatoes, patting them down firmly with a spatula to flatten them and even out the edges. Cook over medium-high heat for about 8 minutes, until the bottom is golden.

Invert the pancake onto a plate and add the remaining 2 tablespoons oil to the skillet to heat. Slide the pancake back into the skillet. Pat it down again with the spatula and cook for another 8 minutes, or until the underside is golden.

Invert onto a platter and cut into the desired number of slices.

THIN POTATO TART

• Makes 4 servings

I love potatoes and find them irresistible in all forms. In this version, they are not peeled (saving you an extra step), but they are still luscious and creamy. The tart can be reheated without losing its crispness.

¾ pound (340 g) Yukon gold potatoes
2 tablespoons extra virgin olive oil
Kosher salt
Freshly ground black pepper

Preheat the oven to 450°F (230°C).

Rinse the potatoes and pat dry. Cut into very thin slices using a mandoline.

Grease a 10-inch (25 cm) nonstick ovenproof skillet with 1 tablespoon of the oil. Starting at the center of the skillet, layer the potatoes in tight overlapping circles until you reach the edge of the pan. Drizzle the remaining oil around the edges of the pan, and season to taste with salt and pepper.

Cook the tart on the stovetop over medium heat for about 10 minutes, until the potatoes have browned on the bottom. Press the potatoes down with a spatula several times as they cook.

Cover the skillet with heavy foil and put it in the oven for 10 minutes. Uncover and bake for another 5 minutes. The bottom will be brown and crisp.

Invert the tart onto a serving plate and cut into wedges.

POTATOES WITH GARLIC AND TARRAGON

• Makes 10 servings

This is a wonderful dish to serve on Friday night or for Passover, when many guests are expected. It is a special favorite with my grandchildren, perhaps because it is so crispy.

4 tablespoons extra virgin olive oil, plus 1 tablespoon for greasing the pan
3½ pounds (1.6 kg) large red-skinned potatoes
3 garlic cloves, thinly sliced
Leaves from 5 tarragon sprigs
Kosher salt
Freshly ground black pepper
1 cup (250 ml) vegetable broth

Preheat the oven to 400°F (205°C). Brush the bottom and the sides of a 9 by 13-inch (23 by 33 cm) baking pan with one tablespoon oil.

Peel the potatoes and cut them into quarters so they will fit through the feed tube of a food processor. If you are not using them immediately, place them in a bowl of cold water to prevent discoloration.

Slice the potatoes, using the medium attachment of the food processor. Spread the sliced potatoes on a dish towel and pat thoroughly to remove the moisture. Transfer the potatoes to a bowl and add the oil, garlic, and tarragon. Season to taste with salt and pepper.

Spread the potatoes in the baking pan and pour the broth over them. Bake for 1 hour. The top layer will be crisp and brown and all the liquid absorbed.

Note: To reheat, warm in a preheated 300°F (150°C) oven for 15 to 20 minutes.

WHITE BEAN AND POTATO PURÉE

• Makes 6 servings

Potato purée is traditionally made with butter and milk or cream. I use beans and soy milk instead, so this version is nutritious as well as delicious and is always a favorite dish. It makes a fine accompaniment to both poultry and meat.

2 medium Idaho baking potatoes (about 1 pound/450 g)
2 garlic cloves, quartered
One 15.5-ounce (440 g) can Goya cannellini beans, drained
2 tablespoons extra virgin olive oil
½ to ¾ cup (120 to 180 ml) soy milk
½ cup (20 g) loosely packed flat-leaf parsley, finely chopped
Kosher salt
Freshly ground black pepper

Peel the potatoes and cut them into thick slices. Steam them until soft, about 10 minutes. Cool.

Place the potatoes in a food processor along with the garlic, beans, and oil, and pulse, slowly adding the soy milk through the feed tube, until the mixture is smooth. Stir in the parsley, and season to taste with salt and pepper.

If not serving right away, transfer the purée to a double boiler to keep warm.

BALSAMIC LENTILS

• Makes 4 servings

Since these lentils do not need to be soaked, only simmered for 20 minutes or so, they always come in handy when I am putting together a quick meal or a last-minute get-together. More reasons to like lentils: They are full of nutrients; they can be used in soups and appetizers as well as in other salads; and they go equally well with meat and poultry.

1 cup (400 g) French green lentils
2 tablespoons extra virgin olive oil
2 red, orange, or yellow bell peppers
¼ cup (10 g) loosely packed flat-leaf parsley, finely chopped
2 tablespoons balsamic vinegar
Kosher salt

Place the lentils in a saucepan. Add cold water to cover and bring to a boil over high heat. Lower the heat to a simmer, and cook, covered, for about 20 minutes, until tender. Drain, transfer to a medium bowl and toss with the oil.

Preheat the broiler.

Set the rack in the broiler pan and cover it completely with heavy foil.

Cut the bell peppers in half lengthwise, then core and seed them. Make a shallow "basket" with a piece of heavy foil, crimping it at the corners so that the liquids don't spill out. (See Notes on Techniques, page 351.) Set the basket on the broiler rack, and arrange the peppers inside, skin side up. Place the broiler pan in the oven (or broiling unit), as close as possible to the heat source. Broil the peppers for about 7 minutes, until the skin is blistered and charred. Cover the peppers with foil and cool. The heat will loosen the skin.

Peel the peppers and cut into small cubes. Combine the peppers with the lentils. Season to taste with the parsley, vinegar, and salt.

PASTA, RICE & GRAINS

DAIRY
LINGUINI WITH PESTO AND ZUCCHINI
ZITI WITH HERBS AND MOZZARELLA
MUSHROOM LASAGNA
RISOTTO

MEAT
SPAGHETTI WITH MEAT SAUCE

PAREVE
RIGATONI WITH BELL PEPPER–TOMATO SAUCE
RIGATONI WITH OLIVES, HERBS, AND ARUGULA
PENNE WITH CAULIFLOWER
PENNE WITH MUSHROOM SAUCE
PENNE WITH UNCOOKED TOMATO SAUCE
FARFALLE WITH PEPPERS AND BASIL
ORECCHIETTE WITH BROCCOLI PESTO
ORECCHIETTE WITH MUSHROOMS AND RADICCHIO
ZITI WITH ROASTED VEGETABLES
SPAGHETTI WITH TUNA
LINGUINI IN OLIVE SAUCE
BARLEY WITH CARROTS, ONIONS, AND PARSLEY
CREAMY COCONUT RICE
SUSHI RICE
QUINOA

TOMATO SAUCES:
WINTER TOMATO SAUCE
MIDSEASON TOMATO SAUCE
SUMMER TOMATO SAUCE

LINGUINI WITH PESTO AND ZUCCHINI

- Makes 6 appetizer servings
- Makes 4 main-course servings

Adding zucchini to this pesto sauce makes an interesting variation on a traditional dish. I like to serve it in the summer at room temperature.

1 cup (40 g) tightly packed fresh basil leaves
2 garlic cloves, quartered
2 tablespoons pine nuts
5 tablespoons extra virgin olive oil
3 medium zucchini
Kosher salt
1 pound (450 g) imported linguini
¾ cup (75 g) grated imported Parmesan cheese
Freshly ground black pepper

Place the basil, garlic, and pine nuts in a food processor. Adding 4 tablespoons of the oil in a stream through the feed tube, pulse until smooth. Transfer to a large bowl.

Trim the ends of the zucchini. Cut the zucchini into strips about 1 inch (2.5 cm) long and ¼-inch (6 mm) thick.

Heat the remaining 1 tablespoon oil in a medium saucepan. Add the zucchini and sauté over high heat for a few seconds. Cool and add to the pesto.

Bring 5 quarts (5 liters) of water to a rolling boil in a large pot. Add 2 tablespoons salt. Add all the linguini at once and stir. Boil briskly, uncovered, for about 5 minutes, until pasta is al dente.

Drain well in a colander. Combine the pasta with the pesto-zucchini sauce. Add the Parmesan. Season to taste with salt and pepper.

ZITI WITH HERBS AND MOZZARELLA

- Makes 6 appetizer servings
- Makes 4 main-course servings

Whenever I make this recipe in the summer, I am always grateful for the freshness of the herbs—basil, parsley, and arugula—that are puréed and tossed with the ziti along with the mozzarella. I serve this dish at room temperature.

4 garlic cloves, unpeeled
2 cups (80 g) tightly packed fresh basil leaves
1 cup (40 g) tightly packed flat-leaf parsley
1 cup (40 g) loosely packed arugula leaves
4 tablespoons extra virgin olive oil
½ pound (227 g) fresh mozzarella
½ teaspoon crushed red pepper
Kosher salt
1 pound (450 g) imported ziti
3 tablespoons freshly squeezed lemon juice
Freshly ground black pepper

Wrap the garlic cloves in foil and bake in a toaster oven at 400°F (205°C) for 15 to 20 minutes, until soft. Cool.

Peel the cloves and place them in a food processor along with the basil, parsley, and arugula. Adding the oil in a stream through the feed tube, pulse until semicoarse. Transfer to a large bowl.

Cut the mozzarella into ½-inch (13 mm) cubes. Add the cheese, along with the crushed pepper, to the herb mixture, and combine.

Bring 5 quarts (5 liters) of water to a rolling boil in a large pot. Add 2 tablespoons salt. Add all the ziti at once and stir. Boil briskly, uncovered, for about 5 minutes, until the pasta is al dente.

Drain in a colander, refresh with cold water, and drain well again. Add the ziti to the herb and mozzarella mixture and combine. Season to taste with the lemon juice, salt, and pepper.

MUSHROOM LASAGNA

• Makes 10 servings

This dish feeds a large, hungry group. The entire dish can be made in advance—in stages or all at once.

TOMATO SAUCE
4 tablespoons extra virgin olive oil
2 medium onions, finely chopped
4 garlic cloves, finely chopped
One 28-ounce (794 g) can imported crushed tomatoes
½ cup (20 g) tightly packed fresh basil leaves, torn into small pieces
¼ cup (10 g) tightly packed flat-leaf parsley, finely chopped
⅛ teaspoon crushed red pepper
Kosher salt
Freshly ground black pepper

FILLING
3 scallions
1 pound (450 g) farmer's cheese
½ pound (227 g) ricotta cheese
½ cup (50 g) grated imported Parmesan cheese
2 large eggs, lightly whisked
½ cup (20 g) tightly packed fresh basil leaves, torn into small pieces
1½ pounds (680 g) white mushrooms
4 tablespoons extra virgin olive oil
Kosher salt
Freshly ground black pepper

1 pound (450 g) imported lasagna
2 tablespoons kosher salt
2 tablespoons unsalted butter
¼ cup (25 g) grated imported Parmesan cheese

TO MAKE THE TOMATO SAUCE: Heat the oil in a medium saucepan. Add the onions and garlic and sauté for about 3 minutes over low heat, until the onions are soft.

Add the tomatoes, basil, parsley, and crushed pepper. Bring to a boil, lower the heat, and simmer, covered, for 20 minutes. Season to taste with salt and pepper. (The tomato sauce can be made in advance and refrigerated or frozen.)

TO MAKE THE FILLING: Finely chop the scallions, including the green part. Combine in a large bowl with the farmer's cheese, ricotta, Parmesan, eggs, and basil.

Wipe the mushrooms with a damp paper towel and cut into thin slices. Heat the oil in a large skillet. Add the mushrooms and stir over high heat until just wilted, about 1 minute. Using a slotted spoon, immediately remove the mushrooms to a small bowl to cool.

Combine the mushrooms with the cheese mixture. Season with salt and pepper. (The filling can be made in advance and refrigerated.)

TO ASSEMBLE: Preheat the oven to 375°F (190°C). Bring 5 quarts (5 liters) of water to a rolling boil in a large pot.

Add the salt and, one by one, the lasagna noodles. Boil briskly, uncovered, for 6 minutes, stirring occasionally. The pasta should be al dente. Drain in a colander and refresh with cold water. Spread the lasagna on a towel in a single layer to dry.

Butter the bottom and sides of a 10 by 15 by 2-inch (25 by 38 by 5-cm) glass, ceramic, or enamel-lined baking pan with 1 tablespoon of the butter. Place a layer of pasta on the bottom of the pan and cover it with half the filling, followed by half of the sauce. Cover with another layer of pasta, the rest of the filling, followed by the rest of the sauce. Top with a final layer of pasta and the remaining butter, cut into small pieces. Sprinkle with Parmesan (see note).

Cover the lasagna with heavy foil and bake 35 to 40 minutes, until it is thoroughly hot.

Notes: It is easier to cut the lasagna with a serrated knife.

If not serving immediately, cover the lasagna with aluminum foil and refrigerate. Before serving, bring it to room temperature and reheat in a preheated 375°F (190°C) oven until hot, about 30 minutes.

RISOTTO

• Makes 4 servings

Most risotto recipes are not only time-consuming to prepare but also intimidating. After many trials, I came up with this version, which is easy and fast and of which I am very proud. You can use it as is, or add just about any vegetable you like, for example mushrooms, asparagus, or green peas.

3 tablespoons (45 g) unsalted butter
4 scallions, including green parts, sliced into thin rounds
1¼ cups (225 g) raw premium-quality Carnaroli or Arborio rice
¾ cup (180 ml) dry white wine
2½ cups (600 ml) vegetable broth
⅓ cup (35 g) grated imported Parmesan cheese, plus more if desired
Kosher salt
Freshly ground black pepper

In a medium enamel-lined saucepan, melt 2 tablespoons (30 g) of the butter. Add the scallions and sauté for 1 minute. Add the rice and keep stirring with a wooden spoon until the rice is coated with butter. Add the wine and stir until all the liquid is absorbed.

In a separate small saucepan, bring the broth to a boil. Add it to the rice. Lower the heat, cover, and cook for 12 to 15 minutes, stirring from time to time. The rice should be a little chewy.

Add the remaining tablespoon (15 g) butter and the Parmesan. Season to taste with salt, pepper, and, if you like, additional Parmesan. Let stand for 2 minutes and serve.

SPAGHETTI WITH MEAT SAUCE

• Makes 6 appetizer servings
• Makes 4 main-course servings

This dish is equally appealing to children and adults. The sauce freezes well, so I always have some on hand.

3 tablespoons extra virgin olive oil
1 onion, finely chopped
4 garlic cloves, finely chopped
½ pound veal (225 g) and ½ pound beef (225 g), ground together
½ cup (125 ml) dry red wine
One 14-ounce (400 g) can peeled imported tomatoes
½ teaspoon crushed red pepper
1 cup (40 g) tightly packed fresh basil leaves, torn in small pieces
1 cup (40 g) loosely packed flat-leaf parsley, coarsely chopped
Kosher salt
Freshly ground black pepper
1 pound (450 g) imported spaghetti

Heat the oil in a large saucepan. Add the onion and garlic and sauté over low heat about 3 minutes, until tender.

Increase the heat, add the meat, and sauté, stirring, until the meat begins to brown. Add the wine and cook over high heat until the wine has evaporated. Add the tomatoes and crushed pepper and simmer, covered, for 20 minutes. Add the basil, parsley, salt, and black papper.

Bring 5 quarts (5 liters) of water to a rolling boil in a large pot. Add 2 tablespoons salt. Add all the spaghetti at once and stir. Boil briskly, uncovered, for about 5 minutes, until pasta is al dente.

Drain well in a colander. Add the spaghetti to the hot sauce and combine. Season to taste.

RIGATONI WITH BELL PEPPER–TOMATO SAUCE

- Makes 6 appetizer servings
- Makes 4 main-course servings

This is a versatile, slightly piquant sauce that you can serve with almost any shape of pasta.

2 red bell peppers
3 tablespoons olive oil
3 garlic cloves, minced
One 14-ounce (400 g) can imported peeled tomatoes
¼ teaspoon crushed red pepper
A few drops of Tabasco sauce
1 tablespoon freshly squeezed lemon juice
Kosher salt
Freshly ground black pepper
1 pound (450 g) imported rigatoni

Preheat the broiler. Set the rack in the broiler pan and cover it with foil.

Cut the peppers in half lengthwise, then core and seed them. Make a shallow "basket" with a piece of heavy foil, crimping it at the corners so that the liquids don't spill out. (See Notes on Techniques, page 351.) Set the basket on the broiler rack, and arrange the peppers inside, skin side up. Place the broiler pan in the oven (or broiling unit), as close as possible to the heat source. Broil for about 7 minutes, until the skin is blistered and charred. Cover the peppers with foil and cool. The heat will loosen the skin.

Peel the peppers, cut them into pieces, and purée in a food processor.

Heat the oil in a large saucepan. Add the garlic and sauté over low heat for a few seconds. Add the pepper purée, tomatoes, and crushed red pepper. Cook for 2 minutes.

Add Tabasco, lemon juice, salt, and black pepper.

Bring 5 quarts (5 liters) of water to a rolling boil in a large pot. Add 2 tablespoons salt. Add all the rigatoni at once and stir. Boil briskly, uncovered, for about 5 minutes, until pasta is al dente.

Drain well in a colander. Add the rigatoni to the sauce and combine. Season to taste.

RIGATONI WITH OLIVES, HERBS, AND ARUGULA

- Makes 6 appetizer servings
- Makes 4 main-course servings

My grandchildren often spend the summer with me, and because pasta is their favorite dish, I have been inspired to create a number of recipes using ziti, spaghetti, penne, and so on. The children love this rigatoni, and since the weather is usually warm when we eat it, I like to serve it at room temperature.

> **3 garlic cloves**
> **Kosher salt**
> **4 tablespoons extra virgin olive oil**
> **⅛ teaspoon crushed red pepper**
> **10 pitted Kalamata olives, coarsely chopped**
> **1 tablespoon small capers**
> **½ cup (20 g) loosely packed flat-leaf parsley, coarsely chopped**
> **1 cup (40 g) loosely packed fresh basil leaves, torn into small pieces**
> **1 pound (450 g) imported rigatoni**
> **1 small bunch arugula, coarsely chopped**
> **3 tablespoons freshly squeezed lemon juice**
> **Freshly ground black pepper**

Coarsely chop the garlic cloves on a cutting board. Sprinkle them with 1 teaspoon kosher salt and, using a knife, crush them into a paste.

Heat the oil in a saucepan. Add the garlic paste and crushed pepper, and stir over low heat for a minute. Add the olives and capers, stir for another minute, and remove from the heat. Add the parsley and basil.

Bring 5 quarts (5 liters) of water to a rolling boil in a large pot. Add 2 tablespoons salt. Add all the rigatoni at once and stir. Boil briskly, uncovered, for about 5 minutes, until pasta is al dente.

Drain well in a colander. Add the rigatoni to the sauce and combine. Add the arugula and toss. Season to taste with lemon juice, salt, and pepper.

PENNE WITH CAULIFLOWER

• Makes 6 appetizer servings
• Makes 4 main-course servings

Since the main ingredient of this dish is available year-round, it is one of my tried-and-true standbys, and you definitely don't have to be a cauliflower-lover to enjoy it. I serve it warm or at room temperature, depending on the season.

1 medium head cauliflower (about 2 pounds/900 g)
⅓ cup (80 ml) extra virgin olive oil
3 garlic cloves, finely chopped
8 flat anchovy fillets, finely chopped
¼ teaspoon crushed red pepper
Kosher salt
1 pound (450 g) imported penne
½ cup (20 g) loosely packed flat-leaf parsley, finely chopped
Freshly ground black pepper

Separate the cauliflower into small florets and steam until tender.

Heat the oil in a large saucepan. Add the garlic and sauté over low heat for a few seconds. Add the anchovies and mash with the back of a spoon until they become paste-like. Combine well with the garlic. Remove from the heat.

Add half of the cauliflower to the saucepan and mash it with a fork. Add the remaining cauliflower and crushed red pepper and combine well.

Bring 5 quarts (5 liters) of water to a rolling boil in a large pot. Add 2 tablespoons salt. Add all the penne at once and stir. Boil briskly, uncovered, for about 5 minutes, until the pasta is al dente.

Drain well in a colander. Add the penne to the sauce and combine. Add the parsley and toss. Season to taste with salt and pepper.

PENNE WITH MUSHROOM SAUCE

- Makes 6 appetizer servings
- Makes 4 main-course servings

I associate mushrooms with cold weather, so I tend to serve this pasta in the late fall and winter. To enhance the flavor, I add dried mushrooms.

¾ ounce (21 g) dried imported porcini mushrooms
¾ cup (180 ml) boiling water
1 pound (450 g) white mushrooms
3 scallions
4 tablespoons extra virgin olive oil
3 garlic cloves, minced
3 tablespoons freshly squeezed lemon juice
Kosher salt
Freshly ground black pepper
1 pound (450 g) imported penne
1 cup (40 g) loosely packed flat-leaf parsley, coarsely chopped

Place the dried mushrooms in a small bowl and pour the boiling water over them. Cover and let stand for 15 minutes.

Remove the reconstituted mushrooms with a slotted spoon. Squeeze all the liquid back into the bowl. Chop the mushrooms coarsely and set aside. Strain the mushroom liquid through a paper-lined sieve into another small bowl and set aside.

Wipe the white mushrooms with a damp paper towel and cut into thin slices. Cut the scallions, including the green part, into thin slices.

Heat the oil in a large saucepan. Add the scallions and garlic and sauté over low heat for a minute. Add all the mushrooms and stir over high heat until the mushrooms begin to wilt. Add the strained mushroom liquid, the lemon juice, salt, and pepper.

Bring 5 quarts (5 liters) of water to a rolling boil in a large pot. Add 2 tablespoons salt. Add all the penne at once and stir. Boil briskly, uncovered, about 5 minutes, until the pasta is al dente.

Drain well in a colander and combine with the sauce. Add the parsley and toss. Season to taste.

PENNE WITH UNCOOKED TOMATO SAUCE

• Makes 6 appetizer servings
• Makes 4 main-course servings

This pasta evokes hot summer days when I am too lazy to cook.

2 pounds (900 g) ripe tomatoes
6 sun-dried tomatoes packed in oil, coarsely chopped
1 cup (40 g) tightly packed fresh basil leaves, torn into small pieces
1 jalapeño pepper
4 tablespoons extra virgin olive oil
3 garlic cloves, finely chopped
Kosher salt
1 pound (450 g) imported penne
2 tablespoons freshly squeezed lemon juice
Freshly ground black pepper

Bring a large pot of water to a boil. Drop the fresh tomatoes into the boiling water; bring the water back to a boil and drain. Core the tomatoes and slip off the skin. Cut the tomatoes in half widthwise and squeeze gently to remove the seeds. (Some seeds will remain.) Cut the tomatoes into large cubes and place them in a large bowl. Add the sun-dried tomatoes and basil and toss.

Cut the jalapeño pepper in half lengthwise. Remove the core and the seeds and chop the pepper finely (see note).

Heat the oil in a small saucepan. Add the jalapeño pepper and garlic and sauté for 1 minute. Combine with the tomatoes and basil.

Bring 5 quarts (5 liters) of water to a rolling boil in a large pot. Add 2 tablespoons salt. Add all the penne at once and stir. Boil briskly, uncovered, for about 5 minutes, until pasta is al dente.

Drain well in a colander. Add the pasta to the sauce and combine. Season to taste with the lemon juice, salt, and pepper.

Note: When seeding jalapeño peppers, I advise wearing thin plastic gloves to avoid irritating your skin or your eyes.

FARFALLE WITH PEPPERS AND BASIL

• Makes 6 appetizer servings
• Makes 4 main-course servings

The combination of peppers, sun-dried tomatoes, basil, and vinegar makes for a light, colorful, and delicious dish. This pasta is equally good served warm or at room temperature.

1 yellow bell pepper
1 red bell pepper
5 sun-dried tomatoes, packed in oil
4 tablespoons extra virgin olive oil
2 cloves garlic, minced
Kosher salt
1 pound (450 g) imported farfalle
1 cup (40 g) tightly packed fresh basil leaves, torn into small pieces
1 to 2 tablespoons balsamic vinegar
Freshly ground black pepper

Preheat the broiler. Set the rack in the broiler pan and cover it with foil.

Cut the peppers in half lengthwise, then core and seed them. Make a shallow "basket" with a piece of heavy foil, crimping it at the corners so that the liquids don't spill out. (See Notes on Techniques, page 351.) Set the basket on the broiler rack, and arrange the peppers inside, skin side up. Place the broiler pan in the oven (or broiling unit), as close as possible to the heat source. Broil for about 7 minutes, until the skin is blistered and charred. Cover the peppers with foil and cool. The heat will loosen the skin.

Peel the peppers and cut them into small cubes. Cut the sun-dried tomatoes into small cubes.

Heat the oil in a large saucepan. Add the garlic and sauté for a few seconds over low heat. Add the peppers and tomatoes, and sauté for another minute.

Bring 5 quarts (5 liters) of water to a rolling boil in a large pot. Add 2 tablespoons salt. Add all the farfalle at once and stir. Boil briskly, uncovered, for about 5 minutes, until the farfalle is al dente.

Drain well in a colander. Add the farfalle to the sauce and combine. Add the basil and toss. Season to taste with the vinegar, salt, and pepper.

Note: In a pinch, you can simplify the recipe by using raw peppers that have been cored, seeded, and cubed.

ORECCHIETTE WITH BROCCOLI PESTO

- Makes 6 appetizer servings
- Makes 4 main-course servings

This recipe combines pasta with calcium-rich broccoli, two of my favorite foods. I think it's best served at room temperature.

1 small bunch broccoli, no more than 1½ pounds/680 g (see note)
1 small garlic clove, quartered
2 tablespoons pine nuts
⅓ cup (80 ml) extra virgin olive oil
1 pound (450 g) imported orecchiette
Kosher salt
2 tablespoons freshly squeezed lemon juice
Freshly ground black pepper

Cut the florets off the broccoli and cut them into small pieces. Peel the stems and cut into small pieces. Steam the florets and stems for about 3 minutes, until crisp to the bite.

Place the broccoli, garlic, and pine nuts in a food processor. Adding the oil in a stream through the feed tube, pulse until coarsely chopped. (This is the pesto.) Transfer to a large bowl.

Bring 5 quarts (5 liters) of water to a rolling boil in a large pot. Add 2 tablespoons salt. Add all the pasta at once and stir. Boil briskly, uncovered, for 5 minutes, or until the pasta is al dente.

Drain well in a colander. Add the orecchiette to the broccoli pesto and combine. Just before serving, season to taste with the lemon juice, salt, and pepper.

ORECCHIETTE WITH MUSHROOMS AND RADICCHIO

- Makes 6 appetizer servings
- Makes 4 main-course servings

The mushroom-radicchio sauce can be prepared in advance. You can serve the pasta warm or, especially when the weather is warm, at room temperature.

1 pound (450 g) white mushrooms
⅓ cup (80 ml) extra virgin olive oil
4 garlic cloves, finely chopped
1 cup (143 g) frozen green peas, defrosted
¼ small radicchio, cut into thin strips
½ cup (20 g) tightly packed flat-leaf parsley, coarsely chopped
Kosher salt
1 pound (450 g) imported orecchiette
3 tablespoons freshly squeezed lemon juice
Freshly ground black pepper

Wipe the mushrooms with a damp paper towel and cut into thin slices.

Heat the oil in a large saucepan. Add the garlic and sauté over low heat for a few seconds. Add the mushrooms and stir over high heat about 1 minute, until the mushrooms are just beginning to wilt. Add the peas, radicchio, and parsley.

Bring 5 quarts (5 liters) of water to a rolling boil in a large pot. Add 2 tablespoons salt. Add all the pasta at once and stir. Boil briskly, uncovered, for about 5 minutes, until the pasta is al dente.

Drain well in a colander. Add it to the sauce and combine. Just before serving, season to taste with the lemon juice, salt, and pepper.

ZITI WITH ROASTED VEGETABLES

• Makes 8 appetizer servings
• Makes 6 main-course servings

This is a dish for all seasons and all tastes, as it is delicious served either warm or at room temperature. Because the vegetables can be roasted ahead of time, this is the perfect pasta to serve when guests are unexpected or preparation time is short.

> **1 pound (450 g) asparagus**
> **2 yellow bell peppers**
> **½ pound (227 g) shiitake mushrooms**
> **1 bunch scallions**
> **4 garlic cloves, peeled**
> **⅓ cup (80 ml) extra virgin olive oil**
> **Kosher salt**
> **Freshly ground black pepper**
> **1 pound (450 g) imported ziti**
> **1 cup (40 g) loosely packed flat-leaf parsley, coarsely chopped**
> **3 tablespoons freshly squeezed lemon juice**

Preheat the oven to 450°F (230°C).

Rinse the asparagus and pat dry. Hold each spear with both hands and snap at the point where it breaks easily. Discard the bottoms and cut the tops on the diagonal into 1-inch (2.5 cm) pieces.

Cut the bell peppers in half lengthwise, then core and seed them. Cut into thin strips. Cut off and discard the mushroom stems. Wipe the caps with a damp paper towel and cut into medium strips. Cut the scallions, including the green part, into thin slices.

Place the asparagus, peppers, mushrooms, scallions, and garlic in a baking pan and toss with the oil. Roast for 10 minutes, or until the vegetables are crisp to the bite. Season generously with salt and pepper. Cover with foil.

Bring 5 quarts (5 liters) of water to a rolling boil in a large pot. Add 2 tablespoons salt. Add all the ziti at once and stir. Boil briskly, uncovered, for about 5 minutes, until pasta is al dente. Drain well in a colander.

Transfer the vegetables to a large bowl. Add the ziti and combine. Add the parsley and lemon juice, and toss. Season to taste with salt and pepper.

SPAGHETTI WITH TUNA

• Makes 6 appetizer servings
• Makes 4 main-course servings

This is a perfect last-minute dish. The ingredients are generally in the cupboard, and except for boiling the pasta, no cooking is required.

3 garlic cloves
Kosher salt
Two 5-ounce (142 g) cans tuna packed in oil
4 tablespoons extra virgin olive oil
1 pound (450 g) imported spaghetti
1 cup (40 g) tightly packed flat-leaf parsley, finely chopped
3 tablespoons freshly squeezed lemon juice
Freshly ground black pepper

Coarsely chop the garlic cloves on a cutting board. Sprinkle them with 1 teaspoon kosher salt and, using a knife, crush them into a paste. Place the garlic paste into a large bowl and set aside.

Drain the tuna and separate it into chunks. Add it to the garlic paste along with the olive oil.

Bring 5 quarts (5 liters) of water to a rolling boil in a large pot. Add 2 tablespoons salt. Add all the spaghetti at once and stir. Boil briskly, uncovered, for about 5 minutes, until the pasta is al dente.

Drain well in a colander. Add the spaghetti to the tuna sauce and combine. Add the parsley and toss. Season to taste with lemon juice, salt, and pepper. Serve at room temperature.

LINGUINI IN OLIVE SAUCE

• Makes 6 appetizer servings
• Makes 4 main-course servings

I developed this recipe because several members of my family are passionate about olives. I serve it at room temperature.

> **1 jalapeño pepper**
> **½ cup (67 g) pitted black olives**
> **½ cup (67 g) pitted green olives**
> **1 teaspoon small capers**
> **5 anchovy fillets**
> **1 garlic clove**
> **¼ cup (25 g) walnuts**
> **4 tablespoons extra virgin olive oil**
> **Kosher salt**
> **1 pound (450 g) imported linguini**
> **2 tablespoons freshly squeezed lemon juice**
> **Freshly ground black pepper**

Cut the jalapeño pepper in half lengthwise, and remove the core and the seeds. Cut it into large pieces (see note).

Place the jalapeño pepper, olives, capers, anchovies, garlic, and walnuts in a food processor. Adding the oil in a stream through the feed tube, pulse the mixture into a coarse paste. Transfer to a large bowl.

Bring 5 quarts (5 liters) of water to a rolling boil in a large pot. Add 2 tablespoons salt. Add all the linguini at once and stir. Boil briskly, uncovered, for about 5 minutes, until the pasta is al dente.

Drain well in a colander. Add the linguine to the sauce and combine. Season to taste with the lemon juice, salt, and pepper.

Note: When seeding jalapeño peppers, I advise wearing thin plastic gloves to avoid irritating your skin or your eyes.

BARLEY WITH CARROTS, ONIONS, AND PARSLEY

• Makes 6 servings

Barley is an underrated grain that I like to serve as an accompaniment to poultry. I think it goes especially well with Roast Capon with Olives (page 214) or Roasted Turkey Breast (page 218).

> 1 cup (200 g) medium pearl barley
> 2 medium carrots
> 1 medium onion
> 2 tablespoons extra virgin olive oil
> 1½ cups (375 ml) vegetable broth
> Kosher salt
> 1½ cups (60 g) loosely packed flat-leaf parsley, finely chopped

Heat a small heavy skillet over high heat, add the barley, and stir with a wooden spoon until the barley turns light brown and smells nutty.

Peel the carrots and finely chop them. Peel and finely chop the onion.

Heat the oil in a saucepan. Add the carrots and onion and sauté, covered, over medium-low heat for about 5 minutes, stirring from time to time, until the vegetables are almost tender.

Add the barley and broth and bring to a boil over high heat. Lower the heat and cook, covered, about 25 minutes, until the liquid is absorbed. If the barley is still not tender at this point, add a few tablespoons of hot water and continue cooking.

Season to taste with salt and stir in the parsley.

CREAMY COCONUT RICE

• Makes 4 servings

This is a delicious and unusual way to prepare rice. With its subtle Thai flavor, it makes a lovely accompaniment to fish dishes like Grey Sole with Cilantro (page 163) or Salmon Teriyaki (page 184).

½ cup (125 ml) unsweetened coconut milk
1 cup (250 ml) water
½ teaspoon kosher salt
1 cup (195 g) raw basmati rice
2 tablespoons slivered or sliced blanched almonds
¼ cup (10 g) loosely packed cilantro leaves

In a small saucepan, combine the coconut milk, water, and salt. Add the rice and bring to a boil. Lower the heat, stir, and simmer, covered, for 20 minutes, or until the rice is tender.

Roast the almonds in a toaster oven on the lowest setting for a minute or two. (Watch them carefully, as they burn quickly.) Fluff the rice with a fork, add the almonds and cilantro, and toss. Season to taste with salt.

SUSHI RICE

• Makes 4 servings

¾ cup (120 g) raw sushi rice
1 cup (250 ml) water
¼ teaspoon kosher salt

Place the rice in a heavy saucepan with the water and salt. Bring to a boil, lower the heat, and simmer, covered, for 8 minutes. Fluff with a fork and serve.

QUINOA

• Makes 4 servings

According to the National Academy of Sciences, quinoa is "one of the best sources of protein in the vegetable kingdom." Quinoa has a delicate taste, and I think it is delicious on its own. But I also like to combine it with many different kinds of vegetables.

1 tablespoon unsalted margarine
½ teaspoon kosher salt
1¼ cups (300 ml) water
1 cup (170 g) quinoa

Put the margarine, salt, and water in a small saucepan, and bring to a boil over high heat. Sprinkle in the quinoa, lower the heat, cover, and cook for 15 minutes, or until all the water is absorbed. If the grains are still not tender at that point, add 1 tablespoon hot water and continue cooking.

Stir with a fork to fluff the grains. Season to taste with salt.

Note: You can serve quinoa combined with parsley as well as almost any vegetable you like. My favorites are steamed broccoli florets or asparagus tips, sautéed mushrooms or sautéed diced leeks.

TOMATO SAUCES

As you will see throughout this book, I have a deep commitment to seasonal produce. As a result, each of these three sauces is different, depending on the tomatoes that are available at a given time of year.

WINTER TOMATO SAUCE

• Makes 2½ cups (600 ml)

⅓ cup (80 ml) extra virgin olive oil
2 medium red onions, thinly sliced
4 garlic cloves, finely chopped
One 28-ounce (794 g) can imported peeled tomatoes
Kosher salt
Freshly ground black pepper

Heat the oil in a heavy-bottomed medium saucepan. Add the onions and garlic and sauté, covered, for 10 minutes over low heat. Pour off most of the juice from the tomatoes and add the tomatoes to the onions and garlic, stirring to break them up.

Simmer, covered, for 30 minutes, stirring from time to time. Season to taste with salt and pepper.

MIDSEASON TOMATO SAUCE

• Makes 2½ cups (600 ml)

1 pound (450 g) ripe plum tomatoes
One 14-ounce (400 g) can imported peeled tomatoes
4 tablespoons extra virgin olive oil
4 garlic cloves, finely chopped
½ teaspoon crushed red pepper
¼ cup (10 g) loosely packed flat-leaf parsley, finely chopped
Kosher salt
Freshly ground black pepper

Bring a large pot of water to a boil. Drop the fresh tomatoes into the boiling water; bring the water back to a boil and drain. Core the tomatoes and slip off the skin. Cut the tomatoes in half widthwise and squeeze gently to remove the seeds. (Some seeds will remain.)

Chop the tomatoes coarsely.

Drain the canned tomatoes and coarsely chop.

Heat the oil in a medium saucepan. Add the garlic and crushed pepper and sauté for a few seconds over low heat. Add all the tomatoes and simmer, uncovered, for 5 minutes. Add the parsley and season to taste with salt and pepper.

SUMMER TOMATO SAUCE

• Makes 3 cups (720 ml)

> **1 pound (450 g) ripe plum tomatoes**
> **1 pound (450 g) ripe tomatoes**
> **2 jalapeño peppers (see note)**
> **3 garlic cloves, quartered**
> **4 tablespoons extra virgin olive oil**
> **¼ cup (10 g) tightly packed flat-leaf parsley, finely chopped**
> **½ cup (20 g) tightly packed basil leaves, torn into small pieces**
> **10 sun-dried tomatoes packed in oil, coarsely chopped**
> **Kosher salt**
> **Freshly ground black pepper**

Preheat the oven to 400°F (205°C).

Rinse the fresh tomatoes and pat them dry. Cut the jalapeño peppers in half lengthwise, then core and seed them (see note).

Spread the jalapeños and garlic on the bottom of a glass, ceramic, or enamel-lined baking pan that is large enough to hold the tomatoes in a single layer. Place the fresh tomatoes on top of the jalapeños and garlic and drizzle over the oil. Roast for 55 minutes, turning the tomatoes once. They will have a charred look. Add the parsley, basil, and sun-dried tomatoes and bake for an additional 5 minutes.

Pass the sauce through a food mill, using the coarse attachment. Season to taste with salt and pepper.

Note: When seeding jalapeño peppers, I advise wearing thin plastic gloves to avoid irritating your skin or your eyes.

FISH

DAIRY
Grey Sole with Cilantro
Halibut with Butternut Squash

PAREVE
Arctic Char with Honey and Wasabi
Glazed Arctic Char
Seared Tuna with Two Sauces
Tuna Burgers
Black Cod with Honey and Soy Sauce
Black Cod with Miso
Black Sea Bass with Potatoes and Tomatoes
Black Sea Bass with Ginger and Scallions
Halibut with Caper Sauce
Halibut Nuggets with Yukon Gold Potatoes
Red Snapper with Coconut Milk
Salmon with Mustard Sauce and Chive Oil
Salmon Burgers with Spinach
Salmon with Orange
Salmon Teriyaki
Marinated Salmon
Marinated Salmon with Mango-Kiwi Relish
Gefilte Fish with Challah

GREY SOLE WITH CILANTRO

• Makes 4 servings

This is a delicious dish, with a subtle but flavorful taste, and even nonfish lovers love it.

3 tablespoons (45 g) unsalted butter
⅓ cup (47 g) pine nuts
2 garlic cloves, quartered
1 tablespoons extra virgin olive oil
¼ cup (60 ml) freshly squeezed lime juice
½ cup (20 g) loosely packed cilantro leaves, plus more for garnish
½ cup (20 g) loosely packed flat-leaf parsley
½ teaspoon kosher salt
Freshly ground black pepper
4 grey sole fillets (about 6 ounces/170 g each)

Preheat the oven to 500°F (260°C). Grease a glass, ceramic, or enamel-lined baking pan with 1 tablespoon (15 g) of the butter.

Place the remaining butter, the pine nuts, garlic, oil, lime juice, cilantro, parsley, salt and pepper in a food procesor and pulse until smooth. Season to taste.

Pat the fillets dry with paper towels and place them on a piece of wax paper. Salt and pepper each side lightly.

Spread the cilantro-parsley mixture on the darker side of the fillet. Fold the narrower third of each piece towards the center, so it covers about half the fillet; fold the other end on top of this, to form a neat, three-layered "packet." Place each packet in the baking pan with the folded side on the bottom. Cover the dish tightly with heavy foil. (The entire dish can be prepared several hours in advance up to this point and refrigerated. Before baking, bring to room temperature.)

Bake in the upper third of the oven for 13 minutes, or until the inside of the fish has just turned opaque. (The fish will continue cooking when it is out of the oven.)

To serve, spoon some of the accumulated juice over each fillet and garnish with cilantro leaves.

HALIBUT WITH BUTTERNUT SQUASH

• Makes 2 servings

This dish has a sweet-and-sour sour taste and a lovely color. It's one of my favorites, as it is so easy and elegant.

> **2 tablespoons (30 g) unsalted butter, plus 1½ teaspoons (7.5 g)**
> **for greasing the baking pan**
> **1 leek**
> **½ pound (227 g) butternut squash**
> **½ cup (125 ml) white wine**
> **1 tablespoon honey**
> **1½ tablespoon freshly squeezed lemon juice**
> **Kosher salt**
> **Freshly ground black pepper**
> **A pinch of cayenne pepper**
> **2 skinless halibut fillets (about 6 ounces/170 g each)**

Preheat the over to 450°F (230°C). Grease a glass, ceramic, or enamel-lined baking pan that can hold the fillets in a single layer with 1½ teaspoons (7.5 g) butter.

Cut off and discard the roots and tough, dark green leaves of the leek. Cut the white and light green parts into ¼-inch (6 mm) cubes. Place in a sieve and rinse thoroughly under cold running water to remove any sand.

Peel the squash and remove the seeds. Cut it into ¼-inch (6 mm) cubes.

Melt 1½ tablespoons (22.5 g) of the butter in a small saucepan. Add the leek and squash, cover, and cook over low heat for about 5 minutes, until soft. Add the wine and honey. Season to taste with the lemon juice, salt, pepper, and cayenne.

Pat the fillets dry with paper towels. Season both sides lightly with salt and pepper and place in the baking pan. Cut the remaining butter in small pieces and spread them on top. Cover the baking pan with heavy foil and bake for 10 minutes, or until the inside of the fish has just turned opaque. (The fish will continue cooking when it is out of the oven.)

TO SERVE: Spoon the vegetable sauce into wide soup bowls or deep dinner plates and place the halibut on top.

ARCTIC CHAR WITH HONEY AND WASABI

• Makes 4 servings

Arctic char is a very light fish, flat like trout and pale pink like salmon. The seasoning gives it a sweet-and-sour flavor with subtle hints of Asia.

4 skinless center-cut arctic char fillets (about 6 ounces/170 g each)
Kosher salt
Freshly ground pepper

MARINADE
1 tablespoon low-sodium soy sauce
1 tablespoon rice vinegar
1 tablespoon extra virgin olive oil
1 tablespoon honey
1-inch (2.5 cm) piece ginger, peeled and grated
2 teaspoons wasabi powder

Pat the fillets dry with paper towels and salt and pepper lightly on both sides. Place in a glass, ceramic, or enamel-lined baking pan.

Combine the marinade ingredients; pour over the fish and coat well. Cover with cling wrap and refrigerate for at least 4 hours. Remove the fillets from the refrigerator and bring back to room temperature.

Preheat the broiler. Set the rack in the broiler pan and cover it completely with heavy foil. Make a shallow "basket" with a piece of heavy foil, crimping it at the corners so that the liquid doesn't spill out. (See "Notes on Technique, see page 351.) Set the basket on the broiler rack and place the fillets, skinned side up, inside. Pour the marinade over them. Put the pan in the oven (or broiling unit), as close as possible to the heat source. Broil the fillets for 6 minutes, without turning, or until the fish has just turned opaque. (It will continue cooking when it is removed from the heat.)

GLAZED ARCTIC CHAR

• Makes 2 servings

This is a delicate flat fish that is a cross between salmon and trout. The glaze gives it a touch of orange and spice.

GLAZE
1 tablespoon orange marmalade
½-inch (13 mm) piece of ginger, peeled and grated
1 garlic clove, minced
2 tablespoons seasoned rice vinegar
2 tablespoons freshly squeezed lemon juice
2 tablespoons freshly squeezed orange juice
1 tablespoon extra virgin olive oil
Kosher salt
Freshly ground black pepper

1 teaspoon extra virgin olive oil for greasing the foil
2 skinless center-cut arctic char fillets (about 6 ounces/170 g each)
Kosher salt
Freshly ground black pepper
Grated zest of 1 navel orange, for garnish

Preheat the broiler.

In an enamel-lined saucepan, combine the ingredients for the glaze—marmalade, ginger, garlic, vinegar, lemon and orange juices, and oil. Bring to a boil.

Cook uncovered over medium-high heat about 10 minutes, until the glaze is reduced by half. (It should be thick enough to coat a spoon.) Season to taste with salt and pepper. Pat the fillets dry with paper towels and season them lightly on both sides with salt and pepper.

Set the rack in the broiler pan and cover it completely with heavy foil. Make a shallow "basket" with a piece of heavy foil, crimping it at the corners so that the liquids don't spill out. (See Notes on Techniques, page 351.) Grease the bottom of the basket with 1 teaspoon oil. Place the fillets in the basket and coat the fish with the glaze. Set the pan in the oven (or broiling unit), as close as possible to the heat source. Broil the fillets for 6 minutes, without turning, until the fish has just turned opaque. (It will continue cooking after it is removed from the heat.)

Garnish with grated orange zest and serve.

SEARED TUNA WITH TWO SAUCES

• Makes 6 servings

Tuna is surely one of America's favorite fish, and it lends itself to many types of preparation, from sashimi to "tuna-fish" sandwiches. The dish that follows calls for the fish to be almost raw; it can be accompanied with one of the Asian-inspired sauces, Ginger or Piquant Asian, that follow.

> **1 teaspoon kosher salt**
> **2 teaspoons freshly ground black pepper**
> **2 pounds (900 g) sashimi-quality tuna**
> **1 tablespoon extra virgin olive oil**
> **Julienned daikon, sliced seeded cucumbers, and strong-tasting salad leaves**
>   **like arugula or watercress, for garnish**
> **Ginger Sauce or Piquant Asia Sauce (page 170), to serve**

Combine salt and pepper in a small bowl.

Pat the tuna dry with paper towels. Heat the oil in a large nonstick skillet over medium heat. Sear the tuna on both sides, then remove from the heat and rub both sides with the salt-pepper mixture.

When cool, wrap the tuna tightly in wax paper, then in foil. Refrigerate it for at least 4 hours or overnight. This will make it firmer and thus easier to slice.

TO SERVE: Cut the fish against the grain in thin slices, and serve accompanied by the suggested vegetables. Serve either of the sauces separately.

GINGER SAUCE

• Makes about ½ cup (125 ml)

2 shallots, finely chopped
3 tablespoons low-sodium soy sauce
2½ tablespoons rice vinegar
2 teaspoons water
½ teaspoon sugar
1-inch (2.5 cm) piece of ginger, peeled and grated
1 generous tablespoon olive oil
1 generous tablespoon sesame oil
½ teaspoon black pepper

Combine the ingredients well, and season to taste.

PIQUANT ASIAN SAUCE

• Makes about 1 cup (250 ml)

¼ cup (10 g) loosely packed cilantro leaves
2 teaspoons wasabi powder
1 tablespoon extra virgin olive oil
¼ teaspoon powdered mustard
3 tablespoons freshly squeezed lime juice
½ cup (78 g) shelled soy beans (edamame), defrosted (see note)
½ cup (125 ml) vegetable broth
Kosher salt
Freshly ground black pepper

Place all the ingredients in a blender and purée until smooth. Strain through a medium-mesh strainer. Season to taste.

Note: Frozen edamame, shelled and unshelled, are available in health-food stores and supermarkets.

TUNA BURGERS

• Makes 4 servings

Instead of buns, I like to serve these burgers over interesting greens, such as Bibb, mâche, frisée, or radicchio, which I dress with a favorite salad dressing like Sesame-Ginger Dressing (page 111) or Balsamic Vinaigrette (page 111). Sometimes I just use a good olive oil and season with salt and pepper.

> **1½ pounds (680 g) sashimi-quality tuna fillet**
> **4 garlic cloves, minced**
> **1-inch (2.5 cm) piece ginger, peeled and grated**
> **3 tablespoons extra virgin olive oil**
> **1 tablespoon low-sodium soy sauce**
> **Kosher salt**
> **Freshly ground black pepper**
> **Dressed greens, for serving**

Cut the tuna into ½-inch (13 mm) slices, then into ½-inch (13 mm) cubes. Place the tuna in a bowl and add the garlic, ginger, 2 tablespoons of the oil, and soy sauce. Combine and season lightly with salt and pepper. After lightly covering your palms with a drop or two of oil, shape the tuna mixture into four patties. (You can make the burgers up to this point and refrigerate them for a few hours. But be sure to bring them back to room temperature before sautéing.)

Coat a nonstick skillet with the remaining 1 tablespoon oil. Heat over high heat and sear the burgers. After 1 minute on each side, they will be brown on the outside and rare on the inside. (Cook longer, according to taste.)

BLACK COD WITH HONEY AND SOY SAUCE

• Makes 2 servings

When black cod is prepared this way, it has a wonderful flavor and a beautiful glaze. Stir-Fried Spinach (page 120) or Chopped Broccoli (page 118) together with Sushi Rice (page 158) make fine accompaniments.

2 skinless black cod fillets (about 6 ounces/170 g each)
Kosher salt
Freshly ground black pepper

MARINADE
1 tablespoon low-sodium soy sauce
1 tablespoon seasoned rice vinegar
1 tablespoon extra virgin olive oil
1 tablespoon honey

Pat the fillets dry with paper towels and place them in a glass, ceramic, or enamel-lined baking pan. Salt and pepper each side lightly.

Combine the marinade ingredients. Pour over the fillets and coat well. Cover the dish with cling wrap and refrigerate for at least 4 hours. Turn the fish once.

Remove the fillets from the refrigerator and bring them back to room temperature.

Preheat the broiler. Set the rack in the broiler pan and cover it with heavy foil.

Make a shallow "basket" with a piece of heavy foil, crimping it at the corners so that the liquid doesn't spill out. Set the basket on the broiler rack, and place the fillets inside it. (See Notes on Techniques, page 351). Pour the marinade on top. Put the pan in the oven (or broiling unit), as close as possible to the heat source. Broil the fillets for about 6 minutes, without turning, until the top is brown and the inside of the fish has just turned opaque. (The fish will continue cooking when it is removed from the heat.)

Remove from the heat, spoon the accumulated juices on top, and serve.

BLACK COD WITH MISO

• Makes 4 servings

Black cod has a wonderful taste, and is thicker, moister, and silkier than regular cod.
I usually serve it with Sushi Rice (page 158).

4 skinless black cod fillets (about 6 ounces/170 g each)

MARINADE
2 tablespoons plus ¾ teaspoon white miso paste
2 tablespoons sugar
¼ teaspoon kosher salt
2 tablespoons mirin
2 tablespoons sake

Pat the fillets dry with paper towels and place in a glass, ceramic, or enamel-lined baking
pan. Combine the marinade ingredients. Pour over the fillets and coat well. Cover the dish
with cling wrap and refrigerate for at least 4 hours. Turn the fish once.

Remove the fillets from the refrigerator and bring them back to room temperature.

Preheat the broiler. Set the rack in the broiler pan and cover it completely with heavy
foil. Make a shallow "basket" with a piece of heavy foil, crimping it at the corners so that
the liquid doesn't spill out. (See Notes on Techniques, page 351.) Set the basket on the
broiler rack, and place the fillets inside. Pour the marinade on top. Put the pan in the
oven (or broiling unit), as close as possible to the heat source. Broil the fillets for about
6 minutes, without turning, until the top is brown and the inside of the fish has just turned
opaque. (The fish will continue cooking when it is removed from the heat.)

Spoon the accumulated juices on top, and serve.

BLACK SEA BASS
WITH POTATOES AND TOMATOES

• Makes 4 servings

This is a one-pot meal that is easy to prepare and quite delicious. It you bake it in an attractive dish, it can go straight from the oven to the table.

4 tablespoons extra virgin olive oil,
  plus 1 teaspoon for greasing the pan
1 pound (450 g) Yukon gold or fingerling potatoes
½ pound (227 g) cherry tomatoes
Kosher salt
Freshly ground pepper
Leaves from 4 rosemary sprigs
4 skin-on sea bass fillets (about 6 ounces/170 g each)
½ cup (125 ml) dry white wine
4 anchovy fillets (optional)

Preheat the oven to 400°F (205°C). Grease a large glass, ceramic, or enamel-lined baking pan with 1 teaspoon of the oil.

Rinse the potatoes, cut them in half horizontally, and steam until tender. Place them in the baking pan. Rinse the tomatoes and cut them in half. Add them to the potatoes and season with salt and pepper. Scatter the rosemary leaves on top.

Pat the fillets dry with paper towels, and season both sides lightly with salt and pepper. Place, skin side up, in a single layer over the potatoes and tomatoes. Pour the wine over the fish and drizzle with the remaining ¼ cup oil. Top with anchovies (optional).

Bake for 15 minutes, or until the inside of the fish has just turned opaque. (The fish will continue cooking when it is removed from the heat.)

BLACK SEA BASS
WITH GINGER AND SCALLIONS

• Makes 2 servings

The lemony sauce gives this light, easy-to-prepare fish a delicate piquancy that my family and guests love. I usually serve it with Sushi Rice (page 158), Chopped Broccoli (page 118) or Stir-Fried Spinach (page 120).

**2 tablespoons extra virgin olive oil,
    plus 1 teaspoon for greasing the pan
2 skinless sea bass fillets (about 6 ounces/170 g each)
Kosher salt
Freshly ground black pepper
2 scallions, including green parts, thinly sliced
½-inch (13 mm) piece ginger, peeled and grated
1 garlic clove, minced
⅛ teaspoon crushed red pepper
2 tablespoons freshly squeezed lemon juice
1 tablespoon low-sodium soy sauce**

Preheat oven to 450°F (230°C). Grease a glass, ceramic, or enamel-lined baking pan with 1 teaspoon of the oil.

Pat the fillets dry with paper towels and lightly season both sides with salt and pepper. Place them in the baking pan.

In a small bowl, combine the remaining 2 tablespoons oil, the scallions, ginger, garlic, crushed pepper, lemon juice, soy sauce, and ½ teaspoon salt.

Spoon the sauce over the fish and bake for 10 minutes, or until the inside of the fish has just turned opaque. (The fish will continue cooking when it is removed from the heat.)

HALIBUT WITH CAPER SAUCE

• Makes 2 servings

Like salmon, halibut lends itself to many different kinds of preparation. This is one of my favorites, as the capers add a piquant flavor. You can also make this dish with red snapper.

1 teaspoon extra virgin olive oil, for greasing the baking pan
2 skinless halibut fillets (about 6 ounces/170 g each)
Kosher salt
Freshly ground pepper
½ cup (20 g) loosely packed flat-leaf parsley, finely chopped, for garnish

CAPER SAUCE
2 tablespoons extra virgin olive oil
2 garlic cloves, minced
1½ tablespoons small capers
¼ cup (60 ml) dry white wine
Kosher salt
Freshly ground pepper

Preheat the oven to 400°F (205°C). Grease a glass, ceramic, or enamel-lined baking pan with 1 teaspoon oil.

Pat the fillets dry with paper towels and season them lightly on both sides with salt and pepper. Place them in the baking pan, cover the pan with heavy foil.

Bake the fish in the upper third of the oven for 13 to 15 minutes without turning, until the inside of the fish has just turned opaque. (The fish will continue cooking when it is out of the oven.)

While the fish is cooking, make the Caper Sauce. Heat the oil in a small pan. Add the garlic and sauté over low heat until just golden. Add the capers and wine and bring to a boil. Remove from the heat. Season to taste with salt and pepper.

TO SERVE: Place a filet on each plate and spoon the hot sauce over it. Sprinkle with the parsley.

HALIBUT NUGGETS
WITH YUKON GOLD POTATOES

• Makes 2 generous servings

This dish is quick to prepare and makes a perfect meal for two. The combination of the halibut and the potatoes is quite delicious.

2 small Yukon gold potatoes (about ¾ pound/340 g), unpeeled
Kosher salt
Freshly ground black pepper
1 pound (450 g) skinless, boneless halibut,
   cut into 2-inch (5 cm) cubes
2 tablespoons extra virgin olive oil
2 garlic cloves, minced
Leaves from 3 mint sprigs, finely chopped,
   plus a few extra leaves for garnish
2 tablespoons freshly squeezed lemon juice

Steam the potatoes for about 30 minutes, until soft. When cool enough to handle, cut into medium slices and season with salt and pepper. Cover with foil to keep warm.

Pat the fish dry with paper towels.

Heat the oil in a wok or skillet over medium heat. Lower the heat, add the fish and garlic, and cook for 3 to 4 minutes, turning several times, until the inside of the fish has just turned opaque. (The fish will continue cooking when it is removed from the heat.)

Remove from the heat, add the mint, and season to taste with the lemon juice, salt, and pepper.

TO SERVE: Place the potatoes in the center of each plate and top with the fish and accumulated juices.

RED SNAPPER WITH COCONUT MILK

• Makes 4 servings

I like to serve this dish on a bed of coconut rice, topped with an Asian-inspired sauce and garnished with bright green cilantro leaves.

4 skinless snapper fillets (about 6 ounces/170 g each)
Kosher salt
Freshly ground black pepper
½ teaspoon curry powder
3 tablespoons freshly squeezed lime juice
Creamy Coconut Rice (page 157), for serving

COCONUT-MILK SAUCE
3 plum tomatoes
2 tablespoons extra virgin olive oil
3 shallots, minced
3 garlic cloves, minced
¾ cup (180 ml) coconut milk
Kosher salt
Freshly ground black pepper
Cilantro leaves, for garnish

Pat the fillets dry with paper towels and lightly season both sides with salt and pepper. Place the fish in a large zip-top plastic bag. In a small bowl, combine the curry powder and lime juice. Pour over the fish. Seal the bag and refrigerate for at least 2 hours. Before cooking bring the fish back to room temperature. Preheat the oven to 450°F (230°C).

TO MAKE THE SAUCE: Bring a pot of water to a boil. Drop in the tomatoes, return the water to a boil, and drain. Core the tomatoes and slip off the skin. Cut tomatoes in half width-wise and squeeze gently to remove the seeds. Dice the tomatoes.

Heat the oil in a small saucepan. Add the shallots and garlic and sauté over low heat until soft. Add the tomatoes and coconut milk. Cook for 5 minutes. Season to taste.

Season the sauce with salt and pepper and bring it to a boil. Pour it into a nonreactive baking pan large enough to hold the fillets in one layer. Spread the sauce, and place the fish on top, of the sauce with the skinned side up. Bake for 8 minutes, or until the inside of the fish has just turned opaque. (The fish will continue cooking when it is removed from the heat.)

TO SERVE: Make a bed of rice in the center of each plate, top with a fillet, then spoon the sauce over it. Garnish with cilantro leaves.

SALMON WITH MUSTARD SAUCE AND CHIVE OIL

• Makes 4 servings

The pinkness of the salmon combined with the yellow of the mustard and the bright green of the chives make this dish beautiful as well as fragrant. I usually serve it at room temperature.

> 1 teaspoon extra virgin olive oil, for greasing the baking pan
> 4 skinless center-cut salmon fillets (about 6 ounces/170 g each)
> Kosher salt
> Freshly ground black pepper
>
> MUSTARD SAUCE
> 2 tablespoons Dijon mustard
> 1 tablespoon rice vinegar
>
> CHIVE OIL
> 1 bunch chives (about ½ cup/20 g), cut into pieces
> ½ cup (125 ml) extra virgin olive oil, chilled for 2 hours

Preheat the oven to 250°F (120°C). Grease a glass, ceramic, or enamel-lined baking pan with 1 teaspoon oil.

Pat the salmon fillets dry with paper towels and lightly season both sides with salt and pepper. Place the fish in the baking pan. Bake for 20 minutes.

TO MAKE THE MUSTARD SAUCE: In a small bowl, whisk the mustard and vinegar.

TO MAKE THE CHIVE OIL: Put the chives in a blender with the oil and purée finely. Strain the oil through a sieve without pressing the chives.

TO SERVE: Spoon a dollop of mustard sauce in the center of each plate and place the fish on top. Drizzle the chive oil around the fish.

SALMON BURGERS WITH SPINACH

• Makes 4 luncheon servings

These burgers, served with dressed baby spinach, can be sautéed an hour in advance. I like to serve them at room temperature over sushi rice.

1 pound (450 g) skinless salmon fillet
8 ounces (227 g) prewashed baby spinach
3 scallions, including green parts, finely chopped
1-inch (2.5 cm) piece ginger, peeled and grated
2 large egg whites, at room temperature
1 tablespoon low-sodium soy sauce
Kosher salt
Freshly ground black pepper
2 tablespoons vegetable oil
Sushi Rice (page 158), for serving

DRESSING FOR THE SPINACH
1 tablespoon freshly squeezed lime juice
1½ teaspoons low-sodium soy sauce
1 tablespoon extra virgin olive oil
1½ teaspoons sesame oil
½-inch (13 mm) piece ginger, peeled and grated
⅛ teaspoon dark brown sugar
Kosher salt
Freshly ground black pepper

Pat the salmon dry with paper towels and cut it into ¼-inch (6 mm) cubes. Place the cubes in a large bowl. Finely chop 5 ounces (140 g) of the spinach and add it to the salmon along with the scallions and ginger.

Whisk the egg whites lightly and add them to the salmon mixture. Add the soy sauce and season to taste with salt and pepper. Combine well and form into 4 rounded burgers.

Coat a 12-inch (30 cm) nonstick skillet with vegetable oil, and heat it over moderate heat. Sauté the burgers for 1 minute on each side. Be careful when turning that the burgers stay intact. Leave in the pan until ready to serve.

In a medium bowl, combine the dressing ingredients well with a wire whisk. Add the remaining 3 ounces (87 g) of spinach and toss.

TO SERVE: Put a serving of rice in the center of the plate and place a burger on top. Surround the burger with the dressed spinach.

SALMON WITH ORANGE

• Makes 2 servings

This dish, with its delicate taste and citrus fragrance, is wonderful warm or at room temperature. I often serve it on Passover because of the simplicity of its ingredients. It goes well with Stir-Fried Spinach (page 120), Spiced Carrots (page 115), and Sweet Potato Fries (page 126).

> **2 skinless center-cut salmon fillets (about 6 ounces/170 g each)**
> **Grated zest of 1 navel orange**
> **1½ teaspoons sugar**
> **1 tablespoon freshly squeezed lemon juice**
> **1 tablespoon olive oil**
> **½ teaspoon kosher salt**
> **½ teaspoon freshly ground black pepper**

Pat the fish dry with paper towels and place it in a large zip-top plastic bag. In a small bowl, combine the remaining ingredients. Add them to the fish in the bag. Seal the bag and refrigerate for at least 2 hours. Before cooking, bring the fish to room temperature.

Preheat the broiler. Set the rack in the broiler pan and cover it with heavy foil.

Make a shallow "basket" with a piece of heavy foil, crimping it at the corners so that the juices don't spill out. (See Notes on Techniques, page 351.) Set the basket on the broiler rack, place the fish inside, and pour the marinade over it. Put the pan in the oven (or broiling unit), as close as possible to the heat source. Broil the fish for 6 minutes, or until the inside has just turned opaque. (It will continue cooking when it is removed from the heat.)

Serve with the accumulated juices.

SALMON TERIYAKI

• Makes 4 servings

No matter how many salmon recipes you have in your repertoire, this one is definitely worth adding. It is easy to prepare and very flavorful, and the ingredients are usually in your cupboard.

4 skinless center-cut salmon fillets (about 6 ounces/170 g each)
Kosher salt
Freshly ground pepper

MARINADE
2 garlic cloves
1 tablespoon dark brown sugar
1-inch (2.5 cm) piece ginger, peeled and grated
2 tablespoons white wine
2 tablespoons low-sodium soy sauce
2 tablespoons extra virgin olive oil
1 tablespoon honey

Pat the fillets dry with paper towels and season lightly on both sides with salt and pepper. Place them in a glass, ceramic, or enamel-lined baking pan.

Coarsely chop the garlic cloves on a cutting board. Sprinkle them with brown sugar and, using a knife, crush them into a paste. Remove the paste to a small bowl and combine it with the ginger, white wine, soy sauce, oil, and honey.

Pour the marinade over the fish, cover with cling wrap, and refrigerate at least 2 hours. Bring the fish and marinade to room temperature.

Preheat the broiler. Set the rack in the broiler pan and cover it with heavy foil.

Make a shallow "basket" with a piece of heavy foil, crimping it at the corners so that the juices don't spill out. (See Notes on Techniques, page 351.) Set the basket on the broiler rack, place the fish inside, and pour the marinade over it. Put the pan in the oven (or broiling unit) as close as possible to the heat source. Broil the fish for about 6 minutes, until the inside has just turned opaque. (It will continue cooking when it is removed from the heat.)

Serve with the accumulated juices.

MARINATED SALMON

• Makes 6 servings

This is a variation on the traditional pickled salmon sold in every Jewish delicatessen. The difference: The salmon is more delicate and less vinegary, and has a richer color. It makes a perfect Sabbath luncheon dish.

> **6 skinless center-cut salmon fillets (about 6 ounces/170 g each)**
> **1 teaspoon extra virgin olive oil for greasing the pan**
> **Kosher salt**
> **Freshly ground black pepper**
>
> **MARINADE**
> **3 tablespoons extra virgin olive oil**
> **4 tablespoons rice vinegar**
> **1½ teaspoons salt**
> **Freshly ground black pepper**
> **1 small red onion, very thinly sliced (see note)**
> **15 dill sprigs, snipped finely with scissors, plus 2 sprigs, snipped, for garnish**

Preheat the oven to 200°F (95°C). Grease a glass or enamel-lined baking pan that can hold the fillets in a single layer.

Pat the fillets dry with paper towels and season them lightly on both sides with salt and pepper. Place them in the dish and bake, uncovered, for 25 to 30 minutes, or until cooked to your taste.

Remove the baking pan from the oven, cover with foil, and let cool completely. (The fish will continue cooking outside of the oven.)

TO MAKE THE MARINADE: In a medium bowl, whisk together the olive oil, vinegar, and salt. Add pepper to taste. Pour the marinade over the salmon, add the onion, and sprinkle with the 15 snipped sprigs of dill.

Cover the dish with wax paper, then foil, and refrigerate for 2 to 3 days without turning.

TO SERVE: Bring the salmon to room temperature. Place on individual plates along with some of the marinade and onions. Garnish with the fresh snipped dill.

Note: I use a mandoline to slice the onion, as it makes the cutting easier.

MARINATED SALMON
WITH MANGO-KIWI RELISH

• Makes 4 servings

This is an easy-to-prepare summer dish that I like to serve at room temperature. The mango, kiwi, and cilantro give it a tropical look and flavor.

4 skinless center-cut salmon fillets (about 6 ounces/170 g each)
Kosher salt
Freshly ground black pepper

MARINADE
1 tablespoon low-sodium soy sauce
1 tablespoon extra virgin olive oil
1 tablespoon honey

MANGO-KIWI RELISH
½ medium mango, peeled and cut in ¼-inch (6 mm) cubes
2 kiwis, peeled and cut in ¼-inch (6 mm) cubes
¼ cup (10 g) loosely packed cilantro leaves
2 tablespoons freshly squeezed orange juice

Dry the fillets with paper towels and season lightly with salt and pepper. Place them in a large zip-top plastic bag.

Combine the marinade ingredients in a small bowl, and season to taste with salt and pepper. Add to the fish in the bag and seal. Marinate for about 10 minutes.

In a medium bowl combine the relish ingredients.

Preheat the broiler. Set the rack in the broiler pan and cover it with heavy foil. Make a shallow "basket" with a piece of heavy foil, crimping it at the corners so that the juices don't spill out. (See Notes on Techniques, page 351.) Set the basket on the broiler rack, place the fish inside, and pour the marinade over it. Put the pan in the oven (or broiling unit), as close as possible to the heat source. Broil the salmon for about 6 minutes, until the inside has just turned opaque. (It will continue cooking when it is removed from the heat.)

Spoon the relish on top of the salmon and serve with the accumulated juices.

GEFILTE FISH WITH CHALLAH

• Makes 12 servings (about 3 dozen ovals)

Gefilte fish, which originated in Eastern Europe, is the most well-known and traditional of all Jewish dishes. Typically, it is the first course served at meals on the Sabbath and on holidays. Making the gefilte ovals is time-consuming but, to me, it is also very satisfying. The ones in this recipe are soft, pale, delicately seasoned, and relatively small, but you can make them any size. (I figure on about three ovals per person.) I always make them a day in advance to allow the aspic to gel. I serve them with fresh Horseradish (page 188), accompanied by Challah (page 189).

FISH STOCK
Frames (heads and bone) and skin from 3 pounds (1.36 kg) whitefish and 3 pounds (1.36 kg) pike (Have the fishmonger bone and skin the fish for you. You will use the fillet to make the ovals, below.)
7 cups (1.75 liters) water
2 onions, quartered
1 carrot, peeled and cut in large pieces
1 tablespoon kosher salt
2 teaspoons sugar
10 peppercorns

FISH OVALS
2 medium onions, quartered
2 hard-boiled large eggs
1 large egg, whisked
6 pounds (2.72 kg) fish fillets (3 pounds/1.36 kg whitefish and 3 pounds/1.36 kg pike, ground together twice (Have the fishmonger fillet and grind the fish for you. See note above.)
2¼ teaspoons sugar
1 tablespoon kosher salt
⅓ cup (80 ml) ice water
Freshly ground black pepper

ASPIC
Strained fish stock, from above
2 onions, finely chopped
3 carrots, peeled and thinly sliced
2 teaspoons sugar
Kosher salt
Freshly ground black pepper

HORSERADISH
1 horseradish root, about 12 inches (30 cm) long
½ cup (125 ml) freshly squeezed lemon juice (2 to 3 lemons)

Challah (recipe follows), for serving

TO MAKE THE FISH STOCK: Rinse the fish frames (heads and bones) and skin well and place in an 8-quart (8 liter) stockpot. Add the water, onions, carrots, salt, sugar, and peppercorns and bring to a boil over high heat. Lower the heat and simmer, covered, for 45 minutes.

When the stock has cooled, double a piece of cheesecloth, wet it with cold water, wring it dry, and place it into a sieve set over a large bowl. Strain the stock through the cheesecloth. Twist the cheesecloth to extract all the liquid and flavor from the fish and vegetables. Discard the cheesecloth and its contents. Rinse the stockpot and pour in the strained fish stock.

TO MAKE THE MIXTURE FOR THE FISH OVALS: Finely grate the onions. (You can do this in a food processor.) Finely grate the hard-boiled eggs. (I use a Mouli grater to do this.). Whisk the fresh egg.

Place the ground fish in the bowl of an electric stand mixer. Add the onions, all the eggs, the sugar, and salt. Using the dough hook, add the ice water, 1½ teaspoons at a time, at very low speed. This may take about 15 minutes. Be patient. Season to taste with salt and pepper. Refrigerate for at least 30 minutes.

TO MAKE THE ASPIC AND THE FISH OVALS: Add the onions, carrots, sugar, salt, and pepper to the strained fish stock. Bring it to a gentle boil.

Place a bowl of cold water nearby. Wet your fingers and, using 2 heaping tablespoons at a time, shape the ground fish mixture into smooth ovals (see note). Drop the ovals into the simmering stock. Bring the stock back to a simmer and poach the ovals, covered, for 1 hour. Shake the pan from time to time. Season to taste. Cool.

Transfer the fish ovals and stock to a container and refrigerate, covered, until ready to serve.

TO MAKE THE HORSERADISH: Trim both ends of the horseradish and peel. Cut it into small pieces and chop finely in a food processor, adding the lemon juice to keep it from darkening. Place it in a container with a tight-fitting lid and refrigerate.

TO SERVE: Place 3 ovals on each plate and spoon over the aspic. Serve the horseradish on the side. Accompany with Challah.

Note: You can also use a #30 oval ice-cream scoop to measure the fish ovals. From time to time, wet the scoop and your fingers in cold water.

CHALLAH

• Makes 3 medium loaves

Challah is the traditional bread eaten on Friday nights and holidays, when it is blessed along with the wine. Homemade challah is so much lighter and airier than even the best store-bought variety that it is definitely worth the effort to make it yourself. While this recipe may at first seem a bit daunting, you will be surprised at how easy it becomes with practice.

YEAST MIXTURE
1¾ cups (420 ml) lukewarm water
2 envelopes active dry yeast (each envelope is 2¼ teaspoons/7 g)
1 tablespoon sugar

DOUGH
½ cup sugar
3 large eggs plus 1 large egg yolk, at room temperature
1 tablespoon salt
½ cup (125 ml) vegetable oil, plus 1 teaspoon for greasing the baking sheet
7½ to 8½ cups (960 to 1090 g) unbleached all-purpose flour

GLAZE
1 large egg, whisked with a fork

TO MAKE THE YEAST MIXTURE: Pour the lukewarm water into the bowl of an electric stand mixer. Add the yeast and sugar and stir lightly. Cover with a towel and place in a warm, draft-free place (such as a food warmer or a warm turned off-oven) for 10 to 15 minutes, until bubbles appear. (This is called proofing the yeast, to make sure it is still active.)

TO MAKE THE DOUGH: Add the sugar, eggs, egg yolk, salt, vegetable oil, and about 7½ cups (960 g) of the flour to the yeast mixture. Fit the dough hook to the mixer and knead the mixture at low speed for about 10 minutes, adding flour as necessary to make the dough smooth and elastic.

Cover the bowl with a towel and again set it in a warm place for about an hour, until the dough doubles in bulk.

Turn the dough out onto a floured pastry board or work surface and divide it into three equal sections. Divide each section into three pieces.

Using your hands, roll each of the nine pieces into strands 10 to 12 inches (25 to 30 cm) long, making them thinner at the ends and thicker in the center. Add more flour as necessary.

Pinch the ends of 3 of the strands together and braid. Do the same with the remaining 6 strands of dough, so that you end up with 3 braided loaves. Place the 3 loaves on a greased baking sheet. Put them in a warm place for 30 minutes so they can rise for the last time.

Meanwhile, preheat the oven to 375°F (190°C).

Brush each of the challah loaves lightly with the glaze and bake for about 30 minutes, until golden.

Note: Challah freezes well. Wrap the loaf in wax paper, then in foil, and place it in a freezer bag. It is not necessary to defrost before serving. Remove the wrappings and place the loaf directly on a shelf in a 200°F (95°C) preheated oven. Bake for about 1 hour, until warm.

POULTRY: CHICKEN, CAPON, TURKEY & DUCK

Chicken with Chestnuts
Chicken with Honey and Mustard
Chicken with Citrus and Tarragon
Chicken Rolls with Mushrooms
Chicken Rolls with Orange Sauce
Chicken with Potatoes and Olives
Chicken Shish Kebabs with Two Marinades
Glazed Chicken with Glazed Mushrooms
Chicken Puttanesca
Sake-Steamed Chicken
Chicken with Rosemary
Curried Chicken
Stir-Fried Chicken with Snow Peas
Roast Capon with Olives
Turkey Scaloppini with Two Sauces
Roasted Turkey Breast
Roast Turkey
Turkey Burgers
Broiled Duck Breasts with Ginger Sauce
Braised Duck

CHICKEN WITH CHESTNUTS

• Makes 8 servings

Chestnuts are often used in Chinese cuisine, and they always add an unusual flavor. Once considered "brain food," they appear most often in dishes that are served in the cold winter months when most of us are in need of energy. Simple white rice or Asian-style rice noodles make a nice complement.

> **2 ounces (57 g) dried shiitake mushrooms**
> **1½ cups (375 ml) boiling water**
> **2 tablespoons vegetable oil**
> **8 chicken legs**
> **8 chicken thighs**
> **Kosher salt**
> **Freshly ground black pepper**
> **1 bunch scallions**
> **2-inch (5 cm) piece ginger, peeled and grated**
> **⅓ cup (80 ml) low-sodium soy sauce**
> **One 14.8 ounce (420 g) jar peeled roasted chestnuts**

Place the dried mushrooms in a small bowl and pour the boiling water over them. Cover and let stand for 20 minutes, or until soft.

Remove the reconstituted mushrooms with a slotted spoon. Squeeze all the liquid back into the bowl and set the mushrooms aside. Strain the mushroom liquid through a paper-lined sieve into another small bowl. Cut off and discard the mushroom stems. Quarter the mushroom caps.

Preheat the oven to 450°F (230°C).

Pat the chicken dry with paper towels. Heat the oil in a heavy-bottomed skillet and sauté the chicken lightly. Transfer to a glass, ceramic, or enamel-lined baking pan that can hold the chicken pieces in a single layer. Season with salt and pepper.

Cut the scallions, including the green part, into thin slices. Reserve some for garnish. To the skillet, add the mushrooms, the strained mushroom liquid, ginger, scallions, soy sauce, and chestnuts. Bring to a boil and pour it over the chicken.

Cover the baking pan with heavy foil and bake for 20 minutes. Uncover and bake for another 20 minutes, or until the chicken is tender.

Season to taste with salt and pepper. Garnish with the reserved scallion rounds.

CHICKEN WITH HONEY AND MUSTARD

• Makes 4 servings

Honey, mustard, and soy sauce make a wonderful combination, and the orange and lemon add a delightful piquancy. I like to serve this moist and flavorful dish at room temperature.

4 boneless, skinless chicken breasts (about 6 ounces/170 g each)

MARINADE
1-inch (2.5 cm) piece ginger, peeled and grated
1½ tablespoons low-sodium soy sauce
2 tablespoons dry white wine
3 tablespoons freshly squeezed orange juice
1 tablespoon freshly squeezed lemon juice
2 tablespoons extra virgin olive oil
2 tablespoons Dijon mustard
1 tablespoon honey
Freshly ground black pepper

Chives, snipped, for garnish

Place the chicken in a glass or nonreactive dish. In a small bowl, combine the marinade well and pour over the chicken. Cover and refrigerate for 3 to 4 hours, turning once.

Preheat the broiler. Set the rack in the broiler pan and cover it completely with heavy foil. Meanwhile, bring the chicken breasts back to room temperature.

Make a shallow "basket" with a piece of heavy foil, crimping it at the corners so that the juices don't spill out. (See Notes on Techniques, page 351.) Set the basket on the broiler rack, place the chicken in the basket, and spoon over half the marinade. Put the pan in the oven (or broiling unit), as close as possible to the heat source. Broil the breasts for 5 minutes. Turn them over, spoon on the remaining marinade, and broil for another 2-3 minutes. The chicken will be slightly pink on the inside.

Remove from the oven, cover the chicken with the lining foil, and let rest for 1 minute so the juices can flow back into the tissues. The chicken will continue cooking.

TO SERVE: Cut the chicken on the diagonal into medium slices and spoon over the accumulated juices. Garnish with snipped chives.

CHICKEN WITH CITRUS AND TARRAGON

• Makes 4 servings

This is a simple, well-seasoned dish that I often serve on Passover because it is quick and easy to prepare, requires little clean up, and tastes delicious at room temperature.

4 boneless, skinless chicken breasts (about 6 ounces/170 g each)

CITRUS-TARRAGON MARINADE
2 garlic cloves
Kosher salt
3 tablespoons extra virgin olive oil
3 to 4 tablespoons freshly squeezed lemon juice
3 to 4 tablespoons freshly squeezed orange juice
Grated zest of 1 navel orange
Leaves from 5 tarragon sprigs, coarsely chopped,
  plus leaves from 2 sprigs for garnish
Freshly ground black pepper

Place the chicken in a glass or nonreactive dish. Coarsely chop the garlic cloves on a cutting board. Sprinkle them with 1 teaspoon kosher salt and, using a knife, crush them into a paste. In a small bowl, combine the garlic paste, oil, lemon and orange juices, orange zest, and chopped tarragon. Season to taste with salt and pepper. Pour the marinade over the chicken. Cover and refrigerate for 3 to 4 hours, turning once.

Preheat the broiler. Set the rack in the broiler pan and cover it completely with heavy foil. Meanwhile, bring the chicken breasts back to room temperature.

Make a shallow "basket" with a piece of heavy foil, crimping it at the corners so that that the juices don't spill out. (See Notes on Techniques, page 351.) Set the basket on the broiler rack, place the chicken in the basket, and pour half the marinade over it. Put the pan in the oven (or broiling unit), as close as possible to the heat source. Broil the breasts for 5 minutes. Turn them over, spoon on the rest of the marinade, and broil for another 2-3 minutes. The chicken will be slightly pink on the inside.

Remove from the oven, cover the chicken with the lining foil, and let rest for 1 minute so the juices can flow back into the tissues. The chicken will continue cooking.

TO SERVE: Cut the chicken on the diagonal into medium slices. Spoon over the accumulated juices and garnish with tarragon.

CHICKEN ROLLS WITH MUSHROOMS

• Makes 4 servings

This is an Asian-inspired dish that I like to serve as either a main course at a dinner party or one of several other dishes on a buffet table. It is beautiful to look at and is equally good hot or at room temperature.

4 boneless, skinless chicken breasts (about 6 ounces/170 g each)
    (Ask the butcher to butterfly the chicken breasts and pound them thin.)
12 large arugula leaves
Kosher salt
Freshly ground black pepper

FILLING
½ pound (225 g) mixed wild mushrooms, including shiitake, chanterelle,
    cremini, or porcini mushrooms
3 tablespoons extra virgin olive oil
2 garlic cloves, minced
1 tablespoon low-sodium soy sauce
1 teaspoon freshly squeezed lemon juice
Kosher salt
Freshly ground black pepper
2 tablespoons fresh marjoram leaves, coarsely chopped

GINGER-SESAME SAUCE
1-inch (2.5 cm) piece of ginger, peeled and grated
1½ tablespoons sesame oil
1½ tablespoons seasoned rice vinegar
¼ cup (60 ml) low-sodium soy sauce
1 tablespoon honey

TO MAKE THE FILLING: Wipe the mushrooms with a damp paper towel. Cut off and discard the shiitake stems, if using. Quarter all the mushrooms and place in food processor. Pulse until coarsely chopped.

Heat the oil in a wok. Add the garlic and sauté over low heat until soft. Add the chopped mushrooms, raise the heat, and stir for 1 minute. Remove to a bowl. Season to taste with the soy sauce, lemon juice, salt, and pepper. Stir in the marjoram and cool.

TO MAKE THE SAUCE: Bring all the sauce ingredients to a boil in a small enamel-lined saucepan and season to taste with salt and pepper. Remove from the heat.

TO MAKE THE ROLLS: Lightly salt and pepper each chicken breast on both sides and place it on a piece of cling wrap. Line the breast with 3 arugula leaves and one-quarter of the filling. Starting with the narrowest end, roll the breast up (not too tight!), until it looks like a log. (I use the cling wrap to facilitate the rolling.) When the breast is rolled and completely enclosed in cling wrap, twist the sides and close with a metal tie. Refrigerate if not cooking right away.

TO COOK THE ROLLS: Bring the chicken rolls back to room temperature, if necessary. Place in the basket of a bamboo steamer. Set the basket over a large pot or wok whose bottom third has been filled with water. Bring the water to a rolling boil. Cover and steam over high heat for 9 to 10 minutes, turning the rolls once. Cook until the chicken has turned pale pink inside. Turn off the heat and let rest, covered, for 1 minute.

TO SERVE: Remove one of the ties and, holding the other end, slip each roll out onto a plate. Pour off the accumulated juices. Cut each roll on the diagonal into three pieces. Place the pieces on a dinner plate or serving dish. Reheat the sauce and spoon the hot sauce over the pieces.

CHICKEN ROLLS WITH ORANGE SAUCE

• Makes 4 servings

This is similar to Chicken Rolls with Mushrooms (page 196), but it has a more distinct Asian flavor. I serve it as the main course for dinner or as one of several dishes on a buffet table.

4 boneless, skinless chicken breasts (about 6 ounces/170 g each)
  (Ask the butcher to butterfly the chicken breasts and pound them thin.)
12 large spinach leaves
Kosher salt
Freshly ground black pepper

FILLING
½ cup (80 g) raw sushi rice
¾ cup (180 ml) cold water
1 tablespoon seasoned rice vinegar
Kosher salt
Freshly ground black pepper

ORANGE SAUCE
1½-inch (4 cm) piece ginger, peeled and grated
3 to 4 tablespoons low-sodium soy sauce
¾ cup (180 ml) freshly squeezed orange juice
1½ tablespoons freshly squeezed lemon juice
1½ tablespoons extra virgin olive oil
1½ tablespoons honey
Kosher salt
Freshly ground black pepper

TO MAKE THE FILLING: Place the sushi rice and water in a small saucepan. Bring to a boil; lower the heat and simmer, covered, for 8 minutes. Remove from the heat and let rest, covered, for 10 minutes. Season with vinegar, salt, and pepper. Mix well and cool.

TO MAKE THE SAUCE: Bring all the sauce ingredients to a boil in a small enamel-lined saucepan. Season to taste with salt and pepper.

TO MAKE THE ROLLS: Lightly salt and pepper each chicken breast on both sides and place it on a piece of cling wrap. Remove the stems from the spinach leaves and flatten the leaves so they will roll easier. Line each breast with 3 spinach leaves and one-fourth of the filling.

Starting with the narrowest end, roll the breast up (not too tight!) until it looks like a log. (I use the cling wrap to facilitate the rolling.) When the breast is rolled and completely enclosed in the cling wrap, twist the sides and close them with a metal tie. Refrigerate if not using right away.

TO COOK THE ROLLS: Bring the chicken rolls back to room temperature, if necessary. Place them in the basket of a bamboo steamer. Set the basket over a large pot or wok, whose bottom third has been filled with water. Bring the water to a rolling boil. Cover and steam over high heat for 9 to 10 minutes, turning the rolls once. Cook until the chicken has turned pale pink inside. Turn off the heat and let rest, covered, for 1 minute.

TO SERVE: Remove one of the ties and, holding the other end, slip each roll out onto a plate. Pour off the accumulated juices. Cut each roll on the diagonal into 3 pieces. Place the pieces on a dinner plate or serving dish. Reheat the sauce and spoon the hot sauce over the pieces.

CHICKEN WITH POTATOES AND OLIVES

• Makes 4 servings

I am always pleased to come up with a dish that is a meal in itself—one that combines either chicken or meat with vegetables. This is one of my favorites. Because it is so easy to make, I often serve it at Passover. I bake it in an attractive casserole so it can go directly from the oven to the table.

> **5 tablespoons extra virgin olive oil**
> **9 garlic cloves**
> **Kosher salt**
> **¼ cup (60 ml) freshly squeezed lemon juice**
> **Leaves from 10 thyme sprigs**
> **Freshly ground black pepper**
> **4 boneless, skinless chicken breasts (about 6 ounces/170 g each)**
> **5 plum tomatoes**
> **1 pound (450 g) Yukon gold potatoes, unpeeled, quartered**
> **½ cup (67 g) pitted black olives, quartered**

Preheat the oven to 450°F (230°C).

With 1 tablespoon of the oil, grease a glass, ceramic, or enamel-lined baking pan that can hold all the vegetables in a single layer .

Coarsely chop 4 of the garlic cloves on a cutting board. Sprinkle with ½ teaspoon salt and, using a knife, crush them into a paste. Place the paste in a small bowl and combine it with the lemon juice, 2 tablespoons of the oil, half of the thyme leaves, and pepper to taste.

Pat dry the chicken breasts with paper towels and season lightly on both sides with salt and pepper. Coat the chicken with the mixture and set aside.

Bring a pot of water to a boil. Drop the tomatoes into the boiling water; bring the water back to a boil and drain. Core the tomatoes and slip off the skin. Cut the tomatoes in half widthwise and squeeze gently to remove the seeds. (Some seeds will remain.) Cut the tomatoes in quarters.

Thickly slice the remaining 5 garlic cloves and spread them in the prepared baking pan along with the tomatoes, potatoes, olives, the rest of the thyme leaves, and the remaining 2 tablespoons oil. Season to taste with salt and pepper. Roast the vegetables, uncovered, for 20 minutes, or until almost tender.

Place the chicken breasts on top of the vegetables and bake, uncovered, for 5 minutes. Turn them over, spoon on some pan juices, and bake for another 5 minutes, or until the chicken is slightly pink on the inside. Cover with foil for 1 minute.

CHICKEN SHISH KEBABS WITH TWO MARINADES

• Makes 8 servings

Chicken on skewers, cooked over hot coals on an outdoor grill, is a favorite hot-weather dish in this country as well as in many parts of the Near, Middle, and Far East. This recipe offers the option of two very different marinades that follow: Sesame-Thyme or Honey-Lemon. If your stove is equipped with a barbecue, you can make this dish at any time of year.

> **8 boneless, skinless chicken breasts (about 6 ounces/170 g each)**
> **8 wooden skewers**
> **Small vegetables, such as mushrooms or onions, or slices of zucchini**
> **   or eggplant (optional)**

Cut each breast into four pieces. Coat the chicken with one of the marinades below, cover, and refrigerate for at least 2 hours.

Soak the skewers in cold water for at least 30 minutes. Prepare the outdoor grill or preheat the indoor grill. Bring the chicken to room temperature. Thread the marinated chicken pieces (and vegetables, if using) onto the wooden skewers.

Grill each skewer for about 2 minutes on each side.

Sesame-Thyme Marinade

• Makes about 1 cup (250 ml) marinade

> **½ cup (60 g) sesame seeds**
> **½ cup (20 g) fresh thyme leaves (about 20 sprigs)**
> **1 teaspoon sea salt**
> **4 tablespoons extra virgin olive oil**
> **4 tablespoons freshly squeezed lemon juice**

Toast the sesame seeds in a dry skillet, over medium heat, until golden. Cool.

Transfer to a spice grinder. (This is available in most kitchen-supply stores.) Add thyme leaves and sea salt and blend to a coarse powder. Transfer to a bowl and add oil and lemon juice.

HONEY-LEMON MARINADE

• Makes about ⅔ cup (160 ml) marinade

3 tablespoons low-sodium soy sauce
3 tablespoons freshly squeezed lemon juice
3 tablespoons extra virgin olive oil
3 tablespoons Dijon mustard
1½ tablespoons honey
3 garlic cloves, minced
Freshly ground black pepper

Combine all ingredients in a small bowl.

GLAZED CHICKEN WITH GLAZED MUSHROOMS

• Makes 4 servings

This is a delicious blend of spicy and sweet flavors. I often serve the chicken over sushi rice, topped with the glazed mushrooms. The arrangement makes an attractive pyramid.

CHICKEN GLAZE
2 tablespoons extra virgin olive oil
2 tablespoons freshly squeezed lemon juice
2 teaspoons Dijon mustard
3 tablespoons honey
2 garlic cloves, minced
1 teaspoon sweet paprika
¼ teaspoon cayenne pepper
Kosher salt
Freshly ground black pepper

MUSHROOM GLAZE
3 tablespoons sake
2 tablespoons low-sodium soy sauce
2 teaspoons sesame oil
2 teaspoons dark brown sugar

1 pound (450 g) shiitake mushrooms
1 tablespoon extra virgin olive oil, plus ½ tablespoon for greasing the pan
Kosher salt
Freshly ground black pepper
4 boneless, skinless chicken breasts (about 6 ounces/170 g each)

Sushi Rice (page 158), for serving
1 bunch chives, finely snipped, for garnish

Preheat the oven to 425°F (220°C).

Combine the ingredients for the chicken glaze in a small bowl. Season to taste with salt and pepper. Set aside.

Combine the ingredients for the mushroom glaze.

Cut off and discard the mushroom stems. Wipe the caps with a damp paper towel and cut into thin slices. Heat a wok and add one tablespoon of olive oil. Stir-fry the mushrooms over high heat until they just begin to wilt.

Pour the mushroom glaze over the mushrooms and continue stirring over medium-heat

SAKE-STEAMED CHICKEN

• Makes 2 servings

Edamame, combined with seasoned sushi rice or rice noodles, makes a fine complement to this delicious and health-conscious dish.

2 boneless, skinless chicken breasts (about 6 ounces/170 g each)
Kosher salt
Freshly ground black pepper

SAKE MARINADE
¼ cup sake
1 tablespoon low-sodium soy sauce
1 tablespoon extra virgin olive oil
2 scallions, including green parts, thinly sliced
¾-inch (2 cm) piece ginger, peeled and grated

½ cup (78 g) shelled soy beans (edamame), defrosted (see note)
Sushi Rice (page 158) or cooked rice noodles, for serving

Pat the chicken breasts dry with paper towels and season lightly with salt and pepper. Place them in a heatproof dish that will fit in the basket of a steamer.

Combine the marinade ingredients in a small bowl. Pour the marinade over the breasts and cover tightly with cling wrap. Refrigerate for at least 2 hours, turning once. Before cooking, bring the chicken back to room temperature.

Place the dish, still sealed with cling wrap, in the steamer basket. Steam, covered, over briskly boiling water for 10 minutes, or until the chicken is pale pink inside. Remove the dish from the steamer and let rest, still covered, for 1 minute.

TO SERVE: Cut each piece of chicken on a diagonal into 3 pieces. Combine the edamame with Sushi Rice or rice noodles and place in a mound in the center of the dinner plate. Top with the sliced chicken and spoon over the accumulated juices.

Note: Frozen endamame, shelled and unshelled, are available in most supermarkets and health-food stores.

CHICKEN WITH ROSEMARY

• Makes 6 servings

This preparation is simplicity itself. Since it doesn't contain any white meat, which tends to become dry when reheated, leftovers can easily be warmed in the oven and served the next day.

6 chicken legs
6 chicken thighs
Kosher salt
Freshly ground black pepper

MARINADE
¼ cup freshly squeezed orange juice
3 tablespoons freshly squeezed lime juice
¼ cup pineapple juice (see note)
2 tablespoons extra virgin olive oil
Leaves from 4 rosemary sprigs, finely chopped
3 garlic cloves, finely chopped
1 teaspoon ground cumin
¾ teaspoon chili powder

Pat the chicken dry with paper towels. Salt and pepper the pieces lightly and place them in a single layer in a glass, ceramic, or enamel-lined baking pan, skin side down.

Combine the marinade ingredients and coat the chicken well. Cover and refrigerate for at least 2 hours.

Preheat the oven to 400°F (205°C). Remove the chicken from the refrigerator and bring it back to room temperature.

Bake the chicken for 15 minutes; turn the pieces over and bake for another 15 minutes, or until the chicken is tender.

TO SERVE: Spoon over the accumulated juices.

Note: Small bottles of pineapple juice are available in most health-food stores.

CURRIED CHICKEN

• Makes 2 servings

This dish, which is simple and quick to make, has a touch of curry, a mix of Indian spices. It looks pretty with the bits of whole-grain mustard on top.

2 boneless, skinless chicken breasts (about 6 ounces/170 g each)
Kosher salt
Freshly ground black pepper

CURRY COATING
1 tablespoon extra virgin olive oil
2 tablespoons freshly squeezed lemon juice
1 tablespoon whole-grain mustard
1 tablespoon honey
½ teaspoon Madras curry powder
¼ teaspoon kosher salt
¼ teaspoon freshly ground black pepper

Preheat the oven to 450°F (230°C). Line a baking pan with foil. Pat the chicken breasts dry with paper towels, season lightly with salt and pepper, and place them in the baking pan.

Mix the ingredients for the curry coating. Cover the chicken with the coating.

Bake for 10 minutes without turning, until they have a trace of pink on the inside. Remove from the oven, cover with the lining foil, and let rest for 1 minute. The chicken will continue cooking.

TO SERVE: Slice the chicken on a diagonal into 3 pieces and spoon over the accumulated juices.

STIR-FRIED CHICKEN WITH SNOW PEAS

• Makes 2 servings

When I want to make a quick and easy dinner for two, I usually think of this tasty Chinese dish, which has a variety of textures, tastes, and colors. I serve it with plain white rice.

2 boneless, skinless chicken breasts (about 6 ounces/170 g each)
6 dried shiitake mushrooms
¼ pound (113 g) snow peas
2 tablespoons vegetable oil
½ teaspoon sugar
½ teaspoon kosher salt
2 tablespoons low-sodium soy sauce

Pat the chicken breasts dry with paper towels. Cut them on the diagonal into 1-inch (2.5 cm) slices and set aside.

Place the dried mushrooms in a small bowl and pour the boiling water over them. Cover and let stand for 20 minutes, or until the mushrooms are soft.

Remove the reconstituted mushrooms with a slotted spoon. Squeeze out all the liquid. Cut off and discard the stems and quarter the caps.

Pinch off both ends of the snow peas and pull off the string running along the straighter edge. Cut the snow peas in half, on the diagonal, and rinse.

Heat a wok over medium heat. Heat 1 tablespoon of the oil. Add the snow peas and cook, covered, for 1 minute, or until they are almost tender. Remove to a bowl.

Add the remaining oil to the wok and heat it. Add the chicken slices and stir-fry them over medium heat until they begin to change color. Add the mushrooms and snow peas and continue stir-frying until the inside of the chicken is slightly pink.

Season with the sugar, salt, and soy sauce.

ROAST CAPON WITH OLIVES

• Makes 10 to 12 servings

Capons have a subtly sweet taste that is quite different from chicken and turkey. The olives add an interesting flavor and give the sauce a delicious taste and texture. I often serve this dish at Passover, and my family and friends (especially the olive lovers) always ask for second helpings.

1 capon, about 9 pounds (4.08 kg)
3 tablespoons freshly squeezed lemon juice
Kosher salt
Freshly ground black pepper
2 onions
1 cup (40 g) tightly packed flat-leaf parsley, coarsely chopped
¾ cup (100 g) pitted Kalamata olives, quartered
3 tablespoons (45 g) unsalted margarine, melted
1 cup (250 ml) dry white wine

Preheat the oven to 350°F (175°C).

Discard any excess fat from the capon. Rinse it inside and out and pat dry with paper towels. Season the inside and out with lemon juice, salt and pepper.

Thinly slice one of the onions and set aside. Quarter the other onion and place it in the cavity along with the parsley and 1 tablespoon of the olives.

Brush the capon with the margarine and place it on its side in a roasting pan. Scatter the sliced onions and the remaining olives around the pan.

Roast the capon for 35 minutes, basting with one-third of the wine.

Turn the capon on its other side and roast for another 35 minutes, again basting with a third of the wine.

Turn the capon breast side up for 15 minutes, basting with the remaining wine.

Turn the breast side down for another 15 minutes. The capon is ready when the drumstick juices run clear. (The total cooking time is about 1 hour and 40 minutes, or about 11 minutes per pound/450 g.)

Remove the capon from the oven and cover it tightly with heavy foil. Let it stand for 20 minutes to let the juices flow back into the tissues. Place it on a cutting board.

Pour the liquid from the baking pan, along with the olives and onions, into a small saucepan. Place the saucepan in the freezer for about 10 minutes, so that the grease can quickly rise to the top. (This makes it easier to remove.)

TO SERVE: Skim off the fat and reheat the sauce. Discard the onion and parsley from the cavity. Cut the breast into thin slices and serve with the sauce.

TURKEY SCALOPPINI WITH TWO SAUCES

• Makes 4 servings

This is a quick and tasty dish that can be served with either of the sauces below. The two tastes are quite different—the Apricot Sauce is sweet and the Caper Sauce is piquant—and both can be prepared ahead of time.

4 turkey scaloppini (about 6 ounces/170 g each)
1 tablespoon unbleached flour
2 tablespoons extra virgin olive oil
Kosher salt
Freshly ground black pepper
Apricot Sauce or Caper Sauce (recipes follow), for serving
¼ cup (10 g) loosely packed flat-leaf parsley, coarsely chopped, for garnish

Pat the turkey dry with paper towels and dredge lightly with flour, shaking off the excess. In a medium nonstick skillet, heat the oil over medium heat. Sauté the scaloppini quickly on each side until there is a slight trace of pink on the inside. Season lightly with salt and pepper. Pour one of the sauces that follow over the scaloppini; garnish with parsley.

APRICOT SAUCE

2 tablespoons extra virgin olive oil
2 small shallots, minced
½-inch (13 mm) piece ginger, peeled and grated
3 dried apricots, cut into ¼-inch (6 mm) cubes
2 tablespoons dried currants
⅓ cup (80 ml) apricot juice
⅓ cup (80 ml) dry white wine
1 tablespoon balsamic vinegar
Kosher salt
Freshly ground black pepper

Heat the oil in a small enamel-lined saucepan. Add the shallots and ginger and cook, covered, over low heat for 3 minutes, or until the shallots are soft. Add the apricots, currants, juice, wine, and vinegar. Bring to a boil, and cook for 1 minute. Season with salt and pepper.

CAPER SAUCE

2 tablespoons extra virgin olive oil
2 small shallots, minced
1 garlic clove, minced
¼ cup (60 ml) dry white wine
2 tablespoons small capers
1 to 2 tablespoons freshly squeezed lemon juice
Kosher salt
Freshly ground black pepper

Heat the oil in a small enamel-lined saucepan. Add the shallots and garlic and cook, covered, over low heat for 3 minutes until soft. Add the wine, capers, and lemon juice. Boil for 1 minute and season to taste with salt and pepper.

ROASTED TURKEY BREAST

• Makes 8 servings

This easy recipe is very versatile. With its well-seasoned and aromatic sauce, it is an excellent main course. It goes especially well with Red Cabbage with Capers (page 119) and Grated Potato Pancake (page 127). And the next day, at lunch, it makes a fine sandwich.

3 tablespoons (45 g) unsalted margarine
1 onion, finely chopped
3 garlic cloves, finely chopped
2 tablespoons whole-grain mustard
3 tablespoons low-sodium soy sauce
One 3-pound (1.36 kg) boneless, skin-on turkey breast, rolled and tied
  (Ask the butcher to do this for you.)
1 cup (250 ml) white wine
¾ cup (180 ml) freshly squeezed orange juice

Preheat the oven to 325°F (165°C).

Melt the margarine in a small saucepan, and sauté the onion and garlic over low heat until soft, about 5 minutes. Remove from the heat, add the mustard and soy sauce, and mix well.

Place the turkey in a roasting pan and coat it with the mustard–soy sauce mixture.

Combine the wine and orange juice in a measuring cup with a spout (this makes pouring easier).

Roast the turkey, uncovered, for 35 minutes, basting frequently with the wine–orange juice mixture. Turn the turkey over and, continuing to baste, roast for another 35 minutes. A meat thermometer inserted in the center should register 160°F (70°C), and the center should still have a touch of pink.

Remove the turkey from the oven and cover with heavy foil. Let it rest for 15 minutes before slicing.

TO SERVE: Place the turkey on a cutting board and cut into ½-inch (13 mm) slices. (An electric knife makes the cutting much easier.) Serve with the accumulated juices.

ROAST TURKEY

• Makes 12 to 14 servings

You do not have to wait for Thanksgiving to serve this dish, as it is surprisingly easy to make and always very tasty. I often serve it when I have many guests to feed.

One 14-pound (6.35 kg) turkey
3 tablespoons freshly squeezed lemon juice
3 tablespoons low-sodium soy sauce
Freshly ground black pepper
1 cup (250 ml) freshly squeezed orange juice
1 cup (250 ml) dry white wine
2 onions
5 sprigs rosemary
5 tablespoons (75 g) unsalted margarine, melted

Preheat the oven to 325°F (165°C).

Discard any excess fat from the turkey. Rinse it inside and out and pat dry with paper towels. Season the skin and the cavity with the lemon juice, soy sauce, and pepper.

Combine the orange juice and wine in a measuring cup with a spout. (This makes pouring easier.)

Thinly slice one of the onions and set it aside. Cut the other onion in quarters and place it in the cavity along with the rosemary sprigs. Brush the turkey with the margarine and place it on its side in a roasting pan. Scatter the sliced onion around the pan.

Roast the turkey for 30 minutes, basting with the orange juice–wine mixture. Turn the turkey on its other side and roast for another 30 minutes, continuing to baste. Turn the turkey breast side up and, continuing to baste, roast for 20 minutes. For the final 20 minutes, place the turkey breast side down. (If the drumsticks begin to get too brown, cover the ends with foil.)

The turkey is ready when the drumsticks move easily in their sockets and the juices run clear. (The total cooking time is about 1 hour and 40 minutes, or about 7 minutes per pound/ 450 g.) A meat thermometer inserted into the thickest part of the breast should read 160°F (70°C).

Remove the turkey from the oven and cover it tightly with heavy foil. Let it stand for 30 minutes. (This allows the juices to flow back into the tissues.) Place it on a cutting board.

Pour the contents of the roasting pan into a small saucepan. Put the saucepan in the freezer for about 10 minutes, so that the grease can quickly rise to the top. (This makes it easier to remove.)

TO SERVE: Skim off the fat and reheat the pan juices. Discard the onion and rosemary from the cavity and carve the turkey. Serve with the juices.

TURKEY BURGERS

• Makes 4 burgers

The combination of mushrooms, mustard, and herbs makes the ground turkey moist and flavorful as well as nutritious. These burgers can be served warm or at room temperature.

½ ounce (14 g) dried porcini mushrooms
¾ cup (180 ml) boiling water
½ pound (227 g) shiitake mushrooms
2 small shallots, quartered
1 pound (450 g) ground turkey, a mix of dark and light
2 teaspoons Dijon mustard
Leaves from 10 thyme sprigs
Kosher salt
Freshly ground black pepper
2 tablespoons extra virgin olive oil

Place the dried mushrooms in a small bowl and pour the boiling water over them. Cover and let stand for 15 minutes, or until the mushrooms are soft.

Remove the reconstituted mushrooms with a slotted spoon. Squeeze out all the liquid (see note). Place the mushrooms in a food processor.

Cut off and discard the shiitake stems, wipe the caps with a damp paper towel, and quarter them. Add to the food processor along with shallots. Pulse, scraping the sides with a rubber spatula, until all the mushrooms are finely chopped.

Transfer the mushrooms to a bowl; add the ground turkey, mustard, and thyme. Season well with salt and pepper. Place a few drops of oil in your palms, and form the mixture into 4 rounded burgers.

Heat the oil in a nonstick skillet. Sauté the burgers over medium heat, covered, for 5 minutes on each side, or until cooked through.

Turn off the heat and let stand, covered, for 1 minute.

Note: Strain the mushroom soaking liquid through a paper-lined sieve and freeze for later use. It makes a wonderful addition to sauces and soups.

BROILED DUCK BREASTS WITH GINGER SAUCE

• Makes 2 servings

The sweet-and-sour sauce complements the rich taste of the duck. My husband loved this dish, and I often prepared it for the two of us as a special-occasion dinner.

GINGER SAUCE
3 tablespoons ginger, orange, or apricot preserves
2 tablespoons freshly squeezed orange juice
Grated zest of 1 lemon
1 tablespoon freshly squeezed lemon juice
1 tablespoon Cognac
1 teaspoon balsamic vinegar
Kosher salt
Freshly ground black pepper

2 boneless, skinless duck breasts (about 6 ounces/170 g each)
1 tablespoon extra virgin olive oil
Freshly ground black pepper

Preheat the broiler.

In a small enamel-lined saucepan, combine ingredients for the sauce—preserves, orange juice, lemon zest and juice, and Cognac. Bring to a boil, lower the heat, and simmer for 1 minute. Season with the vinegar; add salt and pepper to taste. Set aside.

Set the rack in the broiler pan and cover it completely with heavy foil. Make a shallow "basket" with a piece of heavy foil, crimping it at the corners so that that the juices don't spill out. (See Notes on Techniques, page 351.) Set the basket on the broiler rack.

Brush both sides of the duck breasts with oil and season lightly with pepper. (Kosher ducks tend to be salty, so I don't recommend adding salt.)

Arrange the duck breasts inside the foil basket, skin side up. Place the broiler pan in the oven (or broiling unit), as close as possible to the heat source. Broil for 3 minutes. Turn over and broil for another 2 minutes for medium-rare.

Remove the duck from the oven, cover with foil, and let rest for 1 minute so the juices can flow back into the tissues. The duck will continue cooking.

TO SERVE: Slice the breasts on the diagonal into medium slices and arrange on individual dinner plates. Reheat the sauce if necessary and spoon it over the duck.

BRAISED DUCK

• Makes 3 to 4 servings

Braising a duck, as opposed to roasting it, is common in Chinese cuisine. The result is a skinless and completely fat-free duck, with an unusually flavorful sauce. Because this dish is made a day in advance, it is also very convenient. I often serve this dish with plain white rice.

1 duck, about 5 pounds (2.27 kg)
4 tablespoons low-sodium soy sauce
6 scallions
1-inch (2.5 cm) piece ginger, peeled and sliced
2 star anise
1 cinnamon stick
2 tablespoons light brown sugar
3 tablespoons dry white wine
3 cups (720 ml) cold water

Discard the excess fat from the duck. Rinse it well inside and out and pat it dry with paper towels. Rub 2 tablespoons of the soy sauce into the skin. Place the duck in a glass or non-reactive dish and refrigerate, uncovered, overnight.

The next day, place the duck, breast side down, in an enamel-lined Dutch oven.

Cut 3 of the scallions, including the green part, into large pieces. Add them to the duck along with the remaining 2 tablespoons soy sauce, the ginger, star anise, cinnamon, 1 tablespoon of the sugar, the wine, and the water. Bring to a boil over high heat. Lower the heat and cook, covered, for 1 hour.

Turn the duck breast side up, cover, and cook for another hour.

Remove the duck from the pot, place it on a cutting board and let it cool slightly. When it is cool enough to handle, remove and discard the skin. (This process is easier when the skin is warm.)

While the duck is cooling, add the remaining sugar to the liquid in the pan. Boil it down, uncovered, until the liquid is reduced by half. Strain the sauce into a small saucepan and cool. Put the saucepan in the freezer for about 20 minutes, so that the grease can quickly rise to the top. (This makes it easier to remove.)

Coarsely chop the remaining 3 scallions, including the green part. Remove the breast from the bone. Cut the legs and the thighs from the carcass, leaving the drumstick bone in place.

TO SERVE: Skim off the fat from the sauce. Add the chopped scallion to the degreased sauce and heat. Serve the duck with the sauce.

MEAT

Osso Buco (Braised Veal Shanks)

Curried Veal Roast

Veal Stew

Boneless Rack of Veal

Barbecued Split Fillet (London Broil) with Two Marinades

Split Fillet (London Broil) with Port Wine Glaze

Chicken Livers with Vinegar

Pot Roast

Braised Short Ribs of Beef

Hearty Beef Stew

Beef Stew with Thyme

Baked Eggplant with Ground Meat, Tomatoes, and Pine Nuts

Stuffed Cabbage Rolls

Cholent

Meat Chili

Meatloaf

OSSO BUCO (BRAISED VEAL SHANKS)

• Makes 12 servings

Shanks of veal lend themselves to braising. This is a lovely dish, with a thick and aromatic sauce. It is best made a day or two in advance to allow the flavors to blend fully.

> **12 veal shanks, each 1½ inches/4 cm thick**
> **(Ask the butcher to tie the shanks around the middle.)**
> **2 tablespoons unbleached all-purpose flour**
> **4 tablespoons extra virgin olive oil**
> **Kosher salt**
> **Freshly ground black pepper**
> **5 celery stalks, peeled and cut into large pieces**
> **2 large onions, quartered**
> **4 garlic cloves, quarered**
> **3 large carrots, peeled and cut into large pieces**
> **One 35-ounce (992 g) can peeled imported tomatoes**
> **1 cup (250 ml) dry white wine**
> **1 cup (250 ml) chicken broth**
> **Leaves from 10 thyme sprigs**
> **1 cup (40 g) tightly packed flat-leaf parsley, coarsely chopped**

Preheat the oven to 350°F (175°C).

Pat the veal shanks dry with paper towels and dredge them lightly with flour. Shake off the excess.

Heat half the oil in a large nonstick skillet over medium-high heat. Sauté the shanks, four or five at a time, on both sides until lightly brown. Season the shanks lightly with salt and pepper and, as they are done, transfer them to an 8-quart (8 liter) enamel-lined saucepan or Dutch oven with a tight-fitting lid.

Finely chop the celery, onions, garlic, and carrots. You can do this in a food processor, one vegetable at a time: Pulse the celery until fine. Remove to a small bowl. Pulse the onions and garlic together until fine; add them to the celery. Pulse the carrots until fine. (If you chop everything together, the vegetables will become mushy.)

Heat the remaining oil in the skillet. Add the chopped vegetables and sauté over medium heat for a few minutes. Add the vegetables to the meat, along with the tomatoes, wine, broth, thyme, and parsley.

Bring to a boil over medium heat. Cover the saucepan or Dutch oven and bake in the lower third of the oven for 2 hours, or until the meat is tender.

Uncover and cook for another 30 minutes or so to reduce the sauce and thicken it. The shanks are done when the meat comes easily off the bone and is tender enough to be cut with a fork.

Refrigerate the veal shanks in the pot. (You can do this because it is enamel lined.) As the dish chills, the fat will come to the top and can easily be removed.

When ready to serve, remove the fat with a spoon and reheat the dish, covered, over medium heat. Spoon the sauce over each shank.

CURRIED VEAL ROAST

• Makes 6 servings

This is a tasty dish, with lots of vegetables and a flavorful sauce.

3 pounds (1.36 kg) boneless rack of veal, rolled and tied.
  (Ask the butcher to bone and tie the meat for you.)
1¾ teaspoons Madras curry powder
4 tablespoons extra virgin olive oil
¾ pound (340 g) small onions or shallots, peeled (see note)
3 garlic cloves, finely chopped
1 pound (450 g) baby carrots
Kosher salt
Freshly ground black pepper
Leaves from 15 marjoram sprigs, plus 5 sprigs for garnish
¾ cup (180 ml) dry white wine
½ cup (20 g) tightly packed flat-leaf parsley, coarsely chopped

Pat the veal dry with paper towels, place it on a sheet of wax paper and rub it all over with curry powder.

In a heavy 4-quart (4 liter) enamel-lined saucepan, heat the oil over moderate heat until hot but not smoking. Brown the veal on all sides for 4 minutes, turning the piece with tongs. Add the onions, garlic, and carrots. Season the meat and vegetables with salt and pepper. Add the marjoram leaves, wine, and parsley. Bring to a boil. Lower the heat, cover, and simmer for 1 hour, turning twice. (The meat will be pink.)

Remove from the heat and cool.

When the veal has cooled, remove it from the saucepan and place it on a cutting board. Cut it into ¼-inch (6 mm) slices. (An electric knife makes the cutting easier.) Wrap in foil until ready to serve.

Bring the sauce and vegetables to a boil and season to taste with salt and pepper. Serve the meat at room temperature and spoon the boiling sauce and vegetables on top.

Note: The easiest way to peel onions or shallots is to drop them into boiling water and return the water to a boil. Pour them into a strainer and peel. The skin will come off easily.

VEAL STEW

• Makes 6 servings

I prepare all my stews in advance, since doing so gives the flavors a chance to blend nicely. A heavy saucepan is essential for cooking stews, as it allows for slow, even cooking.

3 green bell peppers
4 tablespoons extra virgin olive oil
3 pounds (1.36 kg) boned shoulder of veal, cut into 2-inch (5 cm) pieces
   (Have the butcher remove the gristle and fat, and cut the veal for you.)
2 tablespoons unbleached all-purpose flour
Kosher salt
Freshly ground black pepper
2 onions
2 garlic cloves
One 28-ounce (794 g) can peeled imported tomatoes
15 black olives, pitted and coarsely chopped
½ cup (125 ml) dry white wine
Leaves from 10 thyme sprigs

Preheat the broiler. Set the rack in the broiler pan and cover it with foil.

Cut the peppers in half lengthwise, then core and seed them. Make a shallow "basket" with a piece of heavy foil, crimping it at the corners so that the liquids don't spill out. (See Notes on Techniques, page 351.) Set the basket on the broiler rack, and arrange the peppers inside, skin side up. Place the broiler pan in the oven (or broiling unit), as close as possible to the heat source. Broil for about 7 minutes, until the skin is blistered and charred. Cover the peppers with foil and cool. The heat will loosen the skin. Peel the peppers and cut them into 1-inch (2.5 cm) pieces.

Preheat the oven to 375°F (190°C).

In a large heavy skillet, heat the oil over medium heat. Pat the veal pieces dry with paper towels and dredge them lightly with flour, shaking off the excess. Over medium heat, sauté the meat, several pieces at a time, until browned. As the pieces brown, transfer them with tongs to a 4-quart (4 liter) enamel-lined saucepan or Dutch oven. Season the veal lightly with salt and pepper.

Finely chop the onions and garlic. You can do this in a food processor. Be sure to quarter the onions and garlic first, so that they chop quickly and do not become mushy.

Add the peppers, onions, garlic, tomatoes, olives, wine, and thyme to the veal. Bring to a boil over medium heat. Cover the pan with a tight-fitting lid and bake for 1 hour, or until the meat is tender. Season to taste with salt and pepper.

BONELESS RACK OF VEAL

• Makes 12 generous servings

This is an excellent dish to serve on Passover, as it is easy to prepare and serves many guests. It can be made ahead of time, then sliced and reheated in the sauce.

4 tablespoons extra virgin olive oil
Two 3-pound (1.36 kg) boneless breasts of veal
  (Ask the butcher to bone, roll, and tie the veal for you.)
Kosher salt
Freshly ground black pepper
3 onions
4 garlic cloves
One 28-ounce (794 g) can peeled imported tomatoes
1 cup (250 ml) dry white wine
1 tablespoon double-concentrated tomato paste
1 bunch tarragon

Preheat the oven to 350°F (175°C).

Heat half the oil in a large skillet. Pat the meat dry with paper towels and brown on all sides over medium-high heat. This will take about 4 minutes for each roast. Season with salt and pepper and transfer to an 8-quart (8 liter) enamel-lined roasting pan with a tight-fitting lid.

Finely chop the onions and garlic. You can easily do this in a food processor. Be sure to quarter the onions and garlic first so that they chop quickly and don't become mushy.

Add the remaining oil to the skillet and sauté the onions and garlic for a minute. Add the tomatoes, wine, tomato paste, and three-quarters of the tarragon sprigs. (Leave the rest for the garnish.) Bring to a boil and pour over the meat.

Cover the pan with foil, then with a lid to seal completely. Place in the oven and cook for 45 minutes. Turn meat over and cook for another 45 minutes.

Remove the roasts from the pan and let them cool. Discard the tarragon sprigs.

Remove the strings and cut the meat into ¼-inch (6 mm) slices. (It's easy to do this if you use an electric knife.) Wrap in foil until ready to serve. Pour the sauce into a small saucepan and set aside.

Remove the leaves from the reserved tarragon sprigs and chop coarsely. Before serving, bring the sauce to a boil. Add the chopped tarragon and season to taste with salt and pepper. Place the meat on a serving platter or individual plates and pour the boiling sauce over.

BARBECUED SPLIT FILLET (LONDON BROIL) WITH TWO MARINADES

• Makes 4 to 6 servings

A steak cooked on an outdoor grill is a summertime favorite, but if your stove is equipped with a barbecue, you can make this dish at any time of year. The two marinades below have very different flavors, and both are quite tasty.

2 pounds (900 g) split fillet (London broil)
Basil Marinade or Spicy Marinade (recipes follow), for serving

Place the meat in a glass or nonreactive dish and coat with one of the marinades below. Cover the dish with cling wrap and refrigerate for at least 2 hours, turning the meat once.

Before grilling, bring the meat back to room temperature. Prepare the outdoor grill or preheat the indoor grill. Cook the meat for about 5 minutes on each side for rare. Cover with foil and let rest for 2 to 3 minutes depending on how rare you like your meat.

TO SERVE: Cut the fillet on the diagonal into medium-thin slices.

BASIL MARINADE

• Makes about ¾ cup (180 ml) marinade

1 cup (40 g) tightly packed fresh basil leaves
2 garlic cloves, quartered
3 tablespoons freshly squeezed lemon juice
3 tablespoons extra virgin olive oil
¾ teaspoon kosher salt
Freshly ground black pepper

Place all the ingredients in a food processor and pulse until smooth. Season to taste with pepper.

SPICY MARINADE

• Makes about ⅓ cup (80 ml) marinade

    2 garlic cloves
    1 teaspoon kosher salt
    1 teaspoon chili powder
    1 teaspoon ground cumin
    2 teaspoons Worcestershire sauce
    ¼ teaspoon sugar
    ¾ teaspoon freshly ground black pepper
    3 tablespoons extra virgin olive oil

Coarsely chop the garlic cloves on a cutting board. Sprinkle them with the salt and, using a knife, crush them into a paste. Combine the paste with the other ingredients in small bowl.

SPLIT FILLET (LONDON BROIL) WITH PORT WINE GLAZE

• Makes 4 servings

The delicious glaze brings out the flavor of the meat.

PORT WINE GLAZE
½ cup (125 ml) port wine
¼ cup (60 ml) balsamic vinegar
½ teaspoon Dijon mustard
1½ tablespoons extra virgin olive oil
Kosher salt
Freshly ground black pepper

1½ pounds (680 g) split fillet (London broil)

In a small enamel-lined saucepan combine the wine, vinegar, mustard, and oil. Bring to a boil; lower the heat to medium-high and cook, uncovered, for about 25 minutes, until the liquid is reduced to about 3 tablespoons. Season with salt and pepper. (The glaze can be made in advance and refrigerated until needed. Rewarm it before using.)

Preheat the broiler. Set the rack in the broiling pan and cover it completely with heavy foil. Place the meat on the rack and set the pan in the oven (or broiling unit), as close as possible to the heat source. Broil for 5 minutes on each side for rare.

Remove from the oven and salt and pepper the meat lightly. Cover with foil, and let rest for 2 to 3 minutes, depending on how rare you like your meat, so the juices can flow back into the tissues.

TO SERVE: Cut the fillet on a diagonal into thin slices and spoon the glaze over.

CHICKEN LIVERS WITH VINEGAR

• Makes 6 appetizer servings
• Makes 4 main-course servings

Chicken livers in a vinegary sauce, along with cloves and caramelized onions, is a particularly satisfying dish on a cold, wintry night. Brown rice or Quinoa (page 158) makes a good accompaniment.

CARAMELIZED ONIONS
4 medium onions
3 garlic cloves
4 tablespoons vegetable oil
3 whole cloves

CHICKEN LIVERS
1 teaspoon vegetable oil, for oiling the foil
1¼ pounds (567 g) chicken livers
2 tablespoons unbleached all-purpose flour
Kosher salt
Freshly ground black pepper
1 to 2 tablespoons balsamic vinegar
½ cup (20 g) loosely packed flat-leaf parsley, finely chopped, for garnish

TO MAKE THE CARAMELIZED ONIONS: Cut the onions in thin slices. (I find that this is easier using a mandoline rather than a knife.) Mince the garlic. Heat the oil in a heavy skillet. Add the onions, garlic, and cloves. Cook over medium-low heat until the onions are golden and soft, about 20 minutes. Stir from time to time. This step can be done earlier in the day.

TO MAKE THE CHICKEN LIVERS: Preheat the broiler. Line the rack of the broiler pan with foil and place the rack in the pan. Make a shallow "basket" with a piece of heavy foil, crimping it at the corners so that the liquids don't spill out. (See Notes on Techniques, page 351.) Lightly brush the bottom of the basket with oil.

Remove from the livers any green spots, which are bitter, as well as any fatty particles. Pat the livers dry with paper towels. Combine the flour, salt, and pepper on a piece of wax pepper. Coat the livers with the seasoned flour, and shake off the excess.

Place the livers in the basket and set the broiler pan in the oven (or broiling unit), as close as possible to the heat source. Broil for 4 to 5 minutes without turning, until the livers are seared. Remove the livers with tongs and combine them in a saucepan along with the caramelized onions. Season with the vinegar and salt and pepper to taste. Stir until very hot. Garnish with chopped parsley.

POT ROAST

• Makes 8 to 10 servings

Pot roast made with beef brisket is traditional at holiday dinners because it serves a large number of guests. This flavorful recipe is one of my favorites, and I think it's best when prepared a day in advance and refrigerated, as this makes it easier to slice the meat and degrease the sauce. (If there are any leftovers, you're in luck, as they freeze well.)

4 leeks
5 pounds (2.27 kg) first-cut brisket of beef (Ask the butcher to trim the fat.)
2 tablespoons extra virgin olive oil
¼ cup (60 ml) brandy
Kosher salt
Freshly ground black pepper
4 garlic cloves, finely chopped
6 sun-dried tomatoes, packed in oil, cut into strips
1 cup (250 ml) beef broth
2½ tablespoons whole-grain mustard
2½ tablespoons Dijon mustard

Preheat the oven to 325°F (165°C).

Cut off and discard the roots and tough, dark-green leaves of the leeks. Cut the white and light green parts into thin slices. Place in a sieve and rinse thoroughly under cold running water to remove any sand.

Pat the meat dry with paper towels. Heat the oil over medium heat in an enamel-lined roasting pan and brown the meat on all sides. Pour the brandy over. Transfer the meat to a large plate and season with salt and pepper.

Add the leeks and garlic to the drippings in the roasting pan and sauté for 1 minute. Add the tomatoes, broth, mustards, and meat. Bring to a boil. Cover the pan with heavy foil, then a tight-fitting lid. Place in the oven and braise for 1½ hours.

Turn the meat over and continue cooking for another 1½ hours, or until the meat is tender.

Cool the meat and refrigerate in the roasting pan overnight.

Before serving, remove the meat from the roasting pan and place it on a carving board. Spoon off the fat that has risen to the top of the sauce.

Slice the meat against the grain into ¼-inch (6 mm) slices (you may have to rotate the meat in order to do this) and return them to the roasting pan. Let the sauce gently reheat. Season to taste with salt and pepper.

BRAISED SHORT RIBS OF BEEF

• Makes 6 to 8 servings

This is a very flavorful dish using Chinese ingredients. I prepare it in advance and just reheat. I like to serve this with Parsnip and Potato Purée (page 126), White Bean and Potato Purée (page 131) or Vegetable Medley, Asian Style (page 121).

8 beef spareribs (about 4 pounds/1.80 kg)
   (Ask the butcher to cut the ribs into pieces that are 4 inches long and
   2 inches wide /10 by 5 cm.)
¼ cup (30 g) sesame seeds
1 cup (250 ml) water
8 garlic cloves, finely chopped
2-inch (5 cm) piece ginger, peeled and grated
⅓ cup (67 g) sugar
½ cup (125 ml) low-sodium soy sauce
2 tablespoons sesame oil

Preheat the oven to 400°F (205°C).

Place the ribs in a roasting pan large enough to hold them in a single layer.

Roast the sesame seeds in a toaster oven on the lowest setting for a minute or two, until lightly brown. (Watch them carefully, as they burn quickly.)

Combine the sesame seeds with the water, garlic, ginger, sugar, soy sauce, and sesame oil. Pour the mixture over the meat. Cover the pan with heavy foil and roast for 2½ hours, turning the meat once or twice.

Uncover the ribs and slip the bones out of the meat. Return the pan to the oven to bake for another 20 minutes, until the meat is very tender. Skim off the liquid fat with a spoon.

Note: To reheat, cover the meat and place in a preheated 350°F (175°C) oven for about 15 minutes.

HEARTY BEEF STEW

• Makes 6 servings

This wonderful winter dish, a simplified version of a classic French dish, boeuf bourguignon, is even more flavorful when made a day in advance. Minute steak, the cut of meat I use here, is on the expensive side, but I think it is worth it, particularly for a special occasion. See Beef Stew with Thyme (page 239) for a stew made with a less pricey cut.

3 tablespoons extra virgin olive oil
3 pounds (1.36 kg) minute steak, cut into 2-inch (5 cm) cubes
**   (Ask the butcher to cut the meat for you.)**
2 tablespoons unbleached all-purpose flour
Kosher salt
Freshly ground black pepper
1 cup (250 ml) beef broth
2 tablespoons double-concentrated tomato paste
1 cup (250 ml) dry red wine
Leaves from 10 thyme sprigs
½ pound (225 g) small white pearl onions
1 pound (450 g) small white mushrooms
1 cup (40 g) tightly packed flat-leaf parsley, coarsely chopped

Preheat the oven to 325°F (165°C).

In a large, heavy skillet, heat the oil over medium heat. Pat the meat dry with paper towels and dredge lightly with flour, shaking off the excess. Sauté several pieces of meat at a time until they are light brown. As the pieces brown, transfer them with tongs to a 4-quart (4 liter) enamel-lined saucepan or a Dutch oven. Season lightly with salt and pepper.

Stir in the beef broth, tomato paste, wine, and thyme. Bring to a boil, cover tightly, transfer to the oven, and cook for 45 minutes.

While the meat is cooking, prepare the vegetables. Peel the onions (see note) and wipe the mushrooms with a damp paper towel. Add the onions, mushrooms, and parsley to the meat and continue cooking for another 45 minutes, or until the meat is tender. Season to taste with salt and pepper.

Note: The easiest way to peel onions is to drop them into boiling water and return the water to a boil. Pour them into a strainer and peel. The skin will come off easily.

BEEF STEW WITH THYME

• Makes 8 servings

Like most stews, this dish can almost be a meal in itself. I usually serve it with brown or white rice.

> **4 tablespoons extra virgin olive oil**
> **4 pounds (1.80 kg) first-cut lean brisket of beef, cut into 2-inch (5 cm) cubes**
>   **(Ask the butcher to cut the meat for you.)**
> **2 tablespoons unbleached all-purpose flour**
> **Kosher salt**
> **Freshly ground black pepper**
> **2 onions**
> **5 garlic cloves**
> **¾ pound (340 g) white pearl onions**
> **1 cup (250 ml) dry red wine**
> **One 28-ounce (794 g) can peeled imported tomatoes**
> **Leaves from 14 thyme sprigs, saving some for garnish**
> **1 pound (450 g) baby carrots**

Preheat the oven to 350°F (175°C).

Heat 3 tablespoons of the oil in a heavy skillet over medium heat. Pat the meat dry with paper towels and dredge lightly with flour, shaking off the excess.

Sauté several pieces of meat at a time until light brown. As the pieces brown, transfer them with tongs to a 4-quart (4 liter) enamel-lined saucepan or Dutch oven. Season lightly with salt and pepper.

Finely chop the onions and the garlic. You can easily do this in a food processor. Be sure to quarter the onions and garlic first so that they chop quickly and don't become mushy. Peel the pearl onions (see note).

Heat the remaining tablespoon of oil and sauté the chopped onions and garlic for a minute. Add these to the meat along with the wine, tomatoes, thyme, pearl onions, and carrots. Bring the mixture to a boil, cover the pan, and transfer to the oven. Cook for 2½ hours, or until the meat is tender. Season to taste with salt and pepper.

Serve garnished with thyme.

Note: The easiest way to peel pearl onions is the drop them into boiling water and return the water to a boil. Pour them in a strainer and peel. The skin will come off easily.

BAKED EGGPLANT WITH GROUND MEAT, TOMATOES, AND PINE NUTS

• Makes 8 servings

This dish takes a bit of time to prepare but is well worth it, as it is rich in nutrients as well as flavor. Also appealing: Leftovers (if any) freeze well.

2 medium eggplants (about 1¼ pounds/567 g each)
4 tablespoons extra virgin olive oil, plus 2 tablespoons for greasing the eggplants
Kosher salt
Freshly ground black pepper
2 medium onions
4 garlic cloves
1 pound (450 g) veal and 1 pound (450 g) beef, ground together
One 28-ounce (794 g) can imported crushed tomatoes
3 tablespoons double-concentrated tomato paste
1 cup (40 g) tightly packed fresh basil leaves, torn into small pieces
1 cup (40 g) loosely packed flat-leaf parsley, coarsely chopped
½ cup (70 g) pine nuts

Preheat the broiler. Set the rack in the broiler pan and cover it completely with heavy foil.

Trim the ends of the eggplants, peel, and cut into ¼-inch (6 mm) slices. Arrange the slices on the broiler-pan rack and lightly brush the top of each one with oil. Set the pan in the oven (or broiling unit), as close as possible to the heat source. Broil the eggplant until golden. (You will have to do this in several batches.) Remove the eggplant and set aside on a cookie sheet. Season with salt and pepper.

Finely chop the onions and the garlic. You can easily do this in a food processor. Be sure to quarter the onions and garlic first so that they chop quickly and don't become mushy. In a wok, heat the remaining oil and sauté the onions and the garlic until soft. Add the meat, raise the heat, and stir-fry until it is lightly cooked. Add the tomatoes and tomato paste. Remove from the heat and stir in the basil and parsley. Season to taste with salt and pepper.

Preheat the oven to 375°F (190°C).

Line a glass, ceramic, or enamel-lined baking pan (about 10 by 16 inches/25 by 40 cm) with one third of the eggplant slices and cover with half of the meat. Make another layer of eggplant and add the rest of the meat. Place the remaining eggplant slices on top. Sprinkle with the pine nuts.

Cover the dish with foil and bake for 20 minutes. Uncover and bake for another 15 minutes, or until bubbling and very hot.

TO SERVE: Cut into 8 portions, each about 4 by 5 inches (10 by 13 cm).

STUFFED CABBAGE ROLLS

• Makes about 3 dozen small rolls

In Eastern Europe, stuffed cabbage rolls are traditionally served on Sukkoth. There are many versions of this dish, but this one is a favorite, as it is light and sweet-and-sour. Also, the cabbage rolls are small and thus not too filling. Like all the stuffed cabbage recipes, this is a bit time-consuming, but you can do it in stages, and because it freezes very well, you can make it in advance.

CABBAGE
2 tablespoons kosher salt
2 medium heads cabbage (about 3 pounds/1.36 kg each)

FILLING
1 onion, quartered
2 garlic cloves, quartered
1 Idaho baking potato, peeled and cut in large pieces
1 large egg
1 pound (450 g) veal and 1 pound (450 g) beef, ground together
½ cup (20 g) tightly packed flat-leaf parsley, coarsely chopped
⅓ cup (62 g) raw long-grain white rice
2 tablespoons double-concentrated tomato paste
1 tablespoon low-sodium soy sauce
Kosher salt
Freshly ground black pepper

SAUCE
2 Granny Smith apples
4 carrots, peeled and cut into large pieces
2 onions, quartered
4 tablespoons extra virgin olive oil
1 cup (40 g) tightly packed flat-leaf parsley, coarsely chopped
¾ cup (175 g) golden raisins
6 ounces (170 g) dried apricots, diced
One 35-ounce (992 g) can imported peeled tomatoes
One 28-ounce (794 g) can imported crushed tomatoes
One 15-ounce (425 g) can tomato sauce
2 tablespoons double-concentrated tomato paste
3 tablespoons dark brown sugar, plus more as needed
1 cup (250 ml) chicken broth

TO PREPARE THE CABBAGE LEAVES: Bring a large pot of water to a boil with the salt. With the point of a knife, cut out some of the hard center core of the cabbages. Remove and discard any bruised and discolored leaves. Add the cabbage to the boiling water and boil for a few minutes, turning the cabbage often. Remove the cabbage from the water by piercing the core with a large fork and lifting out the head.

To remove the leaves without damaging them, cut them where they are attached at the core, then peel off. If necessary, return the cabbage to the boiling water to soften the leaves. Shred the small center leaves.

Repeat this process for the second cabbage. (You can do this earlier in the day or the night before. Place the leaves in a tightly sealed zip-top plastic bag and refrigerate until needed.)

TO PREPARE THE FILLING: Place the onion, garlic, potato, and egg in a food processor and pulse until smooth. Transfer to a large bowl and add the meat, parsley, rice, tomato paste, and soy sauce. Mix with your hands to combine well. Season to taste with salt and pepper.

TO FILL THE CABBAGE LEAVES: Spread each cabbage leaf on a cutting board and cut out some of the center rib. Place 2 tablespoons of the filling in the center. Starting from the smaller end, roll the cabbage halfway, fold the sides toward the center, and roll tightly to the end. Continue until all the filling has been used.

TO MAKE THE SAUCE: Peel, core, and quarter the apples. Chop the apples, carrots, and onions in a food processor, one at a time. (Chopping each ingredient separately preserves its distinct texture.)

Heat the oil in a small saucepan. Add the apples, carrots, and onions, and sauté for a few minutes. Remove to a large bowl, and add the parsley, raisins, apricots, peeled and crushed tomatoes, tomato sauce, tomato paste, sugar, and broth.

TO COOK THE ROLLS: Preheat the oven to 350°F (175°C).

Place the rolls close to each other, seam side down, in an enamel-lined saucepan large enough to hold the rolls in two or three layers. Scatter the leftover shredded cabbage on top. Add the sauce. Bring to a slow boil over medium heat. (If the heat is too high, the bottom will burn.)

Cover the pan with heavy foil and a tight-fitting lid. Place in the oven and cook for 1½ hours.

Season the sauce to taste with sugar, salt, and pepper.

CHOLENT

• Makes 8 to 10 servings as a side dish
• Makes 6 servings as a main course

The origin of the word "cholent" comes from the old-French word *chalt*, the modern version of which is *chaud,* meaning "warm." The casserole is cooked overnight in a heavy dish and served at Sabbath lunch. There are many variations of this dish. Mine has Eastern European origins and is a combination of barley, a variety of beans, and meat. Some people also add potatoes.

2 tablespoons vegetable oil
1 onion, finely chopped
3 garlic cloves, finely chopped
6 cups (1.5 liters) cold water
½ cup (100 g) medium pearl barley
½ cup (115 g) dried chickpeas
¾ cup (170 g) dried large lima beans
¾ cup (135 g) dried red kidney beans
1½ pounds (680 g) boneless flanken (Ask the butcher to trim the fat from
the flanken and cut the meat into 1-inch (2.5 cm) pieces.)
Kosher salt
Freshly ground black pepper

The day before Sabbath, preheat the oven to 200°F (95°C).

Heat the oil in an enamel-lined 8-quart saucepan. Add the onion and garlic and sauté for 1 minute.

Add the water, barley, chickpeas, both kinds of beans, and the meat. Bring the mixture to a boil, season with salt and pepper and cook, covered, for 5 minutes.

Place the pan in the oven. (If you are using a slow cooker, transfer everything to the cooker and set it for the appropriate cooking time.) Leave the cholent to cook until the following day, at which point the legumes and the meat will be soft and there will be a nice crust on top.

Before serving, check if the cholent is too dry. If it is, add a little boiling water. Season to taste with salt and pepper.

MEAT CHILI

- Makes 6 generous main-course servings
- Makes 8 generous luncheon servings

This is an easy-to-prepare and easy-to-freeze dish that is tasty and nutritious. I serve it with brown rice and a green salad—perfect winter fare.

One 35-ounce (992 g) can imported peeled tomatoes
2 green bell peppers
2 onions, finely chopped
6 garlic cloves
4 tablespoons extra virgin olive oil
1½ pounds (680 g) center-cut chuck, ground
Two 15.5-ounce (440 g) cans Goya red kidney beans, drained
2 teaspoons chili powder
1 tablespoon Dijon mustard
2 tablespoons double-concentrated tomato paste
¼ teaspoon crushed red pepper
½ cup (20 g) tightly packed flat-leaf parsley, coarsely chopped
2 cups (80 g) tightly packed fresh basil leaves, torn into large pieces
¼ cup (10 g) tightly packed cilantro leaves, plus more for garnish
Kosher salt
Freshly ground black pepper

Pour the tomatoes and their juice into a bowl and crush them with a wooden spoon. Cut the bell peppers in half lengthwise, core and seed them, then cut into small pieces. Finely chop the onions and garlic in a food processor. (Be sure to quarter the onions and garlic first so that they chop quickly and don't become mushy.)

Heat the oil in a large enamel-lined saucepan. Add the onions and garlic and sauté over low heat until the onions are soft, about 5 minutes. Add the meat and sauté over high heat until the meat darkens. Add the tomatoes, beans, chili powder, mustard, tomato paste, and crushed pepper. Bring to a boil over high heat. Lower the heat and simmer for 10 minutes. Add the parsley, basil, and cilantro and cook for another 5 minutes. Season to taste with salt and pepper.

Serve in deep bowls, garnished with cilantro leaves.

MEATLOAF

• Makes 4 servings

This unconventional meatloaf was one of my husband's favorites. Instead of using bread, I add grated potato, which gives the meat a light and moist texture. It is equally good served warm or at room temperature.

> **2 tablespoons vegetable oil, plus 1 tablespoon for greasing the foil**
> **1 medium onion, coarsely chopped**
> **2 garlic cloves, coarsely chopped**
> **1 Idaho baking potato, peeled and cut into large pieces**
> **1 large egg**
> **½ pound (225 g) veal and ½ pound (225 g) beef, ground together**
> **1 tablespoon double-concentrated tomato paste**
> **1 tablespoon ketchup**
> **1 tablespoon low-sodium soy sauce**
> **½ cup (20 g) tightly packed flat-leaf parsley, coarsely chopped**
> **Kosher salt**
> **Freshly ground black pepper**

Preheat the oven to 375°F (190°C). Line a 5 by 9-inch (13 by 23 cm) glass loaf pan with foil. Brush the foil with oil.

In a small skillet, heat the oil over low heat. Add the onion and garlic and sauté until lightly golden, about 3 minutes. Cool.

Place the onion and garlic in a food processor. Add the potato and egg and pulse until very smooth. Transfer to a large bowl. Add the ground meat, tomato paste, ketchup, soy sauce, and parsley. Mix with your hands until thoroughly combined. Season with salt and pepper. Place the meat in the foil-lined pan and smooth the top.

Bake for 55 minutes, or until lightly browned on top. Remove from the oven and let rest for 30 minutes before cutting. (The meatloaf is easier to cut when not very hot.)

LUNCHEON DISHES

DAIRY

Acorn Squash Soufflé

Spinach Pie

Stuffed Portobello Mushrooms

Zucchini Frittata

Eggplant Tart

Eggplant Parmigiana

Sole and Parmesan Soufflé

PAREVE

Southwestern Ratatouille

Tofu with Mushrooms

Mushroom Ragoût

Mushroom Frittata

Bell Pepper and Potato Frittata

Bean and Rice Frittata with Guacamole

Vegetarian Burgers

Barley-Stuffed Cabbage Rolls

Bulgur Chili

White Bean Chili

Black Bean Chili

ACORN SQUASH SOUFFLÉ

- Makes 6 appetizer servings
- Makes 4 luncheon servings

This is a wonderful comfort food. I like it best in winter, when squashes are plentiful.

2 tablespoons (30 g) unsalted butter for greasing the soufflé dish
1 acorn squash (about 2 pounds/900 g)
4 scallions, including the green part, cut into thin slices
3 large eggs, separated, at room temperature
8 ounces (227 g) cottage cheese, at room temperature
Kosher salt
Freshly ground black pepper

Preheat the oven to 375°F (190°C). Line a baking pan with foil. Grease a 1-quart (1 liter) soufflé dish with 1 tablespoon of the butter.

Cut the squash in half and discard the seeds and fiber. Place the halves, skin side up, in the baking pan and bake until the inside is soft, about 40 minutes. Cool.

Heat the remaining butter in a small skillet and sauté the scallions. Remove from the heat.

Scoop the squash from the shells (discard the shells) and place in a medium bowl. Mash coarsely with a fork. Add the scallions, egg yolks and cottage cheese. Combine well and season to taste with salt and pepper.

Beat the egg whites until stiff. With a rubber spatula, combine them gently with the squash mixture. Spoon the mixture into the soufflé dish and bake for 30 to 35 minutes, until the soufflé is puffy and golden on top.

SPINACH PIE

• Makes 6 appetizer servings
• Makes 4 luncheon servings

This is a colorful and easy dish that I make all year round.

1 tablespoon (15 g) unsalted butter, for greasing the pan
2 pounds (900 g) prewashed baby spinach
2 large eggs, at room temperature
One 15-ounce (425 g) container ricotta cheese (see note)
1¼ cups (125 g) grated imported Parmesan cheese
2 tablespoons plain dried breadcrumbs
Kosher salt
Freshly ground black pepper

Preheat the oven to 375°F (190°C). Butter a glass or ceramic flan dish, 10 inches (25 cm) in diameter by 1½ inches (4 cm) high.

Heat a wok or large pot over high heat. Add the spinach in batches and stir with tongs until the spinach is just wilted. Remove each batch to a sieve and drain. Cool. Use your hands to squeeze out all the liquid. (You can do this step in advance.)

Place the spinach in a food processor. Add the eggs and pulse to a fine consistency.

Transfer the mixture to a bowl and combine well with the ricotta, Parmesan, and breadcrumbs. Season to taste with salt and pepper. Spoon into the buttered dish and smooth the top.

Bake for 25 minutes, or until the top feels almost firm to the touch.

If you are not serving the spinach pie right away, cover it with foil. When ready to serve, warm it in a preheated 350°F (175°C) oven for about 15 minutes.

Note: If there is any liquid in the container on top of the ricotta, absorb it with a paper towel.

STUFFED PORTOBELLO MUSHROOMS

• Makes 4 servings

This is an attractive winter luncheon dish in which the mushrooms caps become a saucer-like container for a tasty and nutritious filling. You can assemble the whole dish earlier in the day and bake it when needed. I like to serve these surrounded with dressed greens.

⅓ cup (62 g) raw brown rice (see note)
⅔ cup (160 ml) water
2 poblano peppers
4 tablespoons extra virgin olive oil
5 ounces (142 g) prewashed baby spinach
1 medium onion, finely chopped
4 ounces (113 g) shredded sharp cheddar cheese
¼ cup (10 g) loosely packed cilantro leaves
4 large portobello mushrooms (about 5 inches/13 cm in diameter)
Kosher salt
Freshly ground black pepper
Bibb lettuce or frisée, lightly tossed with dressing (see page 111), for serving

Bring the rice and water to a boil in an enamel-lined saucepan over high heat. Lower the heat and cook, covered, until the rice is soft, about 35 minutes. Transfer to a medium bowl.

Preheat the broiler. Set the rack in the broiler pan and cover it with foil.

Cut the peppers in half lengthwise, then core and seed them. Make a shallow "basket" with a piece of heavy foil, crimping it at the corners so that the liquids don't spill out. (See Notes on Techniques, page 351.) Set the basket on the broiler rack, and arrange the peppers inside, skin side up. Place the broiler pan in the oven (or broiling unit), as close as possible to the heat source. Broil the peppers for about 3-4 minutes, until the skin is blistered and charred. Cover with foil and cool. The heat will loosen the skin.

In a large skillet, heat 1 tablespoon of the oil. Add the spinach and sauté until it is just wilted. Remove to a bowl and cool. When cool, chop the spinach finely, and add it to the rice.

In the same skillet, heat another tablespoon of the oil. Add the onion and sauté until soft. Add it to the rice and spinach and mix well.

When the peppers are cool, peel them, chop them finely, and add to the bowl with the rice mixture. Add the cheese and cilantro, combining them thoroughly. Season to taste with salt and pepper.

Cut off and discard the mushroom stems. Wipe the caps with a damp paper towel and rub them with the remaining 2 tablespoons oil. Season the mushrooms with salt and pepper.

Turn the mushroom caps upside down (gill side up) and spoon one-fourth of the filling in a mound in the center of each cap. (You can make the recipe ahead of time up to this point. Cover the mushrooms with cling wrap and refrigerate. Return the mushrooms to room temperature before baking.)

Preheat the over to 350°F (175°C). Line a baking pan with foil.

Place the caps in the pan and bake for about 30 minutes, or until the filling is thoroughly hot. Serve the stuffed mushrooms on individual plates, surrounded with dressed Bibb lettuce or frisée.

Note: I prefer premium Japanese medium-grain brown rice, as it is much creamier than other varieties.

ZUCCHINI FRITTATA

- Makes 6 appetizer servings
- Makes 4 luncheon servings

A frittata is an open-face Italian omelet that can be prepared with a variety of vegetables, including asparagus, red or green bell peppers, or mushrooms. This dish is tasty and light and, like all frittatas, is equally good served warm or at room temperature.

1 pound (450 g) small zucchini
1 teaspoon kosher salt
3 tablespoons (45 g) unsalted butter
Leaves from 6 marjoram sprigs, chopped
6 large eggs, at room temperature
Freshly ground black pepper

Rinse and dry the zucchini, and trim the ends. Grate the zucchini coarsely in a food processor fitted with a medium grating attachment. Place the grated zucchini in a colander, sprinkle with the salt and let stand for 30 minutes. Use your hands to squeeze out any remaining liquid, then place the zucchini in a small bowl.

Preheat the broiler.

Heat 1 tablespoon of the butter in a 10-inch (25 cm) nonstick ovenproof skillet. Sauté the zucchini over high heat until golden. Return it to the bowl, add the marjoram, and cool.

In a large bowl, whisk the eggs with a fork. Add the zucchini and season to taste with salt and pepper.

Heat the remaining 2 tablespoons (30 g) butter in the same skillet over moderately high heat. Pour in the egg mixture, distributing the zucchini evenly in the pan. Lower the heat and cook for 6 minutes, shaking the pan once or twice until the sides are set but the top is still soft.

Place the frittata in the oven (or broiling unit), as close as possible to the heat source. Broil until the top is set, about 1 minute. Slide the frittata onto a serving platter and cut it into wedges. Serve warm or at room temperature.

EGGPLANT TART

• Makes 8 appetizer servings
• Makes 6 luncheon servings

This is a wonderful vegetarian dish that is delicious warm or at room temperature. It is equally tasty the next day. I like to serve it with dressed mâche.

4 tablespoons extra virgin olive oil,
   plus 2 tablespoons for greasing the baking sheets
2 medium eggplants (about 1¼ pounds/567 g each)
Kosher salt
Freshly ground black pepper
4 garlic cloves, minced
1½ pounds (680 g) cherry tomatoes, halved
¾ cup (30 g) loosely packed fresh basil leaves, torn in small pieces
1 cup (100 g) grated imported Parmesan cheese

Preheat the oven to 400°F (205°C). Grease two large baking sheets with 1 tablespoon of oil each. Line a 10-inch (25 cm) springform pan with wax paper.

Trim the ends of the eggplants, peel the eggplants, then cut them into ¼-inch (6 mm) rounds. Place the slices on the baking sheets. Using a pastry brush, brush the tops of the rounds with 2 tablespoons of the oil. Bake for 10 minutes, or until softened and lightly golden. Season lightly with salt and pepper on both sides.

Heat the remaining oil in a medium saucepan. Add the garlic and tomatoes and cook over medium heat for about 5 minutes, until the tomatoes are soft. Add the basil and season to taste with salt and pepper.

Place one-third of the eggplant slices in tight, overlapping layers in the springform pan. Top with half of the tomatoes and sprinkle over one-third of the Parmesan. Add another layer of eggplant, the remaining tomatoes and half of the remaining Parmesan. Cover with a final layer of eggplant and sprinkle with the rest of the Parmesan.

Bake for 15 minutes, until golden and bubbly. Let the tart stand for 5 minutes. Release the latch on the pan and remove the rim. Invert the tart onto a plate, remove the bottom of the pan and peel off the wax paper. Invert the tart again onto a serving plate. Cut the tart into wedges and serve.

Note: The tart can be warmed in a preheated 300°F (150°C) oven for 10 minutes.

EGGPLANT PARMIGIANA

• Makes 8 appetizer servings
• Makes 6 luncheon servings

This is a light version of the traditional Italian dish. I usually make it in an attractive baking pan that can go directly from my oven to the table. This makes serving (and cleaning up) extra easy. Like all Italian dishes, eggplant parmigiana goes beautifully with a simply dressed salad.

2 medium eggplants (about 1¼ pounds/567 g each)
3 tablespoons extra virgin olive oil
Kosher salt
Freshly ground black pepper

TOMATO SAUCE
3 tablespoons extra virgin olive oil
1 onion, finely chopped
2 garlic cloves, finely chopped
One 14-ounce (400 g) can imported peeled tomatoes
1 cup (40 g) loosely packed fresh basil leaves, torn into small pieces
1 cup (100 g) grated imported Parmesan cheese
½ cup (28 g) panko (Japanese breadcrumbs)

Preheat the broiler. Set the rack in the broiler pan and cover it with foil.

Trim the ends of the eggplants, then peel and cut them into ¼-inch (6 mm) slices. Place the slices on the foil and lightly brush the top of each one with oil. Set the broiler pan in the oven (or broiling unit), as close as possible to the heat source. Broil the eggplant until golden. (You will have to do this in two batches.) Season with salt and pepper. Remove the eggplant and set aside on a cookie sheet.

TO MAKE THE TOMATO SAUCE: Heat the oil in a small saucepan. Add the onion and garlic and cook, covered, over low heat until tender, about 5 minutes. Add the tomatoes and basil and cook, covered, for another 10 minutes, stirring from time to time to break up the tomatoes. Season to taste with salt and pepper.

TO ASSEMBLE AND BAKE THE DISH: Preheat the oven to 375°F (190°C). Spoon a layer of sauce on the bottom of a glass or ceramic baking pan that is 10 inches round and 2 inches deep (25 by 5 cm). Cover with a layer of one-third of the eggplant and sprinkle over it one-third of the Parmesan. Add another layer of sauce, another layer of eggplant and another sprinkling of Parmesan. Finish with a third layer of sauce, eggplant, and Parmesan. Top with the panko. Bake until golden and bubbly, about 20 minutes.

TO SERVE: Cut into wedge-shaped slices.

Note: This dish can be prepared in advance and reheated in a preheated 350°F (175°C) oven for 15 minutes.

SOLE AND PARMESAN SOUFFLÉ

• Makes 4 servings

This is a nonchallenging soufflé that my guests always love. Most of the recipe can be prepared hours in advance.

> **¾ pound (340 g) lemon sole fillets**
> **Kosher salt**
> **Freshly ground pepper**
> **3 tablespoons (45 g) unsalted butter,**
> **   plus 1 tablespoon (15 g) for greasing**
> **3 tablespoons unbleached all-purpose flour**
> **¾ cup plus 2 tablespoons (210 ml) milk**
> **2 large egg yolks, at room temperature**
> **½ teaspoon powdered mustard**
> **Pinch of cayenne**
> **½ cup (50 g) plus 1 tablespoon grated imported Parmesan cheese**
> **5 large egg whites, at room temperature**

Pat the fillets dry with paper towels and season both sides lightly with salt and pepper. Put them in a heatproof dish and place in a steamer. Steam, covered, over briskly boiling water for 5 minutes. Cool the fillets, pour off any accumulated liquid, and flake with a fork.

Preheat the oven to 425°F (220°C).

Grease a 1-quart (1 liter) soufflé dish with 1 tablespoon of the butter.

In a medium enamel-lined saucepan, melt the remaining 2 tablespoons of butter over low heat. Add the flour and mix continuously with a wooden spoon for several minutes, until the butter and flour froth together without coloring. Gradually add the milk and stir continuously over medium heat until the mixture is very thick and bubbles appear. (This is the roux.)

Remove the roux from the heat, add the egg yolks, and mix well. Season with the mustard, ½ teaspoon salt, and the cayenne. The flavor should be strong. Combine with the flaked fish and ½ cup (50 g) of the Parmesan. (This part of the recipe can be prepared in advance.)

In the bowl of an electric stand mixer, use the balloon whip attachment to beat the egg whites over high speed until they form soft peaks.

Take one-quarter of the whites and, using a rubber spatula, delicately combine them with the fish mixture to lighten it. Now reverse the process: Pour the fish mixture into the bowl with the remaining egg whites and gently combine.

Pour into the soufflé dish, sprinkle the remaining tablespoon of Parmesan on top and bake for 10 minutes. Reduce the heat to 400°F (205°C), and bake for another 10 minutes or until top is puffy and brown.

SOUTHWESTERN RATATOUILLE

- Makes 8 appetizer servings
- Makes 6 luncheon servings

This is a typical summer dish full of seasonal vegetables. It can be made a day ahead and served warm over couscous. Add chopped parsley to the couscous to enhance the flavor.

2 red bell peppers
2 jalapeño peppers
5 plum tomatoes
3 medium zucchini
2 red onions
3 garlic cloves
4 tablespoons extra virgin olive oil
Kernels from 3 ears uncooked corn
½ cup (20 g) loosely packed cilantro leaves
Kosher salt
Freshly ground black pepper

Cut the bell peppers in half lengthwise. Remove the core and the seeds, and cut into ½-inch (13 mm) cubes. Cut the jalapeño peppers in half lengthwise. Remove the core and the seeds, and finely chop (see note). If you prefer the ratatouille on the spicier side, do not remove the seeds.

Cut the tomatoes in half widthwise. Remove the cores and, squeezing gently, remove the seeds. (Some seeds will remain.) Cut the tomatoes into ½-inch (13 mm) cubes. Trim the ends and cut the zucchini into ½-inch (13 mm) cubes.

Chop the onions and garlic together in a food processor. (Be sure to quarter the onions and garlic first so they don't become mushy.)

Heat the oil in a medium saucepan. Add the onions and garlic and sauté over medium heat, covered, about 5 minutes, until the onions are soft. Add the bell peppers, jalapeños, tomatoes, zucchini, and corn kernels, and bring to a boil. Lower the heat and cook, covered, over medium heat, for about 5 minutes, until the vegetables are slightly soft. Stir from time to time.

Season to taste with cilantro, salt, and pepper.

Note: When seeding jalapeño peppers, I advise wearing thin plastic gloves to avoid irritating your skin or your eyes.

TOFU WITH MUSHROOMS

• Makes 2 luncheon servings

I love working with tofu. It has a subtle taste, can be prepared in many different ways, and goes with many different ingredients. This nutritious recipe satisfies my winter craving for comfort food.

> **8 shiitake mushrooms**
> **3 scallions**
> **14 ounces (400 g) extra firm tofu**
> **3 tablespoons vegetable oil**
> **2 teaspoons sesame oil**
> **1 tablespoon low-sodium soy sauce**
> **Kosher salt**
> **Freshly ground black pepper**

Cut off and discard the mushroom stems. Wipe the caps with a damp paper towel and cut in thin slices. Cut the scallions, including the green parts, into 2-inch (5 cm) pieces. Cut the pieces into thick strips. Cut the tofu into four equal pieces and dry with paper towels. (Tofu has a high water content, so it is important that it is thoroughly dry before stir-frying.)

Heat 1 tablespoon of the vegetable oil in a wok or skillet over medium heat. Stir-fry the tofu about 5 minutes, until it is lightly golden. Transfer to a bowl and cover.

Heat the remaining 2 tablespoons vegetable oil in the wok. Add the mushrooms and scallions and stir-fry over high heat until the mushrooms are just wilted. Season to taste with the sesame oil, soy sauce, salt, and pepper.

TO SERVE: Place the tofu in the center of the plate and scatter the warm mushroom mixture over it.

MUSHROOM RAGOÛT

• Makes 4 luncheon servings

Mushrooms are always in season. But my favorite time of year to make this ragoût is in winter, when I can serve it over quinoa, couscous, or polenta. I often top it with grated mozzarella or shavings of Parmesan cheese.

> 1½ **pounds (680 g) assorted mushrooms, such as shiitake, cremini, and white**
> ⅓ **cup (80 ml) extra virgin olive oil**
> 6 **garlic cloves, minced**
> 8 **scallions, including green parts, thinly sliced**
> ¼ **cup (60 ml) dry red wine**
> **Kosher salt**
> **Freshly ground black pepper**
> ½ **cup (20 g) tightly packed flat-leaf parsley, finely chopped**

Discard the stems from the shiitakes. Wipe all the mushrooms with a damp paper towel. and cut into quarters.

Heat 2 tablespoons of the oil in a wok or skillet. Add the garlic and scallions and sauté over low heat until softened, about 1 minute.

Add the remaining oil. Add the mushrooms and sauté over high heat, stirring, until the mushrooms are slightly wilted.

Add the wine and cook over high heat, stirring from time to time, until the liquid is almost absorbed.

Season to taste with salt and pepper. Stir in the parsley and serve.

MUSHROOM FRITTATA

- Makes 6 appetizer servings
- Makes 4 generous luncheon servings

This is a fine dish for winter, a time when most varieties of wild mushrooms are plentiful. I like to serve it warm.

¾ pound (340 g) mixed wild mushrooms, such as porcini, shiitake, cremini, or oyster mushrooms
4 tablespoons extra virgin olive oil
1 onion, finely chopped
2 garlic cloves, finely chopped
6 large eggs, at room temperature
Leaves from 4 thyme sprigs
½ cup (20 g) loosely packed flat-leaf parsley, coarsely chopped
Kosher salt
Freshly ground black pepper

If using shiitake mushrooms, cut off and discard the stems. Wipe all the mushrooms with a damp paper towel and trim the ends where needed. Chop the mushrooms coarsely. (You can do this in a food processor, but quarter the mushrooms first.)

Preheat the broiler.

Heat 1 tablespoon of the oil in a 12-inch (30 cm) ovenproof nonstick skillet. Add the onion and garlic and sauté until soft. Transfer to a medium bowl.

In the same skillet, heat another 2 tablespoons of the oil. Add the mushrooms and sauté over high heat for about 4 minutes, until the mushrooms begin to release their juices. Add the mushrooms to the onions and garlic and cool slightly.

Whisk the eggs in a medium bowl. Add the mushroom mixture and stir in the thyme and parsley. Combine well. Season with salt and pepper.

Heat the remaining oil in the skillet over medium-high heat. Pour the egg mixture into the skillet, distributing the vegetables evenly, and lower the heat. Cook the frittata for about 7 minutes, shaking the pan once or twice, until the sides are set but the top is still soft.

Place the frittata in the oven (or broiling unit), as close as possible to the heat source. Broil about 1 minute, until the top is set. Slide the frittata onto a serving platter. Cut it into wedges and serve warm.

BELL PEPPER AND POTATO FRITTATA

- Makes 8 appetizer servings
- Makes 6 generous luncheon servings

Frittatas, which are flat, pancake-like omelets, are a staple of Mediterranean cuisine. Easy to make and always tasty, they are becoming increasingly popular here. I serve them in the summer, with a variety of fillings, as luncheon dishes, appetizers, or even snacks.

2 large Idaho baking potatoes
1 yellow bell pepper
5 scallions
4 tablespoons extra virgin olive oil
5 large eggs, at room temperature
½ cup (20 g) tightly packed flat-leaf parsley, coarsely chopped
Kosher salt
Freshly ground black pepper

Peel the potatoes and cut into ¼-inch (6 mm) cubes. Cut the bell pepper in half lengthwise, then remove the core and seeds. Cut into ¼-inch (6 mm) cubes. Cut the scallions, including the green part, into thin slices.

Preheat the broiler.

Heat 2 tablespoons of the oil in a 12-inch (30 cm) ovenproof nonstick skillet. Add the potatoes and cook, covered, over medium heat for 5 minutes. Add the bell pepper and sauté for a minute. Add the scallions and cook, covered, until the potatoes are just tender. Cool.

Whisk the eggs in a large bowl. Add the vegetables and parsley and season well with salt and pepper.

Add the remaining oil to the skillet and heat over medium heat. Pour in the egg mixture, distributing the vegetables evenly, and reduce the heat to low. Cook the frittata, covered, for 7 minutes, or until the sides are set but the top is still soft. Shake the pan once or twice during this period.

Place the frittata in the oven (or broiling unit), as close as possible to the heat source. Broil about 1 minute, until the top is golden and set. Slide the frittata onto a serving platter. Cut it into wedges and serve warm or at room temperature.

BEAN AND RICE FRITTATA WITH GUACAMOLE

- Makes 6 appetizer servings
- Makes 4 generous luncheon servings

I love this dish because it is so easy to make—I use canned beans rather than dried ones—and so nutritious. The guacamole, which follows, adds a wonderful Mexican flavor.

⅓ cup (62 g) raw brown rice (see note)
½ cup (125 ml) water
1 red bell pepper
1 zucchini
5 tablespoons extra virgin olive oil
1 small red onion, finely chopped
3 garlic cloves, finely chopped
½ teaspoon crushed red pepper flakes
5 large eggs, at room temperature
One 15.5-ounce (440 g) can Goya black beans, drained
½ cup (20 g) loosely packed cilantro leaves
Kosher salt
Freshly ground black pepper
Tabasco sauce
Guacamole (recipe follows), for serving

Bring the rice and water to a boil in an enamel-lined saucepan over high heat. Lower the heat and cook, covered, for 35 minutes, or until the rice is soft. Cool.

Cut the pepper in half lengthwise. Remove the core and the seeds and cut into ¼-inch (6 mm) cubes. Trim the ends of the zucchini and cut into ¼-inch (6 mm) cubes.

Preheat the broiler.

In a 12-inch (30 cm) ovenproof nonstick skillet, heat 4 tablespoons of the oil. Add the onion, garlic, crushed red pepper flakes, and zucchini and sauté for a few minutes. Add the bell pepper cubes and stir well. Transfer the vegetables to a large bowl and cool.

Beat the eggs lightly with a fork. Add them to the vegetables along with the beans, cooked rice, and cilantro. Season well with salt, pepper, and a few drops of Tabasco.

In the same skillet you used for the vegetables, heat the remaining tablespoon of oil over medium heat. Pour in the egg mixture, distributing the contents evenly. Reduce the heat to low and cook for 7 minutes, or until the underside of the frittata is golden and the sides are set, but the top is still soft. Shake the pan once or twice during this time.

Broil the frittata in the oven (or broiling unit), as close as possible to the heat source, about 1 minute, or until the top is golden and set. The center will still be soft.

TO SERVE: Slide the frittata onto a platter and cut into wedges of your choice. Serve warm or at room temperature with the Guacamole, below.

Note: I prefer premium Japanese medium-grain brown rice, as it is much creamier than other varieties.

GUACAMOLE

• Makes about 1 cup (250 ml)

> **2 plum tomatoes**
> **1 firm, ripe avocado**
> **¼ small red onion, minced**
> **1 garlic clove, minced**
> **2 to 3 tablespoons freshly squeezed lime juice**
> **Kosher salt**
> **Freshly ground black pepper**

Cut the tomatoes in half widthwise and remove the core. Squeeze the tomato halves gently to remove the seeds. (Some seeds will remain.) Chop the tomatoes coarsely. Cut the avocado in half and remove the pit. Scoop the flesh into a medium bowl and mash with a fork. Stir in the tomatoes, onion, and garlic. Season with lime juice and salt and pepper to taste.

VEGETARIAN BURGERS

• Makes 6 burgers

These burgers are great on their own, but you can also serve them topped with slices of Parmesan or ricotta salata. Dressed mâche or Boston lettuce makes a fine accompaniment.

½ cup (95 g) raw brown rice (see note)
¾ cup (180 ml) water
¾ pound (340 g) shiitake mushrooms
5 tablespoons extra virgin olive oil
1 medium onion, finely chopped
3 garlic cloves, finely chopped
1 large carrot, peeled and coarsely grated
2 ounces (57 g) walnuts (about ½ cup)
2 large eggs, at room temperature, whisked
4 tablespoons whole-wheat breadcrumbs
Kosher salt
Freshly ground black pepper

Place the rice and water in an enamel-lined saucepan and bring to a boil over high heat. Lower the heat and cook, covered, about 35 minutes, until the rice is soft.

Cut off and discard the mushroom stems. Wipe the caps with a damp paper towel and cut into slices. Heat 1 tablespoon of the oil in a large nonstick skillet over medium-high heat. Add the onions and garlic and sauté over low heat until the onions are soft. Add 3 tablespoons of the remaining oil and increase the heat to high. Add the mushrooms and sauté until they are slightly soft. Remove the skillet from the heat and cool.

Roast the walnuts on the lowest setting of your toaster oven for a minute or two. (Be sure to watch them, as they burn quickly.)

In a food processor, pulse the cooked rice, mushroom mixture, the grated carrots, and walnuts to a medium-coarse consistency. Transfer to a bowl. Add the eggs, then the bread-crumbs, and combine thoroughly. Season well with salt and pepper.

Place a few drops of oil in your palms and form the mixture into six rounded burgers.

Preheat the broiler. Set the rack in the broiler pan and cover it completely with heavy foil. Lightly brush the foil with the remaining 1 tablespoon oil.

Place the burgers on the broiler-pan rack and set the pan in the oven (or broiling unit), as close as possible to the heat source. Broil the burgers 5 minutes per side, or until lightly browned on both sides. Serve warm or at room temperature.

Note: I prefer premium Japanese medium-grain brown rice, as it is much creamier than other varieties.

BARLEY-STUFFED CABBAGE ROLLS

• Makes about 16 rolls

These sweet-and-sour bundles can be served as a main course at lunch or as an appetizer. If you are vegetarian, you can serve these on Sukkoth. Note: These cabbage rolls freeze very well.

CABBAGE
1 medium cabbage (about 3 pounds/1.36 kg)
1 tablespoon kosher salt

FILLING
1½ cups (360 ml) water
¾ cup (150 g) medium pearl barley
½ pound (227 g) white mushrooms
2 tablespoons extra virgin olive oil
2 medium carrots, peeled and grated
½ cup (20 g) tightly packed flat-leaf parsley, finely chopped,
   plus more for garnish
2 garlic cloves, minced
1 large egg, lightly beaten
1 teaspoon kosher salt
Freshly ground black pepper

SAUCE
4 tablespoons extra virgin olive oil
2 medium onions, finely chopped
One 35-ounce (992 g) can peeled imported tomatoes
One 8-ounce (227 g) can tomato sauce
10 sun-dried tomatoes packed in oil, finely chopped
1½ cups (360 ml) vegetable broth
3 tablespoons freshly squeezed lemon juice, plus more as needed
3 tablespoons dark brown sugar, plus more as needed
½ teaspoon kosher salt
Freshly ground black pepper
½ cup (20 g) tightly packed flat-leaf parsley, coarsely chopped, for garnish

TO PREPARE THE CABBAGE LEAVES: Bring to boil a large pot of water with salt. With the point of a knife, cut out some of the hard center core of the cabbage. Remove and discard any bruised and discolored leaves. Add the cabbage to the water and boil for a few minutes, turning the cabbage often. Remove the cabbage from the water by piercing the core with a large fork and lifting out the head.

To remove the leaves without damaging them, cut them where they are attached at the core, then peel off. If necessary, return the cabbage to the boiling water to soften the remaining leaves. Shred the small center leaves.

TO PREPARE THE FILLING: Bring the water to a boil in a small saucepan. Add the barley, lower the heat, and cook, covered, for 15 minutes, or until the grains are firm and the water has been absorbed. Transfer to a medium bowl.

Wipe the mushrooms with a damp paper towel and chop them coarsely. Heat the oil in a small skillet and sauté the mushrooms over high heat until they are dry. Add the mushrooms to the barley along with the carrots, parsley, garlic, and egg. Blend well and season with the salt and pepper to taste.

TO FILL THE CABBAGE LEAVES: Spread each cabbage leaf on a cutting board and cut out some of the center rib. Place 2 tablespoons of the filling in the center. Starting from the smaller end, roll the cabbage halfway, fold the sides toward the center, and roll tightly to the end. Continue until all the filling has been used.

TO MAKE THE SAUCE: Heat the oil in a small skillet. Add the onions, and sauté over low heat for 10 minutes, until the onions are golden. Remove from the heat.

In a bowl, combine the canned tomatoes, tomato sauce, sun-dried tomatoes, vegetable broth, lemon juice, brown sugar, and salt.

TO COOK THE ROLLS: Preheat the oven to 300°F (150°C).

In a large enamel-lined saucepan, place the rolls, seam-side down, very close to each other, in one layer if possible. Scatter the sautéed onions on top. Pour the sauce over the rolls. Scatter the reserved shredded cabbage on top.

Bring to a boil over medium-low heat. Cover, transfer to the oven, and cook for 1 hour, or until the cabbage is soft.

Season to taste with lemon juice, brown sugar, salt, and pepper. Garnish with chopped parsley.

BULGUR CHILI

- Makes 6 as an appetizer or side dish
- Makes 4 generous luncheon servings

This is a wonderful winter luncheon dish that I like to serve with a dollop of ricotta seasoned with salt and pepper or a topping of cubed ricotta salata or any grated cheese, such as mozzarella or cheddar.

2 green bell peppers
2 tablespoons extra virgin olive oil
2 cloves garlic, finely chopped
1 onion, finely chopped
1 pound (450 g) white mushrooms
One 15.5-ounce (440 g) can Goya kidney beans, drained
One 14-ounce (400 g) can imported tomatoes
½ cup (70 g) coarse-grind bulgur
Leaves from 10 thyme sprigs
1 teaspoon ground cumin
1 teaspoon chili powder
½ cup (125 ml) water
Kosher salt
Freshly ground black pepper

Cut the bell peppers in half lengthwise, then core and seed them. Cut into small cubes.

Heat the oil in a medium saucepan. Add the peppers, garlic, and onion, and sauté over low heat about 5 minutes, until the onion is soft.

Wipe the mushrooms with a damp paper towel and cut into thin slices. Add to the saucepan. Increase the heat to medium high and add the beans, tomatoes, bulgur, thyme, cumin, chili powder, and water. Bring to a boil. Lower the heat and cook, covered, for 15 minutes, stirring occasionally.

Season to taste with salt and pepper. Serve in soup bowls.

WHITE BEAN CHILI

• Makes 8 appetizer servings
• Makes 6 luncheon servings

This is an unconventional—and not too spicy—chili recipe, and you don't have to be a vegetarian to love it. I serve it as a luncheon dish accompanied by a salad or as an appetizer course followed by meat or poultry. For a dairy meal, I like to top it with some grated cheese.

1 pound (450 g) dried white beans, such as great Northern or cannellini
3 medium onions
6 garlic cloves
3 medium carrots
3 jalapeño peppers
3 tablespoons extra virgin oil
1 quart (1 liter) vegetable broth
1 tablespoon ground cumin
1 cup (40 g) tightly packed flat-leaf parsley, coarsely chopped
1 cup (40 g) tightly packed cilantro leaves
2 tablespoons freshly squeezed lemon juice
Kosher salt
Freshly ground black pepper

Place the beans into a bowl, cover with cold water, and soak overnight. Drain before using.

Chop the onions, garlic, and carrots. You can do this in a food processor, one vegetable at a time: Quarter the onions and garlic and pulse them together until chopped; remove to a small bowl. Peal the carrots and cut them into large pieces and pulse until chopped. (If you chop everything together, the vegetables will become mushy.) Cut the jalapeño peppers in half lengthwise, then core and seed them. Chop them finely (see note).

Heat the oil over medium heat in a large saucepan. Sauté the onions, garlic, carrots, and jalapeños for a few minutes. Add the beans, vegetable broth, and cumin and bring to a boil. Lower the heat, cover, and cook for about 1 hour, until the beans are tender. (The chili should be slightly soupy.)

Add the parsley and cilantro. Season to taste with the lemon juice, salt, and pepper. Serve in individual soup bowls.

Note: When seeding jalapeño peppers, I advise wearing thin plastic gloves to avoid irritating your skin or your eyes.

BLACK BEAN CHILI

• Makes 8 generous servings

The deep, rich flavor of the black beans lends itself to this spicy chili. It is a wholesome dish to make on cold, wintry days. You can serve it in soup bowls with a dollop of ricotta seasoned with salt and pepper, grated mozzarella or cheddar cheese—or just plain, garnished with cilantro.

> 1 pound (450 g) dried black beans
> 3 medium onions
> 8 garlic cloves
> 1 green bell pepper
> 3 tablespoons extra virgin olive oil
> 5½ cups (1.32 liters) vegetable broth
> 1 tablespoon ground cumin
> 1 tablespoon sweet Hungarian paprika
> ¼ teaspoon cayenne
> 1½ tablespoons chili powder
> 8 sun-dried tomatoes, packed in oil
> One 28-ounce (794 g) can imported tomatoes
> ¼ teaspoon sugar
> 1½ tablespoons apple cider vinegar
> Kosher salt
> Freshly ground black pepper
> 1 cup (40 g) cilantro leaves, plus more for garnish (optional)

Place the beans in a bowl, cover with cold water, and soak overnight. Drain before using.

Chop the onions and garlic in a food processor. (Be sure to quarter the onions and garlic first so that they chop quickly and don't become mushy.) Cut the bell pepper in half lengthwise, then core and seed it. Cut into ½-inch (13 mm) cubes.

Heat the oil over medium heat in a large saucepan. Sauté the onions and garlic for a few minutes. Add the beans and vegetable broth and bring to a boil. Lower the heat, cover, and cook for about 45 minutes.

Heat the cumin in a small skillet over medium-high heat until it begins to smell fragrant. Remove from heat and add the paprika, cayenne, and chili powder. Add to the beans along with the bell pepper, sun-dried tomatoes, canned tomatoes, and sugar and bring to a boil. Lower the heat. Simmer, covered, for 15 minutes, or until the broth is thick and fragrant.

Season with the vinegar and salt and pepper to taste. Before serving, stir in the cilantro.

DESSERTS

DAIRY

CHOCOLATE VELVET CAKE
WARM CHOCOLATE SURPRISES
HAZELNUT BALLS
CHOCOLATE ROLL
WALNUT ROLL
SHORTBREAD BISCUITS
FARMER CHEESE SQUARES
HAMENTASHEN
CITRUS POUND CAKE
TUSCAN CAKE
PEACH ALMOND CAKE
FRUIT LOAF
RICOTTA FLAN WITH RASPBERRY SAUCE
RICOTTA CAKE
APRICOT OR PRUNE CLAFOUTI
PEAR CLAFOUTI
BLINTZES
RUGELACH

PAREVE

CHOCOLATE ALMOND TRUFFLES
FLOURLESS CHOCOLATE NUT TORTE
CHOCOLATE HAZELNUT TORTE WITH RASPBERRY SAUCE
CHOCOLATE ALMOND CAKE WITH ORANGE
CHOCOLATE, PRUNE, AND WALNUT TORTE
WARM CHOCOLATE-COCONUT SURPRISES
CHOCOLATE SOUFFLÉ
EASY BROWNIES
CHOCOLATE MERINGUE SQUARES
PINE NUT BALLS
MOCHA PECAN BALLS
MANDELBROT
HAMENTASHEN
APRICOT SOUFFLÉ
FRUIT CRUMBLE
PEAR TART
MINI FRUIT TRUFFLES
HONEY CAKE
ZUCCHINI CAKE

CHOCOLATE VELVET CAKE

• Makes 12 servings

This cake is a chocolate-lover's delight. It is light, chocolaty, and very moist. It is my granddaughter's absolute favorite dessert.

> **12 tablespoons (180 g) unsalted butter, cut into small pieces, plus 1 tablespoon (15 g) for greasing the pan**
> **12 ounces (340 g) high-quality imported semisweet chocolate, broken into small pieces**
> **¾ cup (150 g) sugar**
> **1½ teaspoons vanilla extract**
> **5 large eggs, separated (see note)**
> **¼ cup (32 g) unbleached all-purpose flour**

Preheat the oven to 350°F (175°C). Grease a 9 by 2½-inch (23 by 6 cm) springform pan with ½ tablespoon (7.5 g) of the butter. Line the pan with wax paper and grease the paper with the remaining ½ tablespoon (7.5 g) of the butter.

Place the chocolate and the remaining 12 tablespoons (180 g) butter in the top of a double boiler. Cover and set over simmering water until the chocolate is melted. Remove the top from the double boiler. Gradually whisk in half of the sugar and the vanilla. Cool a bit. Whisk in one yolk at a time, until the mixture is smooth. Fold in the flour.

Place the egg whites in the bowl of an electric stand mixer. Attach a balloon whisk and beat the whites at high speed until they become foamy. Gradually add the rest of the sugar until soft, stiff peaks form.

With a large rubber spatula, fold half of the whites into the chocolate mixture. Reverse the process and pour the chocolate–egg white mixture back into the bowl with the egg whites. Gently combine the mixtures, making a motion like a figure 8 with the spatula, until all the whites have disappeared. Pour the batter into the springform pan and smooth the top.

Bake on the center shelf of the oven for 28 to 30 minutes. A cake tester inserted into the center should come out moist.

Cool the pan on a wire rack. Remove the rim, invert the cake onto a plate, and discard the wax paper. Invert the cake again onto a serving patter. Slice carefully, as the top will be crumbly.

Note: It is easier to separate the eggs straight from the refrigerator, when they are cold, as the yolks tend to break up as they warm. Make sure the whites have come to room temperature before beating.

WARM CHOCOLATE SURPRISES

• Makes 10 servings

These soufflé-like desserts have a soft (heavenly!) chocolate center and a light crust. They are as delicate as they are delicious, and adults adore them as well as children.

> **7 tablespoons (105 g) unsalted butter, plus 2 tablespoons (30 g)**
>   **for greasing the ramekins**
> **2 tablespoons sugar, plus 2 tablespoons for the ramekins**
> **6 ounces (170 g) high-quality imported semisweet chocolate,**
>   **broken into small pieces**
> **5 tablespoons unsweetened cocoa powder**
> **4 large egg whites, at room temperature**

Preheat the oven to 400°F (205°C). Grease ten ½-cup (125 ml) metal ramekins (oval or round) with 2 tablespoons (30 g) of the butter and sprinkle with 2 tablespoons sugar (see note). Invert the ramekins and tap to remove any excess sugar.

Melt the butter, chocolate, and cocoa in the top section of a double boiler over low heat. Mix until smooth. Remove the top section and cool a bit.

Using the balloon whisk attachment, beat the egg whites in the bowl of an electric stand mixer at high speed until foamy. Gradually add the remaining 2 tablespoons sugar and continue beating the whites until soft, stiff peaks form.

With a rubber spatula, fold one-fourth of the whites into the chocolate mixture. Reverse the process, pouring the chocolate–egg white mixture back into the bowl with the remaining egg whites. Gently combine the two mixtures, making a motion like a figure 8 with the spatula, until all the whites have disappeared. Do not overblend, or the batter will be too heavy.

Spoon the batter evenly among the ramekins and place them on a cookie sheet. Bake for 7 minutes. The top should be slightly set, and the inside will be moist.

Let the ramekins rest for 1 minute before unmolding onto dessert plates.

If not serving the chocolate surprises right away, unmold them onto the cookie sheet. When ready, warm them in a preheated 200°F (95°C) oven for 10 minutes.

Note: If you prefer, you can also use a muffin pan with 12 molds, each of which holds ½ cup (125 ml) of batter.

HAZELNUT BALLS

• Makes 4 dozen cookies

Roasted hazelnuts have a distinct flavor and texture, both rich and subtle. The aroma always reminds me of Italy in the late spring. These delicious balls are easy to make and freeze very well.

> **1 cup (150 g) skin-on hazelnuts**
> **1 cup (128 g) sifted unbleached all-purpose flour, plus more for shaping**
> **3 tablespoons sugar**
> **½ teaspoon vanilla extract**
> **8 tablespoons (120 g) unsalted butter, chilled and cut into small pieces**

Roast the hazelnuts in a toaster oven at 350°F (175°C) for 15 minutes, or until the skins are blistered. While the nuts are still hot, rub them in a dish towel to remove most of their skin. (Some skin will remain.) Cool.

Preheat the oven to 325°F (165°C).

Place the hazelnuts, flour, sugar, vanilla, and butter in a food processor and pulse until the mixture almost forms into a ball. Transfer the dough to a floured pastry board or work surface and shape it into a smooth ball.

Place level teaspoonfuls of dough between the palms of your hands and roll into smooth balls. Place the balls on two ungreased baking sheets with a little space in between. (They will expand as they cook.) Refrigerate for 10 minutes.

Bake one sheet at a time, for 15 minutes, or until the bottoms of the balls are golden.

Place the baking sheet on a wire rack and let the balls cool slightly. Remove them with a metal spatula and place on a wire rack to cool completely. (If not absolutely cool, they will crack.)

Note: To freeze, place them side by side in an air-tight plastic container, with wax paper between the layers.

CHOCOLATE ROLL

• Makes 12 servings

This is a very light dessert that only seems complicated. It is really quite easy to prepare.

CAKE
1 tablespoon vegetable oil, for greasing the pan
1 tablespoon instant coffee powder
¼ cup (60 ml) boiling water
5 ounces (142 g) high-quality imported semisweet chocolate,
  broken into small pieces
5 large eggs, separated (see note)
¾ cup (150 g) sugar

FILLING
1 cup (250 ml) heavy cream, chilled
2 tablespoons confectioners' sugar
1 tablespoon instant coffee powder

2 tablespoons imported unsweetened cocoa powder, for dusting the roll

TO MAKE THE CAKE: Preheat the oven to 400°F (205°C). Brush the bottom and sides of a 10½ by 15½-inch (27 by 40 cm) jelly-roll pan with some of the oil. Line it with enough wax paper to extend several inches beyond the width of the pan. Brush the wax paper with oil.

Combine the coffee powder, boiling water, and chocolate in the top of a double boiler. Cover and set over simmering water. Stir from time to time, until the chocolate is melted and smooth. Remove the top from the double boiler and cool.

Beat the egg yolks in the bowl of an electric stand mixer with a balloon whisk attachment at medium speed, gradually adding the sugar, until the mixture is pale and bubbles begin to appear, about 5 minutes. Lower the speed and slowly add the melted chocolate until the mixture is well combined. Remove to a large bowl.

Wash and dry the balloon whisk and mixer bowl well. Beat the egg whites at high speed until soft, stiff peaks form.

With a large rubber spatula, fold a quarter of the egg whites into the chocolate mixture. Reverse the process, pouring the chocolate–egg white mixture back into the bowl with the egg whites. Gently combine the two mixtures, making a motion like a figure 8 with the spatula, until all the whites have disappeared. Do not overfold, or the roll will be too heavy.

Pour the batter into the jelly-roll pan, tipping the pan to spread the batter evenly. Smooth the top.

Place the pan on the middle shelf of the oven and immediately lower the temperature to 350°F (175°C). Bake for 15 to 20 minutes, until the top is slightly firm and the inside is still moist.

Remove from the oven, cover with a damp dish towel, and cool in the refrigerator for 30 minutes.

After removing the pan from the refrigerator, remove the towel and leave the cake at room temperature for 15 minutes. (This makes it easier to peel off the wax paper.)

TO MAKE THE FILLING: Place the cream, sugar, and coffee powder in a chilled metal bowl. (I keep mine in the freezer for 10 minutes.) Whip the mixture with the balloon whisk attachment of the electric stand mixer until stiff peaks form.

TO ASSEMBLE THE ROLL: Line a large board with wax paper. Invert the cake onto the board. Remove the pan and gently peel off the wax paper lining.

Spread the cream evenly over the cake. Using the wax paper, roll the cake loosely like a jelly roll, adjusting the shape as needed. (Don't worry about any cracks that may appear.)

With the help of the wax paper, carefully transfer the roll onto a serving platter. If you have difficulty with this step, slide a spatula under each end and lift it. Sprinkle the top of the roll with cocoa powder.

If you do not serve the chocolate roll right away, cover it loosely with wax paper and refrigerate.

Serve at room temperature.

Note: It is easier to separate the eggs straight from the refrigerator, while they are cold, as the egg yolks tend to break up as they warm. Make sure the whites have come to room temperature before beating.

WALNUT ROLL

• Makes 12 servings

This is a flourless dessert—light, luscious, and festive.

CAKE
1 tablespoon vegetable oil, for greasing the pan
1¼ cups (125 g) walnuts
6 large eggs, separated (see note)
¾ cup (150 g) sugar
1 teaspoon baking powder
¼ teaspoon almond extract

FILLING
1 cup (250 ml) heavy cream, chilled
2 tablespoons confectioners' sugar, plus 1 tablespoon for dusting the roll
1 tablespoon powdered instant coffee

TO MAKE THE CAKE: Preheat the oven to 350°F (175°C). Brush the bottom and sides of a 10½ by 15½-inch (27 by 40 cm) jelly-roll pan with some of the oil. Line it with enough wax paper to extend several inches beyond the width of the pan. Brush the wax paper with oil.

Chop the walnuts in a food processor until medium-fine.

Place the egg yolks in the bowl of an electric stand mixer. Using a balloon whisk attachment, beat the yolks at medium speed, gradually adding the sugar, until the mixture is pale and bubbles begin to appear, about 5 minutes.

Lower the speed. Add the baking powder and almond extract and beat until thoroughly combined. Remove to a large bowl.

Wash and dry the balloon whisk and mixer bowl well. Add the egg whites and beat at high speed until soft, stiff peaks form.

With a large rubber spatula, fold a quarter of the whites and half of the walnuts into the yolk mixture. Repeat with another quarter of the whites and the remaining walnuts. Reverse the process, pouring the nut mixture into the bowl with the egg whites. Gently fold the two mixtures, making a motion like a figure 8 with the spatula, until all the whites have disappeared. Do not overfold or the roll will be too heavy.

Pour the batter into the pan, tipping the pan to spread the batter evenly. Smooth the top. Bake for 20 minutes, or until the cake is springy to the touch. Cover the roll with a dry dish towel and cool on a wire rack.

TO MAKE THE FILLING: Place the cream, sugar, and coffee powder in a well-chilled metal bowl. (I keep mine in the freezer for 10 minutes.) Whip the mixture with the balloon whisk attachment of the electric stand mixer until stiff peaks form.

TO ASSEMBLE THE ROLL: Line a large board with wax paper. Invert the cake onto the board. Remove the pan and gently peel off the wax paper lining.

Spread the cream evenly over the cake. Using the wax paper, roll the cake loosely like a jelly roll, adjusting the shape as needed. (Don't worry about any cracks that may appear.)

With the help of the wax paper, carefully transfer the roll onto a serving platter. If you have difficulty with this step, slide a spatula under each end and lift it. Dust the reserved sugar on the top of the roll.

If you do not serve the walnut roll right away, cover it loosely with wax paper and refrigerate.

Serve at room temperature.

Note: It is easier to separate the eggs straight from the refrigerator, while they are cold, as the yolks tend to break up as they warm. Make sure the whites have come to room temperature before beating.

SHORTBREAD BISCUITS

• Makes 3 dozen 2-inch (5 cm) rounds

English shortbread inspired these biscuits. Mine are smaller, thinner, and less buttery (also less fattening)—but still quite scrumptious. They also freeze beautifully.

16 tablespoons (240 g) unsalted chilled butter, plus 1 tablespoon (15 g)
 for greasing the baking sheets
½ cup (100 g) sugar
1 teaspoon vanilla extract
1⅓ cup (170 g) unbleached all-purpose flour
½ cup (80 g) white rice flour (see note)

Grease each of two 11 by 18-inch (28 by 46 cm) baking sheets with ½ tablespoon (7.5 g) of the butter and line them with wax paper.

Place the remaining butter, the sugar, vanilla extract, all-purpose flour, and rice flour in a food processor and pulse until the dough just comes together. Turn out the dough on a lightly floured pastry board or work surface and knead it a little until it is smooth and well blended.

Cut the dough into four pieces and shape each into a ball. As you work with each ball, keep the others in the refrigerator.

On a floured piece of wax paper, roll out one ball of the dough to a thickness of ¼ inch (6 mm). Use a 2-inch (5 cm) round cookie cutter to cut out the biscuits, occasionally dipping the cutter in flour to avoid sticking. Use all the scraps of dough. Place the rounds on the prepared baking sheets with a little space in between. Refrigerate for about 1 hour.

Preheat the oven to 325°F (165°C).

Bake the biscuits for 17 minutes, or until they are lightly golden. Let them rest for 1 minute before removing them with a metal spatula to a wire rack to cool completely.

Notes: White rice flour is available in most health-food stores.

These biscuits freeze well. Place them side by side in an air-tight plastic container, with wax paper between the layers.

FARMER CHEESE SQUARES

• Makes about 2 dozen 1½-inch (4 cm) squares

This is an Eastern European version of a light cheesecake. The dough is baked, then filled with cheese and other delicacies and baked again. I always serve it on Shavuot, but it is wonderful any time.

DOUGH
1½ cups (192 g) unbleached all-purpose flour, plus more for shaping and rolling
½ cup (75 g) blanched almonds, finely ground (see note)
¼ cup (50 g) sugar
1 large egg, separated
2 tablespoons freshly squeezed orange juice
10 tablespoons (150 g) unsalted butter, chilled and cut into small pieces

FILLING
1¾ pounds (795 g) farmer cheese
Generous ½ cup (120 g) sugar
3 large eggs, separated (see note)
1 tablespoon vanilla extract
Grated zest of 1 lemon
1 tablespoon freshly squeezed lemon juice
½ cup (115 g) seedless golden raisins (see note)

TO MAKE THE DOUGH: Pulse the flour, almonds, and sugar in a food processor to combine. Combine the egg yolk and the orange juice and add to the food processor along with the butter. (Set aside the egg white to use later.) Pulse until the dough clings to the blade but before it forms a ball.

Turn out the dough onto a lightly floured work surface or pastry board and knead it with your hands into a smooth, flat rectangle about 4 by 6 inches (10 by 15 cm). Wrap it in wax paper, then foil, and refrigerate for several hours or overnight.

TO ROLL OUT THE DOUGH: Remove the dough from refrigerator. When it is malleable, lightly flour it on both sides and roll it between two sheets of wax paper. You should end up with a rectangle about 11 by 15 inches (28 by 38 cm). The dough will spread more easily if you occasionally turn it over, lift the top wax paper, and flour the dough lightly.

Peel off the top sheet of wax paper and gently flip the dough into a 9 by 13 by 2-inch (23 by 33 by 5 cm) ungreased baking pan. Peel off the remaining piece of wax paper and fit the dough firmly into the edges of the pan, fixing any cracks with your fingers. Shape the sides so that they are about 1½ inches (4 cm) high. Prick the bottom of the dough lightly with a fork and refrigerate for 1 hour.

Preheat the oven to 350°F (175°C).

Whisk the reserved egg white lightly with a fork and brush it on the bottom and sides of the dough. Bake the dough on the lowest shelf of the oven for 25 minutes, or until it is golden and the crust shrinks from side of pan. Cool.

TO MAKE THE FILLING: Preheat the oven to 350°F (175°C). Place the farmer cheese, sugar, egg yolks, vanilla, lemon zest, and lemon juice in a food processor and pulse until just combined. (The filling should have a coarse texture.) Transfer to a bowl and add the raisins.

Beat the egg whites until stiff and gently fold them into the cheese mixture. Spread the filling in the shell and smooth the top.

Bake the filled shell on the lowest shelf of the oven for 35 minutes, or until the top feels firm. Cool on a wire rack.

Notes: I use a Mouli julienne grater to finely grind such a small amount of nuts. It's a nice gadget to have on hand.

It is easier to separate the eggs straight from the refrigerator, when they are cold, as the yolks tend to break up as they warm. Make sure the whites have come to room temperature before beating.

If you prefer, you can substitute ½ cup (60 g) of blanched slivered almonds for the raisins. Or you can mix raisins and almonds for a total of ½ cup (115 g).

HAMENTASHEN

• Makes about 3 dozen hamentashen

Purim commemorates the Jews' escape from certain death at the hands of the Persian nobleman, Haman. While there are many versions of how this traditional Purim delicacy got its name, the one I learned from my mother is that the pastry resembles Haman's three-cornered hat. (A pareve recipe for Hamentashen appears on page 326.)

DOUGH
2 cups (255 g) unbleached all-purpose flour, plus more for shaping and rolling
⅓ cup (65 g) sugar
10 tablespoons (150 g) unsalted butter, chilled and cut into small pieces
Grated zest of 1 lemon
1 large egg plus 1 large egg yolk (see note)
2¼ teaspoons distilled white vinegar
2¼ teaspoons cold water

FILLING
2 ounces (57 g) high-quality imported semisweet chocolate
½ cup (125 ml) milk
Generous ¼ cup (60 g) sugar
1¼ cups (180 g) ground poppy seeds (see note)
2 tablespoons (30 g) unsalted butter, cut into small pieces, at room temperature

GLAZE
1 large egg, lightly beaten

TO MAKE THE DOUGH: Pulse the flour and sugar in a food processor to combine. Add the butter and lemon zest and pulse until the mixture resembles coarse crumbs. Add the egg and egg yolk. Mix the vinegar and water, and add to the mixture. Pulse again until the dough clings to the blade but before it forms into a ball.

Turn out the dough on a lightly floured work surface or pastry board and shape it into a smooth ball. Dust the dough lightly with flour, wrap in wax paper and foil, and refrigerate for 30 minutes or overnight (see note).

TO MAKE THE FILLING: Grate the chocolate with a Mouli grater. In a small enamel-lined saucepan, bring the milk and sugar to a boil over medium heat. Add the poppy seeds, lower the heat, and simmer for 3 minutes, stirring constantly with a wooden spoon.

Remove from the heat and stir in the butter and chocolate. Cool (see note.).

TO FORM AND BAKE THE HAMENTASHEN: Preheat the oven to 350°F (175°C).

Cut the dough into 6 pieces, but work with one piece at a time and keep the rest in the refrigerator.

Roll out each piece of dough between two sheets of wax paper, lightly flouring the dough on both sides. The dough should end up as a thin circle, 7 to 8 inches (18 to 20 cm) in diameter. (From time to time, to make it easier to roll the dough, lift the top wax paper, sprinkle the dough lightly with flour, put back the wax paper, and turn the dough packet over.)

With a 3-inch (8 cm) round cookie cutter, cut out 5 circles. From time to time, dip the cookie cutter into flour, as this will keep the dough from sticking. Refrigerate the scraps so they can be reused.

Lightly brush the edges of each circle with egg, then place a level teaspoon of poppy seed filling in the center. Pinch the dough together at three equidistant points on the circle so you form a triangle.

Put the hamentashen on wax paper and brush the dough with the glaze, then place them on cookie sheets. (You will need two cookie sheets.) Repeat with the other scraps of dough: Reroll, cut, fill, shape, and glaze.

Bake for 18 minutes, until the pastry is lightly golden. Remove to wire rack to cool.

Notes: It is easier to separate the eggs straight from the refrigerator, when they are cold, as the yolks tends to break up as they warm.

Ground poppy seeds are obtainable by mail order, and can be frozen.

You can make the dough in advance and freeze it. Defrost it in the refrigerator before using.

You can make the poppy-seed filling several days ahead and refrigerate or freeze it. Defrost the filling in the refrigerator before using.

To freeze the baked hamentashen, place them side by side in an air-tight plastic container, with wax paper between the layers.

CITRUS POUND CAKE

• Makes 2 loaves, 14 servings each

If you like sweets with a lemony flavor, you will love this pound cake. It is wonderful as a midday snack (I often have a slice with my tea), and it also makes a lovely light dessert, served with berries, ice cream, or sorbet.

CAKES

16 tablespoons (240 g) unsalted butter, at room temperature,
   plus 1 tablespoon (15 g) for greasing the pans
3 cups (385 g) unbleached all-purpose flour,
   plus 2 tablespoons for dusting the pans
½ teaspoon baking powder
½ teaspoon baking soda
1½ cups (300 g) sugar
4 large eggs, at room temperature
1 tablespoon grated orange zest
2 teaspoons grated lemon zest
¾ cup (185 g) plain yogurt, at room temperature
¾ cup (180 ml) freshly squeezed orange juice

LEMON SYRUP

¼ cup (50 g) sugar
1 tablespoon freshly squeezed lemon juice

TO MAKE THE CAKES: Preheat the oven to 350°F (175°C). Grease two 5 by 9-inch (13 by 23 cm) loaf pans with ½ tablespoon (7.5 g) butter each, then dust with 1 tablespoon flour each. Invert the pans and tap to shake out the excess flour.

In a medium bowl, combine the flour, baking powder, and baking soda.

Place the butter in the bowl of an electric stand mixer. Using the balloon whisk attachment, beat the butter at medium speed. Gradually add the sugar and continue beating about 5 minutes, until the mixture is pale and fluffy. On low speed, add 1 egg at a time, beating after each addition. Increase the speed and beat another 5 minutes until the mixture is thick and creamy. Using a rubber spatula, stir in the orange and lemon zests.

In a small bowl, mix the yogurt and orange juice.

At low speed, add small amounts of flour to the butter mixture, alternating with spoonfuls of the yogurt mixture and ending with the flour, until the ingredients are well blended. Occasionally scrape down the sides of the bowl.

Spoon the batter into the two loaf pans and smooth the tops.

Bake for 50 to 55 minutes, until a cake tester inserted into the center comes out dry.

Cool on a wire rack for only 10 minutes. Run a metal spatula around the sides of the pans to make sure the cakes don't stick. Unmold onto the wire rack.

TO MAKE THE SYRUP: Heat the sugar and lemon juice, stirring constantly over low heat until the sugar is dissolved.

With the cake tester, poke holes in the top of the warm cakes. Using a pastry brush, brush the syrup all over the top. You may have to do this several times until all the syrup has soaked in. Cool.

Note: These cakes freeze well. Wrap them individually in wax paper, then in foil, and place in plastic freezer bags.

TUSCAN CAKE

• Makes 16 servings

This is a great summer cake that looks beautiful on a buffet table. Berries, sorbet, or ice cream are perfect accompaniments. As strange as it may seem, this cake improves with time—refrigerated, of course. If there are any leftovers, they can be toasted.

> **16 tablespoons (240 g) unsalted butter,**
>   **plus 2 tablespoons (30 g) for greasing the pan**
> **2½ cups (320 g) unbleached all-purpose flour,**
>   **plus more for dusting the pan**
> **1 envelope active dry yeast (2¼ teaspoons/7 g)**
> **4 whole large eggs, at room temperature**
> **2 cups (400 g) sugar**
> **Grated zest of 1 lemon**
> **3 tablespoons freshly squeezed lemon juice**
> **¾ cup (105 g) pine nuts**

Preheat the oven to 350°F (175°C). Grease a 12 inch by 2½-inch (30 by 6 cm) springform pan with 1 tablespoon (15 g) of the butter and line it with wax paper. Grease the wax paper with another 1 tablespoon (15 g) butter and dust it with flour. Invert the pan and tap out the excess flour.

Melt the remaining 16 tablespoons (240 g) butter in small saucepan. Remove from the heat, cool to lukewarm, and stir in the yeast.

Place the eggs in the bowl of an electric stand mixer. Using the balloon whisk attachment, beat the eggs at medium speed until well mixed. Gradually add the sugar and beat about 5 minutes, until the mixture is pale and bubbles appear.

With a rubber spatula, mix the butter-yeast mixture into the eggs along with the lemon zest, lemon juice, and flour. Combine all ingredients well.

Pour the batter into the prepared pan and scatter the pine nuts on top.

Bake for 35 to 40 minutes, until a cake tester inserted in the center comes out clean.

Cool on a wire rack. Remove the rim and invert the cake onto a plate. Remove the wax paper and invert again onto a serving platter.

PEACH ALMOND CAKE

• Makes 8 servings

This is a delicious dessert that I love to make in summer, when peaches are at their best. You can serve it warm or at room temperature, topped with ice cream or sorbet.

**4 tablespoons (60 g) unsalted butter,
   plus 1 tablespoon (15 g) for greasing the pan**
½ pound (225 g) blanched almonds
½ teaspoon vanilla extract
1 teaspoon almond extract
3 peaches
Boiling water, as needed
Generous ½ cup (115 g) sugar
½ cup (64 g) unbleached all-purpose flour
5 large egg whites (see note)

Preheat the oven to 400°F (205°C). Grease a 9 by 2½-inch (23 by 6 cm) springform pan with 1 tablespoon (15 g) of the butter.

Chop the blanched almonds in a food processor to a semifine texture.

In a small saucepan melt the remaining 4 tablespoons (60 g) butter. Add the vanilla and almond extracts and cool.

Peel the peaches by placing them in a bowl and pouring boiling water over them. Drain and slip off the skin. Cut the peaches in half, remove the pits and slice into ¼-inch (6 mm) wedges.

In a medium bowl, combine the almonds, sugar, and flour. Stir in the melted butter mixture.

Place the egg whites in the bowl of an electric stand mixer. Using the balloon whisk attachment, beat them at high speed until stiff. With a rubber spatula, fold half of the egg whites into the flour mixture. Reverse the process and pour the egg white–flour mixture into the bowl with the remaining whites. Combine gently and thoroughly.

Spoon the batter into the springform pan, distributing the batter evenly. Arrange the peach slices on top in overlapping concentric circles.

Bake on the middle shelf of the oven for 30 minutes, until a cake tester inserted in the center comes out clean.

Cool on a wire rack. Remove the rim and unmold.

Note: It is easier to separate the eggs straight from the refrigerator, when they are cold. Make sure the whites have come to room temperature before beating.

FRUIT LOAF

• Makes 14 servings

This is really a pound cake filled with dried fruits. Delicious, nutritious, and easy to make, it is a hostess's dream. A few days later, I like to slice it thin and toast it. It also freezes well (see note).

12 tablespoons (180 g) unsalted butter, at room temperature,
   plus ½ tablespoon (7.5 g) for greasing the pan
1½ cups (192 g) unbleached all-purpose flour,
   plus 1 tablespoon for dusting the pan
½ cup (75 g) dried currants
½ cup (80 g) dried apricots, cut into ¼-inch cubes
½ cup (50 g) walnuts, coarsely chopped
Scant ¾ cup (140 g) sugar
3 large eggs, at room temperature

Preheat the oven to 350°F (175°C). Grease a 5 by 9-inch (13 by 23 cm) loaf pan with ½ tablespoon (7.5 g) of the butter and dust it with 1 tablespoon of the flour. Invert the pan and tap to shake out any excess flour.

In a small bowl, combine the fruits with the nuts.

Place the remaining 12 tablespoons (180 g) butter in the bowl of an electric stand mixer. Using a balloon whisk attachment, beat the butter at medium speed, gradually adding the sugar. Beat for about 5 minutes until pale yellow and fluffy. Lower the speed and beat in 1 egg at a time, Mix in the flour until the ingredients are just combined.

Fold the fruits and nuts into the batter with a spatula.

Spoon the batter into the pan and smooth the top.

Bake the cake on the middle shelf of the oven for 55 to 60 minutes, until a cake tester inserted into the center comes out clean.

Cool on a wire rack. Run a metal spatula around the sides of the pan to release the cake and unmold.

Note: To freeze the cake, wrap it in wax paper, then in foil, and place in a plastic freezer bag.

RICOTTA FLAN WITH RASPBERRY SAUCE

• Makes 8 to 10 servings

I love to serve this light dessert with an easy-to-make raspberry sauce and fresh raspberries. You can bake it a day in advance and refrigerate it. It is wonderful warm, cold, or at room temperature.

FLAN
1 tablespoon (15 g) unsalted butter, for greasing the pan
1 cup (150 g) blanched almonds
4 large eggs, at room temperature
½ cup (100 g) plus 1 tablespoon sugar
1 teaspoon vanilla extract
Grated zest of 2 lemons
One 15-ounce (425 g) container ricotta cheese, at room temperature
Confectioners' sugar, for dusting the flan
Fresh raspberries, for garnish

RASPBERRY SAUCE
One 12-ounce (340 g) package unsweetened frozen raspberries, defrosted
1 tablespoon Cognac (optional)
2 tablespoons confectioners' sugar, or to taste (see note)

TO MAKE THE FLAN: Preheat the oven to 325°F (165°C). Grease a 10 by 1½-inch (25 by 4 cm) flan dish with the butter.

Roast the almonds in a toaster oven at 350°F (175°C) for 5 minutes, until golden. Cool. Finely grind them in a food processor.

In a medium bowl, whisk the eggs, adding the sugar gradually until well combined. Add the vanilla, lemon zest, ricotta, and almonds. Mix well.

Pour the mixture into the prepared dish and bake for 30 to 40 minutes, until the center feels slightly springy to the touch. Place on a wire rack to cool.

TO MAKE THE SAUCE: Purée the raspberries in a blender until smooth. Strain through a medium-mesh sieve. Push the solids through the sieve with the back of a spoon to obtain as much purée as possible. Stir in the Cognac. Sweeten to taste with sugar.

TO SERVE: Spoon the raspberry sauce on individual plates, and place slices of the flan on top. Dust with confectioners' sugar and garnish with fresh raspberries.

Note: To serve on Passover, use superfine sugar rather than confectioners sugar.

RICOTTA CAKE

• Makes 12 servings

This is a crustless, light version of an Italian cheesecake. I find that baking it a day in advance and refrigerating it is not only convenient, but it also makes cutting a bit easier. Ricotta cake goes beautifully with any kind of berry.

> **Two 15-ounce (425 g) containers whole-milk ricotta**
> **1 tablespoon (15 g) unsalted butter, for greasing the pan**
> **2 tablespoons flour, plus 1 tablespoon for dusting the pan**
> **4 large eggs, separated (see note)**
> **Grated zest of 1 lemon**
> **½ cup (70 g) pine nuts**
> **½ cup (100 g) sugar**

Before using the ricotta, it is important to get it as dry as possible. To do this, place the ricotta in a fine-mesh sieve set over a bowl. Cover with cling wrap and set a heavy can on top to weigh it down. (This helps the draining process.) Refrigerate for several hours.

Preheat the oven to 350°F (175°C). Grease a 9 by 2-inch (23 by 5 cm) springform pan with the butter and dust it with 1 tablespoon of the flour. Invert the pan and tap to shake out excess flour.

In a large bowl, combine the ricotta, the remaining 2 tablespoons flour, the egg yolks, lemon zest, and pine nuts.

Place the egg whites in the bowl of an electric stand mixer. Using the balloon whisk attachment, beat the whites at high speed until soft, stiff peaks form. Gradually beat in the sugar until the egg whites are stiff.

With a rubber spatula, fold half the whites into the ricotta mixture. Reverse the process and pour the ricotta mixture into the bowl with the remaining whites. Gently blend the ingredients, making a motion like a figure 8 with the spatula, until the egg whites are well combined.

Spoon the batter into the prepared pan and smooth the top. Place the pan on a sheet of aluminum foil on the middle shelf of the oven (in case the batter drips). Bake for 40 to 45 minutes, until the middle of the cake is firm to the touch and the top is golden.

Cool on a wire rack. The cake will fall a bit. Loosen the cake around the edges with a metal spatula, and remove the rim. Cover the cake with cling wrap and refrigerate.

Note: It is best to separate the eggs straight from the refrigerator, while they are still cold, as the egg yolks tends to break up as they warm. Make sure the whites have come to room temperature before beating.

APRICOT OR PRUNE CLAFOUTI

• Makes 6 servings

This dessert could not be simpler to make and is always a satisfying way to end a meal.

1 tablespoon (15 g) unsalted butter for greasing the pan
¾ cup (120 g) dried California apricots (see note) or pitted prunes
1 tablespoon brandy
3 large eggs, at room temperature
¼ cup (50 g) sugar
⅓ cup (43 g) unbleached all-purpose flour
1 cup (250 ml) milk, at room temperature
1 teaspoon vanilla extract

Preheat the oven to 375°F (190°C). Grease a 10 by 1½-inch (25 by 4 cm) flan dish with the butter.

Cut the apricots or prunes into ¼-inch (6 mm) cubes. Place them in a small bowl and combine them with the brandy.

In a medium bowl, whisk the eggs and sugar until well combined. Gradually add the flour and whisk until smooth. Whisk in the milk and vanilla.

Scatter the apricots or prunes evenly in the bottom of the flan dish and pour the batter over them.

Bake the clafouti for 25 to 30 minutes, until the sides are puffed and golden and the center is just set.

Before serving, warm for 10 minutes in a preheated 300°F (150°C) oven.

Note: I always use California apricots when I make this because they are less sweet than other varieties.

PEAR CLAFOUTI

• Makes 8 servings

 If you make this elegant dessert earlier in the day, just reheat it before serving, as it is best when warm. Baked in an attractive flan dish, it can go straight from the oven to the table.

> **6 tablespoons (90 g) unsalted butter,**
>   **plus 1 tablespoon (15 g) for greasing the flan dish**
> **¾ cup (130 g) blanched, sliced almonds**
> **½ cup (100 g) sugar, plus 1 tablespoon for sprinkling on top**
> **¾ cup (96 g) unbleached all-purpose flour**
> **4 firm ripe medium Bosc pears**
> **2 tablespoons freshly squeezed lemon juice**
> **3 large eggs, at room temperature**
> **¾ cup (180 ml) milk, at room temperature**
> **½ teaspoon vanilla extract**
> **½ teaspoon almond extract**

Preheat the oven to 400°F (205°C).

 Melt 6 tablespoons (90 g) of the butter. Transfer to a medium bowl. With the remaining butter, grease a 10 by 1½-inch (25 by 4 cm) flan dish.

 Grind ½ cup (85 g) of the almonds finely in a food processor, reserving the rest for the topping. Transfer the ground almonds to a bowl and mix in the sugar and the flour.

 Peel, quarter, and core the pears. Cut each quarter in half. Arrange the pears in the flan dish and sprinkle with the lemon juice.

 Add the eggs, milk, and vanilla and almond extracts to the melted butter and whisk. Add the almond mixture and combine well until smooth. Pour the batter over the pears. Sprinkle with the remaining almonds and 1 tablespoon sugar.

 Bake on the center shelf for 35 minutes, or until the top is golden and the crust has begun to pull away from the side of the dish.

 Before serving, warm the clafouti for 10 minutes in a preheated 300°F (150°C) oven.

BLINTZES

• Makes 12 to 14 crêpes, about 6 servings

These are small, light, and not overly sweet crêpes with a delicate cheese filling. I usually make them for Shavuot, but like all of the traditional desserts, I serve them year-round. Berries make a lovely accompaniment.

CRÊPE BATTER
2 large eggs, at room temperature
⅛ teaspoon salt
3½ tablespoons unbleached all-purpose flour
½ cup (125 ml) ice water
1 tablespoon (15 g) unsalted butter, melted, for greasing the crêpe pan

FILLING
¾ pound (340 g) farmer cheese
1 large egg yolk (see note)
½ teaspoon vanilla extract
Grated zest of 1 lemon
2 tablespoons sugar, or to taste

2 tablespoons (30 g) unsalted butter, for browning the blintzes
Confectioners' sugar, for dusting

TO MAKE THE BATTER: Place the eggs, salt, flour, and water in a blender and mix at high speed until the batter is very smooth. (Be sure to scrape down the sides of the blender jar with a spatula.) Pour the mixture into a measuring cup with a spout. Cover with cling wrap and refrigerate overnight.

TO MAKE THE FILLING: Put the farmer cheese, egg yolk, vanilla, lemon zest, and sugar in a medium bowl and mix with a fork until well combined. The mixture will have a coarse texture.

TO MAKE THE CRÊPES: Bring the batter to room temperature and stir well. Heat a 6½-inch (16 cm) crêpe pan over medium heat and brush lightly with butter. (To test if the pan is hot enough, pour a drop of batter on it; if it sizzles, the pan is ready.)

Pour in just enough batter so that when you swirl the pan, the bottom is coated. Immediately pour off any excess, no matter how little. (The goal is to make the crêpe as thin as possible.) Cook the crêpe on both sides until lightly golden. Put finished crêpes on wax paper, with sheets of wax paper in between the layers.

Repeat the process until you have used up all the batter. You do not have to grease the pan each time.

TO ASSEMBLE THE BLINTZES: Place about 1½ tablespoons of the filling in the bottom third of each crêpe and roll it over. Continue rolling the crêpe loosely to the end.

Melt the butter in a skillet and brown the blintzes lightly. (You can keep them warm in a preheated 200°F/95°C oven.)

Before serving, sprinkle with confectioners' sugar.

Notes: It is easier to separate the egg straight from the refrigerator, when it is cold, as the yolk tends to break up as it warms.

You can make the crêpes in advance. Put them in an air-tight plastic container lined with wax paper, separating the layers with wax paper. Refrigerate overnight or freeze. Defrost frozen crêpes in the refrigerator. Whether refrigerating or freezing, bring the crêpes to room temperature before filling.

Blintzes can be made in advance if you omit the browning. Defrost frozen blintzes in the refrigerator. Whether refrigerated or frozen, bring them to room temperature and brown as described above. Sprinkle with confectioners' sugar and serve warm.

RUGELACH

• Makes 32 rugelach

These Eastern European specialty cookies are a favorite at my home, so I always have some on hand. They look like mini croissants, with their flaky dough and delicate taste. They can be made with different fillings, but since my favorites are walnut and chocolate, that is the recipe that follows.

DOUGH
8 tablespoons (120 g) chilled unsalted butter, cut into pieces
3 ounces (85 g) chilled cream cheese, cut into pieces
1 cup (128 g) unbleached all-purpose flour, plus more for kneading

FILLING
1 cup (100 g) walnuts
4 ounces (113 g) high-quality imported semisweet chocolate,
** broken into small pieces**
½ cup (100 g) sugar
1 teaspoon ground cinnamon

TO MAKE THE DOUGH: Place the butter, cream cheese, and flour in a food processor and pulse until the dough clings to the blade. Turn out the dough onto a lightly floured work surface or pastry board and knead into a smooth ball.

Divide the dough into two balls, dust them lightly with flour and flatten. Wrap each in wax paper, then in foil, and place in a plastic bag. Refrigerate for 6 hours or overnight.

Before baking, remove the dough from the refrigerator and wait until it is malleable.

TO MAKE THE FILLING: Chop the walnuts in a food processor until coarse. Transfer to a medium bowl. Chop the chocolate until coarse. Add to the walnuts along with the sugar and cinnamon. Combine well.

TO FILL AND BAKE: Preheat the oven to 375°F (190°C).
Work with one ball of dough at a time, keeping the other refrigerated. On a lightly floured surface, roll out the ball to a circle about 16 inches (40 cm) in diameter. Sprinkle half of the filling over the circle. Cut the circle into 16 wedge-shaped pieces. Roll each wedge tightly from the widest part to the point. Bend it slightly into a curve, like a croissant. Place each of the rugelach on a cookie sheet. (You may need two cookie sheets.) Repeat the process with the other ball. Bake in the upper third of the oven for about 20 minutes, until light brown. Cool on a wire rack.

Note: Rugelach freeze well. Place them side by side in an air-tight plastic container, separating the layers with wax paper.

CHOCOLATE ALMOND TRUFFLES

• Makes 4 dozen truffles

These little balls improve with time, so do make them in advance so you can always have some on hand. No baking required. They are ideal for Passover.

1 cup (142 g) skin-on almonds
¼ pound (113 g) high-quality imported semisweet chocolate,
   broken into small pieces
½ cup (100 g) superfine sugar
2 large egg yolks (see note)
1½ tablespoons dark rum
3 tablespoons unsweetened imported cocoa powder

Roast the almonds in a toaster oven at 350°F (175°C) for 10 minutes. Cool.

Place the almonds, chocolate, and sugar in a food processor and pulse to a coarse texture. Add the egg yolks and rum. Continue pulsing to a fine texture.

Sprinkle the cocoa on a sheet of wax paper. Put a level teaspoon of the chocolate-almond mixture in the palm of your hand, shape it into a ball and roll in the cocoa powder to coat well. Continue until all the mixture has been used.

Notes: It is easier to separate the eggs straight from the refrigerator, when they are cold, as the yolks tend to break up as they warm.

Truffles freeze beautifully. Place them side by side in an air-tight platic container, with wax paper between the layers.

FLOURLESS CHOCOLATE NUT TORTE

• Makes 12 servings

Moist and full of nuts, this cake has a delightful chocolate texture. It is wonderful on any occasion and at any time of year, but I especially recommend it for Passover.

¼ **pound (113 g) blanched almonds**
¼ **pound (113 g) skin-on hazelnuts**
5 tablespoons (75 g) unsalted margarine, plus 1 tablespoon (15 g)
   for greasing the pan, at room temperature
2 tablespoons potato starch, for dusting the pan (see note)
¼ **pound (113 g) high-quality imported unsweetened chocolate,**
   broken into small pieces
3 tablespoons imported unsweetened cocoa powder
1 teaspoon vanilla extract
6 large eggs, separated (see note)
Grated zest of 1 navel orange
⅔ **cup (120 g) semisweet chocolate chips**
1 cup (200 g) sugar

Roast the almonds in a toaster oven at 350°F (175°C) for 10 minutes. Cool. Finely grind them in a food processor. Roast the hazelnuts in a toaster oven at 350°F (175°C) for 15 minutes, or until the skins are blistered. While the nuts are still hot, rub them in a dish towel to remove most of their skin. (Some skin will remain.) Cool. Chop them in a food processor until coarse.

Preheat the oven to 350°F (175°C). Grease a 9 by 2½-inch (23 by 6 cm) springform pan with 1 tablespoon (15 g) of the margarine. Dust the pan with potato starch, then invert and tap it to shake out any excess starch.

Place the chocolate and the remaining 5 tablespoons (75 g) margarine in the top of a double boiler, cover, and set over simmering water. Stir from time to time until the chocolate is melted, about 5 minutes. Remove the top from the double boiler and add the cocoa and vanilla. Cool.

Place the egg yolks in the bowl of an electric stand mixer. Using the balloon whisk attachment, beat the yolks at medium speed, gradually adding the sugar, for about 5 minutes, until they are pale and bubbles appear. With a rubber spatula, fold the yolks into the chocolate. Add the almonds, hazelnuts, orange zest, and chocolate chips. Combine well.

Wash and thoroughly dry the mixer bowl and balloon whisk attachment. Beat the egg whites at high speed until soft, stiff peaks form. (To test that the whites are sufficiently beaten, gently tip the bowl to one side. If the whites do not slide, they are ready. If not, continue beating.)

TO SERVE: Cut the torte into wedges, place on individual dessert plates, and spoon some raspberry sauce around the torte.

Notes: It is easier to separate the eggs straight from the refrigerator, when they are cold, as the yolks tend to break up as they warm. Make sure the whites have come to room temperature before beating.

If you are not serving the torte at Passover, you can use 1 tablespoon of unbleached all-purpose flour rather than potato starch to dust the pan.

CHOCOLATE ALMOND CAKE WITH ORANGE

• Makes 12 servings

This cake is good to keep in your repertoire for Passover, or at any other time of year. Though delicious, it is not too sweet or rich and keeps well frozen. I like to serve it with chocolate sorbet, raspberries, and raspberry sauce.

> **1 tablespoon (15 g) unsalted margarine, for greasing the pan**
> **1 tablespoon unbleached all-purpose flour, for dusting pan (see note)**
> **1¼ cups (180 g) skin-on almonds**
> **Scant 1 cup (200 g) sugar**
> **6 ounces (170 g) high-quality imported semisweet chocolate,**
>   **broken into small pieces**
> **½ cup (64 g) unsweetened imported cocoa powder**
> **6 large eggs, separated (see note)**
> **½ cup (125 ml) freshly squeezed orange juice**
> **2 teaspoons grated zest of a navel orange**
> **1 teaspoon vanilla extract**
> **Raspberry Sauce (page 301), for serving (see note)**

Preheat the oven to 350°F (175°C). Grease a 10 by 2½-inch (25 by 6 cm) springform pan with the margarine. Dust with the flour. Invert the pan and tap to shake out the excess flour.

Place the almonds and ¼ cup (50 g) of the sugar in a food processor and pulse until the almonds are finely ground. Transfer to a bowl.

Place the chocolate in the food processor and pulse until finely ground. Combine with the nuts and sugar. Add the cocoa powder and mix well.

Place the egg yolks in the bowl of an electric stand mixer. Using the balloon whisk attachment, beat the yolks at medium speed for about 5 minutes, gradually adding ½ cup (100 g) of the sugar, until pale and bubbles appear. With a rubber spatula, blend in the almond-chocolate mixture. Add the orange juice, orange zest, and vanilla and combine well.

Wash and thoroughly dry the mixer bowl and the balloon whisk attachment. Beat the egg whites at high speed, until soft peaks form. Gradually add the remaining ¼ cup (50 g) sugar, beating until the whites are stiff.

With a large rubber spatula, fold half of the whites into the chocolate mixture. Reverse the process, pouring the chocolate mixture into the bowl with the egg whites. Gently fold the two mixtures together, making a motion like a figure 8 with the spatula, until just combined. Pour the batter into the prepared pan and smooth the top.

Bake on the middle shelf of the oven for 30 minutes. A cake tester inserted into the center should come out a little moist.

Note: When making the torte for Passover, use potato starch instead of flour and omit the dusting with confectioners' sugar.

It is easier to separate the eggs straight from the refrigerator, when they are cold. Make sure the whites have come to room temperature before beating.

WARM CHOCOLATE-COCONUT SURPRISES

• Makes 6 servings

You can prepare this dessert earlier in the day and warm it just before serving. I like to serve it with sliced mango, pineapple, or kiwi, and chocolate or coconut sorbets.

> **4 tablespoons (60 g) unsalted margarine, at room temperature,**
> **plus 1½ tablespoons (22 g) for greasing the ramekins**
> **⅓ cup (43 g) unbleached all-purpose flour,**
> **plus 1 tablespoon for dusting the ramekins**
> **½ cup (35 g) unsweetened shredded coconut**
> **3 ounces (85 g) high-quality imported semisweet chocolate,**
> **broken into small pieces**
> **½ cup (100 g) sugar**
> **2 large eggs, at room temperature**
> **2 tablespoons dark rum**
> **½ teaspoon vanilla extract**

Preheat the oven to 350°F (175°C). Grease and flour six ½-cup (125 ml) metal ramekins with 1½ tablespoons (22 g) of the margarine and 1 tablespoon of the flour. Invert the ramekins and tap to shake out the excess flour. (You can also use a muffin pan with 12 molds, each of which holds ½ cup/125 ml batter.)

Toast the coconut in a toaster oven on the lowest setting for about a minute. (Watch it carefully, as it burns quickly.)

Place the chocolate and the remaining 4 tablespoons (60 g) margarine in the top of a double boiler, cover, and set over simmering water. Stir occasionally until the chocolate is melted.

Remove the top from the double boiler and gradually whisk in the sugar. Whisk in 1 egg at a time. Add the coconut, rum, vanilla, and flour, continuing to whisk.

Spoon the batter evenly among the ramekins and place them on a cookie sheet. Bake on the middle shelf of the oven for 12 to 13 minutes, until the top feels lightly firm yet springy to the touch. The inside will still be moist.

Let the dessert rest for no more than 2 minutes, then unmold onto individual plates. Serve warm.

Note: You can make the surprises earlier in the day, unmold them onto a cookie sheet, and cover with cling wrap. Before serving, warm in a preheated 200°F (95°C) oven for 5 to 10 minutes. If you freeze the surprises after unmolding, place them on a cookie sheet in a preheated 200°F (95°C) oven for about 15 to 20 minutes without defrosting.

CHOCOLATE SOUFFLÉ

• Makes 6 servings

This soufflé is a chocolate lover's (and a hostess's) dream—scrumptious, light, and easy to make ahead of time. You can use a soufflé dish or individual round or oval ramekins. Note that the soufflé goes straight from the refrigerator to the oven.

>   1½ **tablespoons (22 g) unsalted margarine,**
>   **for greasing the soufflé dish or ramekins**
>   ⅓ **cup (67 g) sugar, plus 2 tablespoons for dusting the soufflé dish or ramekins**
>   **2 ounces (57 g) high quality imported semisweet chocolate,**
>   **broken into small pieces**
>   **3 large eggs, separated (see note)**
>   ¼ **teaspoon cream of tartar**

Grease a 1-quart (1 liter) soufflé dish or six ½-cup (125 ml) ramekins with the margarine and sprinkle with 2 tablespoons sugar. Invert and tap to remove excess sugar.

Melt the chocolate in the top of a double boiler.

Place the egg yolks in the bowl of an electric stand mixer. Using the balloon whisk attachment, beat them at medium speed for about 5 minutes, gradually adding all but 1 tablespoon of the sugar, until the mixture becomes pale and bubbles appear.

Lower the speed and beat in the melted chocolate. Remove to a large bowl.

Wash and thoroughly dry the mixer bowl and the balloon whisk attachment. Put the egg whites in the mixer bowl and beat them at high speed until foamy. Add the cream of tartar and the remaining tablespoon sugar, and beat the egg whites until stiff and glossy.

With a rubber spatula, fold one fourth of the egg whites into the chocolate mixture. Reverse the process, pouring the chocolate mixture into the bowl with the egg whites. Fold the two mixtures together, making a motion like a figure 8 with the spatula, until the ingredients are well combined.

Spoon the batter into the soufflé dish or ramekins, cover with cling wrap, and refrigerate until ready to bake. (If you are using ramekins, after spooning in the batter, place them on a cookie sheet. Cover with cling wrap and refrigerate until ready to bake.)

Preheat the oven to 350°F (175°C).

Place the soufflé dish (or the cookie sheet with the ramekins) in the oven straight from the refrigerator, and bake until the center is almost set, about 20 minutes. (If you are using ramekins, bake them for 14 to 15 minutes.)

Serve right away.

Note: It is easier to separate the eggs straight from the refrigerator, when they are cold, as the yolks tend to break up as they warm. Make sure the whites have come to room temperature before beating.

EASY BROWNIES

• Makes 7 dozen 1-inch (2.5 cm) squares

These fudgy bite-size brownies are always a hit. You can cut them to any size.

16 tablespoons (240 g) unsalted margarine, at room temperature,
   plus 1 tablespoon (15 g) for greasing the pan
1 cup (128 g) unbleached all-purpose flour,
   plus 1 tablespoon for dusting the pan
5 ounces (142 g) good-quality imported semisweet chocolate,
   broken into small pieces
Scant 1¾ cups (325 g) sugar
4 large eggs, at room temperature
1 teaspoon vanilla extract
Generous 1 cup (113 g) walnuts, coarsely chopped

Preheat the oven to 350°F (175°C). Line a 9 by 13 by 2-inch (23 by 33 by 5 cm) baking pan with wax paper. Grease the paper with 1 tablespoon (15 g) of the margarine and dust it with 1 tablespoon of the flour. Invert and tap the pan to shake out the excess flour.

Place the remaining margarine and the chocolate in the top of a double boiler. Cover and set over simmering water. Stir from time to time until all is melted.

Remove the top from the double boiler. Using a wooden spoon, gradually add the sugar, stirring continuously until the chocolate is smooth. Stir in 1 egg at a time until well mixed. Add the vanilla and flour and blend well. Stir in the chopped nuts.

Pour the batter into the prepared pan, tilting the pan to spread the batter evenly. Bake on the middle shelf of the oven for 20 minutes, or until the top is slightly firm to the touch and a cake tester inserted in the center comes out moist.

Cool on a wire rack. Run a metal spatula around the sides of the pan to loosen the brownies. Invert the pan onto a board and cut into squares.

Note: These brownies freeze well. Place them side by side in an air-tight plastic continer, with wax paper between the layers.

CHOCOLATE MERINGUE SQUARES

• Makes 3½ dozen 1½-inch (4 cm) squares

These meringue squares are like cookies, but they are light, chocolaty, and surprisingly low in calories. I often serve them at Passover.

1 tablespoon (15 g) unsalted margarine, for greasing the pan
½ pound (225 g) blanched almonds
6 ounces (170 g) good-quality imported semisweet chocolate,
  broken into small pieces
8 large egg whites (see note)
1 cup (200 g) sugar

Preheat the oven to 350°F (175°C). Line a 9 by 13 by 2-inch (23 by 33 by 5 cm) baking pan with wax paper and grease the paper with the margarine.

Chop the almonds in a food processor, in two batches, until medium-fine. Transfer to a bowl. Chop the chocolate in the processor until fine, and combine with the almonds.

Place the egg whites in the bowl of an electric stand mixer. Using the balloon whisk attachment, beat at high speed until foamy. Gradually add the sugar and beat until stiff.

With a large rubber spatula, gently fold the chocolate-almond mixture into the egg whites, making a motion like a figure 8 with the spatula. Do not overmix.

Spoon the batter into the prepared pan and smooth the top. Bake on the middle shelf of the oven for 25 to 30 minutes, until a cake tester inserted in the center comes out almost dry.

Cool on a wire rack. Invert onto a cutting board and peel off the paper. Cut into 1½-inch (4 cm) squares.

Notes: It is easier to separate the eggs straight from the refrigerator, when they are cold. Make sure the whites have come to room temperature before beating.

To freeze the squares, place them side by side in an air-tight plastic continer, with wax paper between the layers.

PINE NUT BALLS

• Makes about 6 dozen balls

I always like to have sweets on hand that are nutritious as well as delicious, and these bite-size nut balls fit the bill perfectly. They are ideal for Passover.

¼ pound (113 g) skin-on hazelnuts
½ pound (225 g) blanched almonds
2 large egg whites (see note)
½ cup (100 g) sugar
4 tablespoons (60 g) unsalted margarine, cut into small pieces,
  at room temperature
Grated zest of 2 navel oranges
½ pound (225 g) pine nuts

Roast the hazelnuts in a toaster oven at 350°F (175°C) for 15 minutes, or until the skins are blistered. While the nuts are still hot, rub them in a dish towel to remove most of their skin. (Some skin will remain.)

Roast the almonds in a toaster oven at 350°F (175°C) for 10 minutes, until slightly golden. Cool.

Chop the hazelnuts and the almonds separately in a food processor until medium-coarse. Transfer them to a medium bowl.

Preheat the oven to 400°F (205°C). Line two baking sheets with wax paper.

Beat the egg whites with a fork. To the nut mixture, add the beaten egg whites, the sugar, margarine, and orange zest. Combine well with a wooden spoon.

Place the pine nuts on a piece of wax paper. Put a level teaspoon of the hazelnut-almond mixture in the palm of your hand, shape it into a smooth ball, and roll it in the pine nuts, pressing down so the pine nuts adhere well. Continue until all the mixture and all the pine nuts have been used. Arrange the cookies on the baking sheets.

Bake for 11 minutes, or until golden around the edges. Cool for 1 minute, then transfer them with a metal spatula to a wire rack to cool completely.

Notes: It is easier to separate the eggs straight from the refrigerator, when they are cold. Make sure the whites have come to room temperature before beating.

Pine nut balls keep well in the refrigerator or freezer. Put them side by side in an air-tight plastic container lined with wax paper and separate the layers with wax paper.

MOCHA PECAN BALLS

• Makes 4 dozen balls

If you like pareve sweets with a touch of coffee and nuts, you will love these cookies.

> ¼ **pound (113 g) pecans**
> **8 tablespoons (120 g) unsalted margarine, at room temperature**
> ¼ **cup (50 g) granulated sugar**
> **1 teaspoon vanilla extract**
> **1½ teaspoons instant espresso powder**
> **2 tablespoons imported unsweetened cocoa powder**
> **Scant 1 cup (120 g) unbleached all-purpose flour**
> **3 tablespoons confectioners' sugar**

Chop the pecans in a food processor until medium-fine.

Place the margarine in the bowl of an electric stand mixer. Using the balloon whisk attachment, cream the margarine at medium speed. Gradually add the granulated sugar and beat about 5 minutes, until the mixture is pale and bubbles appear. Add the vanilla, espresso powder, and cocoa powder and stir to combine. Scrape down the sides of the bowl as you go along. Using a rubber spatula, add the flour and pecans and combine.

Put a level teaspoon of dough in your palm and roll it into a smooth ball, then place each one on an ungreased baking sheet. Continue making the balls until all the mixture has been used. Refrigerate for at least 30 minutes.

Meanwhile, preheat the oven to 375°F (190°C).

Bake the cookies for 12 minutes, or until they are just firm to the touch. Remove from the oven and cool on a wire rack for 5 minutes.

Place the confectioners' sugar on a piece of wax paper and roll the warm balls in the sugar until they are coated well. Transfer to a wire rack to cool completely. Sprinkle with any remaining confectioners' sugar.

Note: Mocha pecan balls freeze beautifully. Place them side by side in an air-tight plastic container, with wax paper between the layers.

MANDELBROT

• Makes about 5 dozen slices

Mandelbrot, which means "almond bread" in German, look like biscotti. It is the combination of nuts and long, slow baking that gives these cookies their wonderful crunch.

> **2 tablespoons vegetable oil, for greasing the pan**
> **½ cup (64 g) unbleached all-purpose flour,**
>   **plus 1 tablespoon for dusting pan**
> **½ pound (225 g) skin-on hazelnuts**
> **½ pound (225 g) skin-on almonds**
> **½ pound (225 g) dark raisins**
> **½ cup (100 g) sugar**
> **1½ teaspoons ground cinnamon**
> **½ teaspoon powdered ginger**
> **3 large eggs, whisked well**

Preheat the oven to 325°F (165°C). Grease a 9-inch (23 cm) square baking pan with 1 tablespoon of the oil. Line it with wax paper, which should extend about 1 inch (2.5 cm) over the sides. Grease the paper with the remaining tablespoon of oil and dust it with 1 tablespoon of the flour. Invert the pan and tap to shake out excess flour.

Chop the hazelnuts coarsely in a food processor and transfer to a large bowl. Do the same with the almonds and add them to the hazelnuts. Add the raisins, flour, sugar, cinnamon, and ginger and stir with a wooden spoon to combine. Stir in the eggs. Use your hands to combine the ingredients thoroughly.

Press the mixture into the pan and flatten the top with your hands until it feels firm. Place the pan on the middle shelf of the oven and immediately reduce the heat to 300°F (150°C). Bake for 1 hour.

Remove the pan from the oven and reduce the oven heat to 200°F (95°C). Invert the mandelbrot onto a wire rack. Peel off the wax paper and cool for a minute.

Invert the mandelbrot again onto a cutting board, and while still warm, divide with a serrated bread knife into three equal parts, 3 by 9 inches (8 by 23 cm). Cut each part into ¼-inch (6 mm) slices (or thinner, if you like).

Arrange the mandelbrot slices on a cookie sheet. Bake for 45 minutes at 200°F (95°C). Turn the slices over and bake for 45 minutes more. The mandelbrot should be very dry. Cool on wire rack.

Note: Mandelbrot keeps well in an airtight tin container in a cool place.

HAMENTASHEN

• Makes about 3 dozen hamentashen

In Eastern Europe, where I was born, poppy seeds and chocolate are the favorite filling for hamentashen, but prune and apricot are also popular. This delicious pastry is traditionally exchanged on Purim, the joyous holiday that celebrates the Jews' escape from certain death at the hands of the villainous Haman, as described in the Book of Esther. (For a dairy recipe for Hamentashen, see page 292.)

3 large eggs, at room temperature
½ cup (100 g) sugar
4 tablespoons vegetable oil
Grated zest of 1 lemon
1 tablespoon freshly squeezed lemon juice
½ teaspoon vanilla extract
½ teaspoon baking powder
2¼ to 2½ cups (288 to 320 g) unbleached all-purpose flour
Apricot butter or prune butter, as needed (see note)

TO MAKE THE DOUGH: Using a balloon whisk attachment, beat 2 of the eggs in the bowl of an electric stand mixer at medium speed. Add the sugar gradually while beating for about 5 minutes, until the mixture becomes thick. Slowly beat in the oil, lemon zest, lemon juice, and vanilla.

Stop the mixer and switch to the dough hook attachment. At low speed, mix in the baking powder and enough of the flour to make a stiff dough.

Turn out the dough onto a lightly floured work surface or pastry board. Using your hands, shape it into a smooth ball.

TO FORM AND BAKE THE HAMENTASHEN: Preheat the oven to 350°F (175°C). Cut the dough into 6 pieces, but work with one piece at a time and keep the rest in the refrigerator.

Roll out each piece of dough between two sheets of wax paper, lightly flouring the dough on both sides. The dough should end up as a thin circle, 7 to 8 inches (18 to 20 cm) in diameter. (From time to time, to make it easier to roll the dough, lift the top wax paper, sprinkle the dough lightly with flour, put back the wax paper, and turn the dough packet over.)

With a 3-inch (8 cm) round cookie cutter, cut out 5 circles. From time to time, dip the cookie cutter into flour, as this will keep the dough from sticking. Refrigerate the scraps so they can be reused.

Whisk the remaining egg until just mixed. Lightly brush the edges of the circles with egg, then place ½ teaspoon of apricot or prune butter in the center of each circle. Pinch the dough together at three equidistant points on the circle so that you form a triangle.

Put the hamentashen on wax paper and brush the dough with the egg, then place them on cookie sheets. (You will need two cookie sheets.) Repeat with the other scraps of dough: Reroll, cut, fill, shape, and glaze.

Bake for 18 minutes, until the pastry is lightly golden. Remove to a wire rack to cool (see note).

Notes: Apricot butter and prune butter come in 10.5-ounce (298 g) glass jars and are available in many specialty food stores.

Hamentashen keep well in the refrigerator. Place them side by side in an air-tight plastic container, with wax paper between the layers.

APRICOT SOUFFLÉ

• Makes 8 servings

Soufflés have a reputation for being difficult to make at the last minute. I think this recipe represents something of a breakthrough. You can prepare part of the dessert well in advance, and another part half an hour before baking. And it's well worth the effort, as this is a heavenly dish—light, not too sweet, and very special.

¼ pound (113 g) dried California apricots (see note)
1¼ cups (300 ml) cold water
7 tablespoons (90 g) sugar
1½ tablespoons freshly squeezed lemon juice
2 tablespoons (30 g) unsalted margarine, for greasing the ramekins
3 large egg whites (see note)
Boiling water, as needed

Place the apricots and water in a medium enamel saucepan. Bring to a boil, lower the heat, and cook, covered, for 15 minutes or until the apricots are soft. Cool a bit.

Purée the mixture in a blender until very smooth. Add 4 tablespoons of the sugar and 1 tablespoon of the lemon juice and blend. Pour the mixture into a container and refrigerate for at least 1 hour. (You can also do this the day before you will be baking the soufflés.)

Grease eight ½-cup (125 ml) ramekins with the margarine and sprinkle them with 2 tablespoons of the sugar (see note). Invert the ramekins and tap to remove the excess sugar. Place them in a 9 by 13 by 2-inch (23 by 33 by 5 cm) baking pan and refrigerate for at least 30 minutes.

Meanwhile, preheat the oven to 375°F (190°C).

Place the egg whites in the bowl of an electric stand mixer. Using the balloon whisk attachment, beat at high speed until foamy. Gradually add the remaining tablespoon of sugar and the remaining ½ tablespoon of lemon juice. Continue beating until the egg whites form stiff, shiny peaks.

With a rubber spatula, fold half of the whites into the apricot purée. Reverse the process, pouring the apricot purée into the bowl with the egg whites. Gently fold the two mixtures together, making a motion like a figure 8 with the spatula, until most of the whites have disappeared. Take care not to overblend.

Spoon the batter into the prepared ramekins. If you are not baking the soufflés immediately, they will keep for half an hour in the refrigerator.

When ready to bake, pour enough boiling water into the baking pan to reach one-third of the way up the sides of the ramekins. Bake the soufflés on the middle shelf of the oven for 15 minutes.

If you are not serving them right away, you can leave them in the turned-off oven for about 10 minutes.

Notes: I always use California apricots when I make this dish because they are less sweet than other varieties.

It is easier to separate the eggs straight from the refrigerator, when they are cold. Make sure the whites have come to room temperature before beating.

You can also bake the soufflé in a 1-quart (1 liter) soufflé dish. Grease the dish, sprinkle it with sugar, and place in a baking pan. After filling it with the batter and pouring the boiling water as described above, bake for 22 minutes.

FRUIT CRUMBLE

• Makes 6 servings

The best time to make this dessert is in the summer, when you can use fresh peaches, nectarines, and plums. But it is also delicious in winter with pears and apples. More reasons to love fruit crumble: You can bake it in one dish or individual ramekins; you can serve it warm or at room temperature, topped with sorbet.

> **8 tablespoons (120 g) chilled margarine cut into ½ inch cubes,**
> **plus 1 tablespoon (15 g) for greasing the ramekins or flan pan**
> **¾ cup (96 g) unbleached all-purpose flour**
> **Generous ⅓ cup (75 g) sugar**
> **½ cup (75 g) blanched almonds**
> **1½ pounds (680 g) plums, peaches, or nectarines, not overly ripe,**
> **or 3 apples or 3 Bosc pears**
> **1 tablespoon Cognac or fruit-flavored brandy**

Preheat the oven to 425°F (220°C). Grease six ½-cup (125 ml) ramekins with 1 tablespoon (15 g) of the margarine and set them on a cookie sheet. Or you can use a 10 by 1½-inch (25 by 4 cm) flan dish.

Place the flour, sugar, and almonds in a food processor and pulse until the nuts are slightly chopped. Add the margarine and pulse until the mixture is very coarse. Refrigerate until needed.

If you are using plums, peaches, or nectarines, do not peel the fruit but remove the pits and cut the fruit into ½-inch (13 mm) cubes. If you are using apples and/or pears, peel and remove the core, then cut the fruit into ½-inch (13 mm) cubes. Place the fruit in a bowl and toss with the liqueur of your choice.

Arrange the fruit in the bottom of the ramekins. Sprinkle with the topping mixture. Bake on the middle shelf of the oven until the topping is golden brown, about 25 minutes. Serve warm.

Note: This crumble can be assembled a few hours in advance, refrigerated, and baked straight from the refrigerator.

PEAR TART

• Makes 10 to 12 servings

This is a light, attractive, easy winter dessert, when pears are at their best. No rolling of the dough is required.

> **8 tablespoons (120 g) unsalted margarine, at room temperature,**
> **   plus 1 tablespoon (15 g) for greasing the pan**
> **¾ cup (96 g) unbleached all-purpose flour,**
> **   plus 1 tablespoon for dusting the pan**
> **4 ripe, but firm, medium Bosc pears**
> **1 tablespoon freshly squeezed lemon juice**
> **½ cup (100 g), plus 1 tablespoon sugar**
> **2 large eggs, at room temperature**
> **1 teaspoon baking powder**
> **1 teaspoon vanilla extract**
> **1 teaspoon ground cinnamon**

Preheat the oven to 350°F (175°C). Grease a 10 by 2½-inch (25 by 6 cm) springform pan with 1 tablespoon (15 g) of the margarine and dust it with 1 tablespoon flour. Invert and tap the pan to shake out the excess flour.

Peel, quarter, and core the pears. Cut each quarter into in half, place in a bowl, and sprinkle with the lemon juice.

Place the remaining 8 tablespoons (120 g) margarine in the bowl of an electric stand mixer. Using the balloon whisk attachment, beat at medium speed, gradually adding ½ cup (100 g) of the sugar, until light and fluffy, about 5 minutes. Scrape down the sides of the bowl as you go along.

Add 1 egg at a time, whisking after each addition. Add the baking powder and vanilla. With a rubber spatula, fold in the ¾ cup (96 g) of flour and combine well.

Using the spatula, spread the dough evenly over the bottom of the pan. Arrange the pears, round side up, in overlapping circles on the dough, so all the dough is covered.

Combine the remaining tablespoon sugar with the cinnamon and sprinkle over the top. Bake the tart for 45 minutes, or until a cake tester inserted in the dough comes out clean.

Remove the rim, and serve warm or at room temperature.

MINI FRUIT TRUFFLES

• Makes 4 dozen truffles

These nutritious fruit morsels require no baking and are wonderfully easy to make. They are ideal for Passover.

¼ pound (113 g) dried California apricots (see note)
¼ pound (113 g) walnuts
¼ pound (113 g) pitted dates
¼ pound (113 g) dried currants
2 tablespoons apple juice
1 tablespoon superfine sugar, for dusting (see note)

Place the apricots in a food processor and pulse until coarsely chopped. Add the walnuts and pulse to chop. Add the dates and pulse, then add the currants. Add the apple juice and pulse until the mixture sticks to the blade.

Place a teaspoon of the mixture in the palm of your hand and roll it into a smooth ball. Continue until all the mixture has been used.

Before serving, dust the truffles lightly with sugar.

Notes: I always use California apricots when I make this recipe because they are less sweet than other varieties.

These truffles can be refrigerated or frozen. Put them side by side in an air-tight plastic container, with wax paper between the layers.

If you are not serving for Passover, you can roll the truffles in confectioners' sugar instead of granulated sugar.

HONEY CAKE

• Makes 2 loaves, each serving 12

I could not resist sharing this heirloom honey cake recipe with you. Following tradition, I make this every Rosh Hashana. It is moist, light, and not too sweet. When refrigerated, it stays fresh for many days.

2 tablespoons (30 g) unsalted margarine, for greasing the pans
2⅓ cups (298 g) sifted unbleached all-purpose flour,
 plus 2 tablespoons for dusting the pans
2 large eggs, at room temperature
Scant ⅔ cup (130 g) sugar
1 cup (250 ml) strong brewed tea (made with 3 tea bags), cooled
⅓ cup (80 ml) vegetable oil
1 cup (250 ml) honey
½ medium-ripe banana, thoroughly mashed
Grated zest of 1 navel orange
½ teaspoon ground cinnamon
⅛ teaspoon ground cloves
1 teaspoon baking powder
1 teaspoon baking soda

Preheat the oven to 325°F (165°C). Grease two 5 by 9-inch (13 by 23 cm) loaf pans with margarine and dust with 2 tablespoons of the flour. Invert the pans and tap to shake out the excess flour.

Place the eggs in the bowl of an electric mixer bowl. Using the balloon whisk attachment, beat them at medium speed, gradually adding the sugar until the mixture is pale and bubbles appear, about 5 minutes. Lower the speed and beat in the tea, oil, honey, banana, orange zest, cinnamon, and cloves. Combine thoroughly.

With a rubber spatula, gradually fold in the flour, baking powder, and baking soda, combining well after each addition. No traces of flour should be visible.

Pour the batter evenly into the two pans. Bake the pans side by side, without touching, on the middle shelf of the oven for 15 minutes.

Increase the heat to 350°F (175°C) and bake for another 30 minutes, or until a cake tester inserted into the center comes out clean.

Cool the cakes on a wire rack. Run a metal spatula around the sides of the pans to loosen the cakes. Invert each pan onto a serving plate.

Note: These cakes freeze well. Wrap them individually in wax paper, then in foil, and place in plastic freezer bags.

ZUCCHINI CAKE

• Makes 12 servings

A moist and delicious cake that also freezes very well, this is perfect when a surprise visitor pops in and you want to serve a light snack with your tea.

¼ **pound (113 g) skin-on hazelnuts**
½ **cup (125 ml) vegetable oil, plus 1 tablespoon for greasing pan**
2 cups (256 g) sifted unbleached all-purpose flour,
   plus 1 tablespoon for dusting the pan
1 teaspoon baking soda
¾ **teaspoon baking powder**
Generous ¾ cup (160 g) sugar
2 large eggs, at room temperature
2 teaspoons grated zest from a navel orange
⅓ **cup (80 ml) freshly squeezed orange juice**
1½-inch (4 cm) piece ginger, peeled and grated
1 teaspoon vanilla extract
1 medium zucchini (not more than ½ pound/225 g), coarsely grated

Roast the hazelnuts in a toaster oven at 350°F (175°C) for about 15 minutes, or until the skins are blistered. While the nuts are still hot, rub them in a dish towel to remove most of their skin. (Some skin will remain.) Cool. Chop them in a food processor until coarse.

Preheat the oven to 350°F (175°C). Grease a 5 by 9-inch (13 by 23 cm) loaf pan with 1 tablespoon of the vegetable oil. Dust the pan with 1 tablespoon of the flour, then invert and tap the pan to shake out any excess flour.

Place the 2 cups (256 g) flour in a large bowl and add the hazelnuts, baking soda, baking powder, and sugar. In a smaller bowl, whisk the ½ cup (125 ml) oil, the eggs, orange zest, orange juice, ginger, and vanilla. With a rubber spatula, combine the wet ingredients with the flour mixture. Fold in the zucchini.

Spoon the batter into the prepared pan and smooth the top. Bake on the middle shelf of the oven for about 60 minutes, until a cake tester inserted in the center comes out clean.

Cool on a wire rack. Run a metal spatula around the sides of the pan to loosen the cake. Invert the loaf pan onto a serving plate.

HELPFUL TIPS

Read a recipe at least twice before making it.

Check the accuracy of your oven with an oven thermometer. Knowing if your oven is too hot or too cool allows you to adjust the cooking time accordingly. (This is especially important when you are making desserts.) If necessary, have the oven adjusted professionally.

Set your timer to less time than the recipe specifies when baking. Each oven is different, and if a dish comes out underdone, you can still fix it.

To rescue a soup or stew that is too salty, add a raw potato.

Rinse strawberries before removing the stems. Otherwise, the berries will become soggy.

Raspberries don't need to be rinsed.

Always try to buy fresh white mushrooms that are firm and have no separation between the stem and the cap.

Don't rinse mushrooms, just wipe them with a damp paper towel.

Don't rinse dill. Wrap it in a paper towel, place in a plastic bag, and refrigerate. Note that dill loses its aroma after a few days.

Chopping cilantro takes away its aroma. It's better just to remove the leaves from the stem.

Basil leaves discolor if they are chopped. It is best to tear them to the desired size.

After washing and drying greens, if you are using them within the next few hours, place them in a bowl and refrigerate them *uncovered*. If not using them until the following day, wrap them in paper towels and place in a plastic bag. Most greens will remain very crisp for several days. The exceptions are arugula, watercress, and mâche, which should be used rather soon.

If tomatoes or other fruits are not sufficiently ripe, place them in a brown paper bag in a dark place.

The best way to remove cucumber seeds is to cut the cucumber in half lengthwise and scoop out the seeds with a spoon.

Keep nuts, especially hazelnuts, walnuts, and pine nuts, in the freezer. This prevents the oil in them from becoming rancid.

Chop large quantities of nuts in a food processor, using the steel blade. **Grate small amounts** with a Mouli grater.

Grate large amounts of Parmesan cheese in a food processor, using the steel blade. (Be sure to cut the cheese into small pieces first.) **Grate small amounts** with a Mouli grater.

Wrap cheeses in wax paper, then in foil, and refrigerate. Bring them to room temperature before serving.

Ground coffee keeps best in the freezer. Use it straight from the freezer.

To measure flour, even off the top with a knife.

Whip cream when it's cold. It is also helpful to use a very cold bowl. (I keep mine in the freezer for about 10 minutes.)

Separate eggs when they are cold. This prevents the yolks—which add flavor, color, texture, and binding quality—from breaking.

Beat egg whites at room temperature. This allows more air to get into them and thus bring more lightness to your cakes.

If egg whites do not get stiff quickly, add a pinch of salt.

To test if whites have been beaten enough, slowly tilt the bowl that contains them. If they are ready, they will stay in the bowl even if it is turned upside down.

Keep dark brown sugar in the freezer once you've opened the box. This prevents it from hardening.

Always wear thin plastic gloves when you work with beets, as this avoids staining your fingers with beet juice, which can be hard to remove.

When seeding jalapeño peppers, I advise wearing thin plastic gloves to avoid irritating your skin or your eyes.

NOTES ON INGREDIENTS

BROTH: CHICKEN AND VEGETABLE I use both of these broths as bases for soups and stews. Good-quality chicken broth is available in all kosher supermarkets. Low-sodium vegetable broth without MSG is available in the organic department of supermarkets and health-food stores.

BUTTER Sweet unsalted butter is an essential ingredient for cooking. I use it for everything, especially baking. It freezes well.

BULGUR Also called cracked wheat, this is a wonderful alternative to rice. It is available in most supermarkets as well as in health-food and other specialty stores. It comes in three textures: coarse, medium, and fine. I prefer the medium, which has the most taste and texture.

CAPERS Packed in brine, these have a spicy, piquant flavor much like olives. I prefer the small size because they don't require chopping.

CHOCOLATE I use best-quality imported chocolate in all my recipes. For fine-grinding small amounts of chocolate, I use a Mouli grater. For larger amounts and for coarse grinding, I recommend a food processor. Be sure to break the chocolate into small pieces first and grind it in batches, removing one before adding the next.

COCOA POWDER Look for an imported brand, as the quality is usually better.

DAIKON Not strong like red or black radishes, this long white Japanese radish makes a wonderful garnish.

DRIED BEANS AND LENTILS While these are sold in all types of food stores, I prefer to buy them in health-food and specialty markets, as I think they are fresher.

EGGS All the recipes in this book were tested using large eggs. I don't think it makes a difference if they are brown or white. Two tips: Separate eggs while they are cold so that the yolk remains whole. Beat egg whites when they are at room temperature, as they can absorb more air; this makes the dish lighter.

FETA CHEESE This comes in many strengths, from mild (which I prefer) to strong. Whichever variety you buy, it keeps fresher if you place it in water and refrigerate it. Be sure to change the water every day or so.

FRISÉE Also known as French chicory, this is a faintly bitter salad green that makes an excellent garnish on its own or combined with other greens.

GINGER ROOT Look for fresh, firm young ginger that has a pale tan color and a smooth, tight skin. Ginger keeps well for several weeks, wrapped in cling wrap and refrigerated.

HERBS Most supermarkets and specialty stores carry fresh cilantro, dill, chives, basil, tarragon, thyme, parsley, and mint. Dried herbs are not really a good substitute, but if you have no choice, rub the pieces between your fingers to release more flavor.

BASIL is a versatile herb for cooking and garnishing and is excellent in sauces, stews, soups, salads, and roasts. Before using, rinse and spin-dry the leaves and spread them on a piece of paper towel to air-dry completely. Basil keeps for a few days in the refrigerator, wrapped in a paper towel and placed in a plastic bag. When needed, tear the leaves rather than cut them.

CHIVES are slender green shoots of the onion family, and they make a wonderful flavoring or garnish for soups, salads, vegetables, sauces, and fish. They do not require rinsing, and only need to be kept dry. Wrap them in a paper towel and refrigerate in an airtight plastic bag or container. When ready to use, snip with scissors rather than cut with a knife.

CILANTRO, also known as Chinese parsley or coriander, is a pungent seasoning or garnish. It is sold in bunches like parsley, but unfortunately does not keep like parsley, and loses its fragrant aroma after a day or so. Rinse and spin-dry cilantro, as you would basil. Do not chop the leaves; just leave them whole.

DILL is a wonderful herb that is used in soups, vegetables, salads, sauces, and fish dishes. Fortunately, it is available throughout the year. Do not wash dill. Keep it dry by wrapping it in a paper towel, then place it in a plastic bag and refrigerate. When needed, snip it with scissors, rather than cutting with a knife.

MINT, with its unmistakable fragrance and flavor, is excellent in soups, salads, and sauces. It also makes a lovely garnish for desserts, and, of course, tea. You do not have to wash it; just keep it dry.

PARSLEY comes in two varieties: the familiar curly kind used as a garnish and the Italian flat-leaf kind. I only use the latter, as it has a subtler, more refined flavor. Rinse and spin-dry thoroughly; wrap in a paper towel and place in a plastic bag. It keeps for several days, refrigerated.

TARRAGON is one of my favorite herbs. The pointed leaves have a delicate flavor of anise and add a delicious note to any number of poultry, meat, and fish dishes, as well as eggs, sauces, and salads. Tarragon requires no rinsing; just wrap it in a paper towel and place in a plastic bag. It refrigerates well for several days.

THYME Next to parsley, this is the most popular herb for stocks, stews, bouquets garnis, soups, roasts, and braised dishes. It also requires no rinsing, just keeping dry.

KOSHER SALT A coarse salt without any preservatives that tastes less salty than the regular (table) variety. I use it in cooking, but not baking.

MARGARINE Pareve Fleischmann's unsalted margarine works very well for baking.

MIRIN A sweet Japanese rice wine that you can easily find in health-food stores and most supermarkets.

MISO A Japanese paste made from fermented soy beans; available in different colors and salt levels, in health-food stores and Asian markets.

MUSHROOMS I use both dried and fresh mushrooms in soups, sauces, stews, and pasta. Dried mushrooms, which have a more intense taste than fresh ones, are sold by weight, packaged in cellophane bags. Before using, they must be soaked in boiling water.

SHIITAKE MUSHROOMS are tree fungi with a rich, meaty taste. The caps, which have striated indentations on the surface and curl under, are usually 2 inches (5 cm) or more in width and lend themselves to broiling and stir-frying over high heat.

PORCINI AND POLISH MUSHROOMS grow wild in many parts of Europe, and their rich, intense taste is totally different from the white or cultivated mushrooms that are most often seen in supermarkets.

NUTS Today most nuts are sold shelled. I prefer to buy them in health-food or specialty stores, as they seem to be fresher. All nuts freeze very well, and I think they keep better whole. Bring to room temperature before using. If you need chopped or ground nuts, process only the amount you need. For fine-grinding small amounts, I recommend using a Mouli grater. Otherwise a food processor is fine.

OILS I use a variety of oils, depending on whether I want a flavor to be strong or subtle.

OLIVE OIL is my default oil, the one I use most often for cooking chicken, meat, and fish dishes, as well as for salads, vegetables, and sauces. Whenever possible, I buy oil that is extra-virgin, first-pressed, and imported, as I think it is well worth the extra cost.

SESAME OIL is made from roasted sesame seeds. The pure Asian variety, which I prefer, has a thick, nutty flavor and a light brown color.

TRUFFLE OIL is now available with kosher certification. It makes a delicious enhancement for soups, salads, and pastas.

VEGETABLE OIL is preferable for some baking, stir-frying, or deep-frying or for dishes where a neutral flavor is called for.

PASTA I use only imported Italian pasta with the kosher certification. The premium brands are now available all over the country.

SALAD GREENS There are so many wonderful varieties, such as endive, mâche, watercress, arugula, Boston, Bibb, baby spinach, baby arugula, frisée, and many more.

SESAME SEEDS Tiny flat seeds that come either white or dark; the white ones are hulled. They are sold by weight, freeze very well, and are available in specialty and health-food stores.

SHALLOTS More pungent than onions—whose family they belong to—and more delicate than garlic, they have a thousand uses in stews, soups, sauces, and braised dishes.

SOY SAUCE I use the low-sodium variety.

STAR ANISE A brown, licorice-flavored spice that looks like a star with eight points.

TOMATOES Unless tomatoes are fully ripe and not at all mealy, don't use them in cooking. I think canned imported peeled tomatoes are definitely preferable. If possible, buy the variety from the San Marzano region of Italy.

SUN-DRIED TOMATOES Spicy and concentrated, these add a wonderful tomato flavor to almost any dish. They come semidry or packed in oil; I prefer the oil-packed variety, as they do not require reconstituting. They are sold by weight and keep very well refrigerated.

VINEGAR I use a variety of vinegars in addition to white distilled vinegar and apple cider vinegar.

RICE AND SEASONED RICE VINEGARS are amber–colored, mild, and sweet.

BALSAMIC VINEGAR, both dark and light, now comes in kosher varieties. I use the light one for dishes where I would like to preserve the original color. Brown balsamic has a richer and deeper taste.

WASABI This powdered Japanese horseradish has a pungent flavor. It comes in a small can and has a long shelf life.

WONTON WRAPPERS Thin squares of dough made from wheat flour, egg, and water. I use them to make different kinds of hors d'oeuvres.

NOTES ON EQUIPMENT

BLENDER I use it for puréeing soups and sauces to a silky consistency. When puréeing, be sure the ingredients are slightly cool and do not fill the blender all the way to the top; otherwise the lid will pop.

CAKE TESTER A thin metal skewer inserted into the center of a cake that indicates how moist a cake is.

COOKIE SHEETS Buy sheets of good quality and heavy gauge so they will not warp and will conduct heat well. I prefer sheets that are nonstick.

DOUBLE BOILER Very useful to have for melting chocolate, butter, and margarine, and for keeping puréed food warm.

ELECTRIC MIXER I have had my KitchenAid stand mixer for many, many years and find it extraordinarily useful for beating, whipping, and kneading. I recommend buying an extra mixer bowl and balloon whisk.

ELECTRIC KNIFE Comes in handy for slicing meat and turkey evenly and quickly.

FLOUR SIFTER To aerate and combine flour and other dry ingredients.

FOOD MILL This is a simple hand-operated device that comes with three discs. It is good for puréeing soups and sauces.

FOOD PROCESSOR This is an essential piece of kitchen equipment. Learn the difference among the various discs and blades for chopping, grating, and shredding vegetables, nuts, and cheese. Be sure to cut vegetables and cheese into smaller pieces before you put them in the processor so the blades don't mush or mutilate the food. (When working with small amounts of nuts or seeds, I prefer using a Mouli grater, see below.)

KNIVES There is a knife for every kitchen purpose. Some of the essential knives are a paring knife, a chopping French chef's knife, a slicing knife, a boning knife, a cleaver, and a bread knife. Buy the best-quality stainless-steel knives you can afford and choose one with a comfortable handle. Care for them properly: Always wash them by hand, never in the dishwasher.

MANDOLINE A cutting device that is one of my most-used kitchen utensils. It comes with four stainless-steel blades and does a wonderful job slicing and julienning vegetables

and fruits to the desired thinness and shape. My favorite is a very inexpensive Japanese one made by Benriner.

MEASURING CUPS These typically come in plastic, aluminum, and glass. Cups for liquids have a pouring spout. Passing a knife over the top of metal cups can level sugar and flour.

MEASURING SPOONS Look for stainless-steel spoons, preferably with long handles, as they make scooping easier. Buy them in sizes from 1/8 teaspoon to 1 tablespoon.

MEAT THERMOMETER This is very useful to have on hand when you are roasting a turkey or other poultry. It saves much guessing.

MOULI GRATER A small hand-cranked grater, perfect for small amounts of nuts, chocolate, or cheese.

OVEN I have an electric oven and find it very good for baking. But when it comes to broiling, it is less reliable than gas. Since I broil a lot because it is quicker, healthier, requires less fat, and is less messy than sautéing, I have learned that it is important to learn your oven's pluses and minuses, what it can do and what it can't.

The **BROILER PAN AND RACK INSERT** that come with the oven are important cooking tools. The rack, which is flush with the top of the broiler pan, allows the meat, fish, or vegetable to be cooked as close as possible to the source of heat. This lets it sear more quickly, thereby retaining more moisture. To save clean-up time, I always cover the rack and pan with foil.

OVEN THERMOMETER I use an oven thermometer from time to time to check the accuracy of my oven's temperature. Many a cake has been ruined from not checking. The Taylor thermometer is the brand I find most reliable.

PASTRY BRUSHES Nonsynthetic (natural bristle) flat brushes are my preference. I have them in various sizes and use them to brush on melted butter or margarine, to coat pie crusts with egg white, to grease baking pans, and so on. Brushes should be washed in warm, soapy water, then flicked dry and left to air-dry completely.

POULTRY SHEARS These are special scissors designed to cut through the joints of a chicken, duck, turkey, or capon.

SALAD SPIN-DRYER This is a wonderful gadget that makes it easy to dry salad greens, spinach, and herbs such as parsley or basil. You place the rinsed greens in the slotted basket that fits in the plastic bowl. When the basket spins, the water on the leaves is thrown into the outer bowl. Do not pack too many greens at one time, and empty the water after each spin. To make sure that no traces of moisture remain after spinning, place the leaves on paper towels for a few minutes to air-dry.

SAUCEPANS Many cooks like stainless-steel or aluminum pans. But I prefer enamel-lined cast-iron ones, such as Le Creuset, because they distribute heat evenly and can be used both on the top of the stove and in the oven. Unlike aluminum pans, they are nonreactive so you can put them in the refrigerator without concern that the flavor and color of the food inside will be changed. Also, they clean easily and well. They come in many sizes and colors—which makes it easy to distinguish meat from dairy—and are pretty to look at. The only disadvantage: Enamel-lined cast-iron pots are heavy and may chip if dropped.

SCISSORS This is an all-purpose kitchen tool that can cut wax paper, foil, string, herbs, artichoke leaves, and even dough. Choose a pair of good quality that is also rustproof.

SIEVES AND STRAINERS I use stainless-steel mesh sieves, fine and medium, for straining soups, sauces, and puréed fruits.

SKILLETS For sautéing, a nonstick heavy-gauge good-quality skillet is essential. Look for one that has a metal handle—so you can place it under the broiler when making frittatas or other dishes—and comes with a cover.

SPATULAS There are various sizes available in rubber, metal, or wire, depending on their function.

RUBBER SPATULAS are excellent for folding, blending, and combining ingredients, especially batter with beaten egg whites. They are also useful for scraping the last bit of mixture from bowls and jars.

METAL SPATULAS have wooden handles and are 1 inch (2.5 cm) wide and about 12 inches (30 cm) long. They are indispensable for lifting cookies and releasing the sides of cakes.

WIRE SPATULAS, also called skimmers, are used to lift sautéed or fried or stir-fried foods.

STEAMERS Many different kinds of steamers are on the market, metal as well as bamboo. The easiest and least expensive are stainless-steel collapsible baskets with three legs that fit into any saucepan or a wok. They come in two sizes and can be found in hardware stores. I also like the French Le Creuset steamer, made like the top of a double boiler, and the bamboo (Chinese) variety. The latter has many tiers of baskets, and you can steam different foods in each compartment.

TONGS These come in various sizes and are helpful when sautéing poultry or meat, for turning the food, and removing it from the pan.

WHISKS For mixing, these come in many sizes and qualities. Choose heavy stainless-steel whisks, the best you can afford, and buy at least two sizes. They will not rust or bend.

WIRE RACKS They come in various sizes, and I use them for cooling breads, cakes, pastries, and so forth. They are also useful when I want to warm foods in the oven that I do not want to get soggy, such as potato latkes, curried wontons, and pearl tidbits, among many others.

WOK I find the wok to be the most useful of all cooking vessels. I use it for stir-frying, deep-frying, and, with a rack insert, for steaming. It heats very quickly and is easy to clean (Wash it with soap and water, not detergents or scouring pads, and rub with oil.) I prefer those with wooden, rather than metal, handles, as they do not get hot. I also like woks with flat bottoms.

WOODEN SPOONS Their uses are many: for stirring, especially in enamel-lined saucepans, since they do not scratch; for mixing ingredients; for pushing vegetables or potatoes through a sieve; and for creaming ingredients when baking.

NOTES ON TECHNIQUES

BLANCH means to expose foods, such as peaches, tomatoes, or nuts, to boiling or roasting in order to loosen the skin and facilitate peeling.

> TO **BLANCH ALMONDS:** Drop them into boiling water, return the water to a boil, and drain immediately. While the almonds are still hot, slip off their skins by pressing them between your thumb and index finger. Dry on paper towels before using.

> TO **BLANCH HAZELNUTS:** Spread them in a baking pan and place them in a 350°F (175°C) toaster oven for 15 minutes. This will blister the skin. While still hot, wrap the nuts in a dish towel and rub the towel against a hard surface such as a table. Most of the skin will come off; don't worry if some skin remains on the nuts.

> TO **BLANCH TOMATOES:** Drop the tomatoes into boiling water. Return the water to a boil and drain. Loosen the tomato skin and slip it off.

BRAISE means to cook food in liquid, in a covered pot. The amount of liquid is usually very small, often only the natural juice of the meat or vegetable.

BROIL means to cook meat, fish, or vegetables in the oven (or broiling unit), as close as possible to the source of heat, so that the food sears quickly and retains moisture. Most ovens are equipped with a special broiler pan with a rack insert for this purpose.

> **Special broiling tip**: When broiling chicken, fish, or vetetables with sauces, I make a shallow "basket" using heavy foil so that that the juices don't spill out. (See photograph below.) First, set the rack in the broiling pan and cover it completely with heavy foil. Next, form a rectangular basket, about one inch (25 mm) high, which will hold the food in a single layer. Crimp the foil at the edges so that is is leakproof. Place the basket on the broiler rack, and arrange the food inside. Put the pan in the oven (or broiling unit), as close as possible to the heat source, for the time specified in the recipe.

DICE means to cut food, usually fruit, vegetables, or cheese into ¼-inch (6 mm) cubes.

JULIENNE means to cut food into matchstick pieces, usually ⅛ to ¼-inch (3 to 6 mm) wide, and whatever length the recipe calls for.

MINCE means to chop very fine.

PURÉE means to reduce the food to a smooth consistency. Depending on the consistency you want, smooth or semismooth, you may do this process in a blender, food mill or food processor.

SAUTÉ means to cook food for a very short time over relatively high heat in a small amount of hot fat such as butter, oil, or margarine.

To **SEED TOMATOES:** After blanching the tomatoes (see above), core them, cut them in half widthwise, and squeeze each half gently until the seeds pop out.

SIFT means to put dry ingredients, such as flour, baking powder, baking soda, or cornstarch, through a sifter to remove lumps and to make the ingredients light. A cup of sifted flour is lighter and contains less flour than a cup of unsifted flour.

To **SKIN PEPPERS:** Set the rack in the broiler pan and cover it completely with foil. Place the peppers on the rack and place it in the oven (or broiling unit), as close as possible to the heat source. Broil the peppers for about 7 minutes, or until the skin is blistered and charred. Cover the peppers with foil. The heat will loosen the skin. When the peppers are cool, slip or rub off the skins; do not rinse the peppers under running water, as this removes much of the flavor.

STEAM means to cook foods, covered, in the steam rising from briskly boiling water in the pan beneath it. The food may be placed in a separate steaming basket or on a heatproof dish set in a steaming basket.

STIR-FRY means to cook foods very quickly in a small amount of hot oil, stirring and tossing the food continuously as it cooks. Stir-frying may be done in a skillet, but the best utensil is a wok because it is deep and heats very quickly, thus making stirring so much easier.

STRAIN means to remove solid particles from liquid.

ACKNOWLEDGMENTS

First and foremost I am indebted to my assistant, Anna Blanarova. Without her patience, support, enthusiasm, and devotion, this book would not have been possible.

My children, Pamela, Joshua, Beth, and George, and my grandchildren, Rebecca, Daniella, Alexander, Nina, Samantha, and Jason tasted many of these recipes in their earliest incarnations and gave me excellent feedback and encouragement.

My sister-in-law, Caryl Englander, provided constant enthusiasm, as did my brother Israel Englander (whose taste buds are, not surprisingly, very much like mine) and all my nieces and nephews.

Kitty Ross shepherded the book along from beginning to end. She encouraged me, brought out the best in me with sympathy and intelligence, and has become a treasured friend. I will have fond memories of the pleasurable time we spent working on the book.

I could not have done without the sound advice, encouragement, and kind words of Dr. Judith Ginsberg.

For practical assistance at all stages, I am indebted to Robin Levine. I am grateful to Joan Rosenbaum for her early encouragement, Carolyn Hessel for her constructive suggestions during the beginning stages, and Yvette Schops for her organizational skills.

Judith Thurman's guidance and advice have been invaluable.

Peter Mayer, the legendary publisher and CEO of Overlook Press, offered input at every step of the way. His encouragement and advice have been invaluable. George Davidson at Overlook has managed all phases of the book's production with wisdom, kindness, and professionalism. I am also grateful to his Overlook colleague Jack Lamplough and to Rachel Tarlow Gul at Over the River Public Relations for their publicity talents.

I thank Deborah Thomas, the designer, for her excellent work, dedication, and unflagging good cheer. Thanks also to Ann Stratton, for her beautiful photography, and to Carrie Purcell, Sarah Abrams, and Denise Carter, her wonderful staff.

I have relied on Michael Kane at Park East Kosher Butcher in New York City throughout this project.

I have leaned on many indulgent friends during the testing and retesting process, especially Fanya Heller, Carol Saper, Lili Assa, Joan Grubin, Eve Grubin, David Grubin, Clemence Boulouque, Marlene Meyerson, Dr. Maria Padilla, Dr. Paul Meyers, Dr. Owen Lewis, Dr. Paul LeClerc, Susan Rai, Dr. Kanti Rai, and Michele Harkins. Their enthusiasm has been priceless.

INDEX

Dairy recipes are indicated by (D), meat recipes by (M), and pareve recipes by (P).
Page numbers in italics indicate photographs.

A

Acorn Squash Soufflé (D), 249
Acorn Squash, Sweet-and-Sour (P), *113*, 124, *125*
Almond and Green Bean Soup (P), 83
Almond Peach Cake (D), 298
Almonds, blanching, 351
Anna's Coleslaw (P), 98
Appetizers
   Baked Baby Artichokes (P), 43
   Beets with Ginger (P), *31*, *40*, 41
   Beets with Walnuts (P), 42
   Cauliflower with Capers (P), 44
   Ceviche (P), 33
   Eggplant Relish (P), 50
   Eggplant with Mushrooms (P), 52
   Eggplant with Tahini Dressing (P), 48, *49*
   Haricots Verts with Mustard Dressing (P),
     38, *39*
   Herring Salad (P), 38
   Mushroom Tarts (P), 46
   Oriental Eggplant (P), 51
   Roasted Bell Peppers (P), 45
   Salmon Tartare (P), 34
   Sautéed Baby Artichokes (P), 43
   Tuna Tartare (P), 35
   Tuna Tartare with Avocado (P), 36, *37*
Apricot or Prune Clafouti (D), 303
Apricot Sauce for Turkey Scaloppini (P), 216
Apricot Soufflé (P), *328*, *329*
Arborio Rice, 141
Arctic Char, Glazed (P), 167
Arctic Char with Honey and Wasabi (P), 166
Artichokes, Baked Baby (P), 43
Artichokes, Sautéed Baby (P), 43
Asian Cabbage Salad (P), *100*, 101
Asian Sauce, Piquant (P), 170
Asian-Style Vegetable Medley (P), 121
Asparagus Soup (M), *53*, *64*, 65

B

Baby Artichokes, Baked (P), 43
Baby Artichokes, Sautéed (P), 43
Baked Baby Artichokes (P), 43
Baked Eggplant with Ground Meat, Tomatoes,
   and Pine Nuts (M), *240*, 241
Balsamic Lentils (P), 132
Balsamic Vinegar, uses, 344
Balsamic Vinaigrette (P), 111
Barbecued Split Fillet (London Broil) with Two
   Marinades (M), 230
Barley Salad (P), 106
Barley Soup with Miso (P), 80, *81*
Barley with Carrots, Onions, and Parsley (P), 156
Barley-Stuffed Cabbage Rolls (P), 272
Basil Garnish (P), 74, *75*
Basil Leaves, handling, 337, 340
Basil Marinade for Split Fillet (P), 230
Basmati Rice, 157
Bean and Rice Frittata with Guacamole (P), 268
Beans, Dried, where to buy, 339
Beef Dishes
   Baked Eggplant with Ground Meat,
     Tomatoes, and Pine Nuts (M), *240*, 241
   Barbecued Split Fillet (London Broil) with
     Two Marinades (M), 230
   Beef Stew with Thyme (M), 239
   Braised Short Ribs of Beef (M), *223*, 236, *237*
   Cholent (M), 244
   Hearty Beef Stew (M), 238
   Meat Chili (M), 245
   Meatloaf (M), 246
   Pot Roast (M), 235
   Split Fillet (London Broil) with Port Wine
     Glaze (M), *232*, 233
   Stuffed Cabbage Rolls (M), 242
Beef Stew, Hearty (M), 238
Beet Salad, Raw (P), 103
Beet Soup (P), *76*, 77
Beets with Ginger (P), *31*, *40*, 41
Beets with Walnuts (P), 42
Beets, working with, 338

Bell Pepper and Potato Frittata (P), *247*, 266, *267*

Bell Pepper and Tomato Soup with Basil Garnish (P), 74, *75*

Bell Peppers and Basil Sauce for Farfalle (P), 148, *149*

Bell Peppers, removing the skin, 352

Bell Peppers, Roasted (P), 45

Brussels Sprouts, Roasted (P), 115

Black Bean and Quinoa Salad (P), 105

Black Bean, Chicken, and Corn Salad (M), 96

Black Bean Chili (P), 276

Black Bean Salad (P), 104

Black Cod with Honey and Soy Sauce (P), 172

Black Cod with Miso (P), 173

Black Sea Bass with Ginger and Scallions (P), 175

Black Sea Bass with Potatoes and Tomatoes (P), 174

Blanch, how to, 351

Blender, 345

Blintzes (D), 305

Boneless Rack of Veal (M), 229

Braise, how to, 351

Braised Duck (M), 222

Braised Short Ribs of Beef (M), *223*, 236, *237*

Braised Veal Shanks (Osso Buco) (M), 225

Breads

    Challah (P), 189

    Potato Bread (P), 22

Broccoli, Chopped (P), 118

Broccoli Pesto for Orecchiette (P), *150*, 151

Broccoli with Panko (P), 116, *117*

Broil, how to, 351

Broiled Duck Breasts with Ginger Sauce (M), 221

Broiler Pan, 347; rack insert for, 347, *351*

Broth, Chicken (M), 60; uses, 339

Broth, Vegetable, uses 339

Brown Sugar, Dark, storing, 338

Brownies, Easy (P), 320

Brussels Sprouts, Roasted (P), 115

Bulgur and Chickpea Salad (P), 97

Bulgur Chili (P), 274

Bulgur, uses, 339

Burgers, Salmon with Spinach (P), 182

Burgers, Tuna (P), 171

Burgers, Turkey (M), 220

Burgers, Vegetarian (P), 270, *271*

Butter, cooking with, 339

Butternut Squash, Roasted (P), 124

Butternut Squash with Halibut (D), *161*, *164*, 165

C

Cabbage and Mushroom Soup (M), 66

Cabbage, Red, with Capers (P), 119

Cabbage Rolls Stuffed with Barley (P), 272

Cabbage Rolls Stuffed with Veal and Beef (M), 242

Cabbage Salads

    Anna's Coleslaw (P), 98

    Asian Cabbage Salad (P), *100*, 101

    Napa Cabbage Salad (P), 99

    Savoy Cabbage Salad (P), 98

Cake Tester, 345

Cakes and Tortes

    Chocolate Almond Cake with Orange (P), 313

    Chocolate Hazelnut Torte with Raspberry Sauce (P), 311

    Chocolate, Prune, and Walnut Torte (P), 315

    Chocolate Velvet Cake (D), 279

    Citrus Pound Cake (D), 294

    Honey Cake (P), 334

    Peach Almond Cake (D), 298

    Ricotta Cake (D), 302

    Tuscan Cake (D), 296, *297*

    Zucchini Cake (P), 335

Cannellini Bean and Porcini Soup (M), 62

Cannellini Bean Salad (D), 89

Carnaroli Rice, 141

Caper Sauce for Halibut (P), 176

Caper Sauce for Turkey Scaloppini (P), 217

Capers, uses, 339

Capon, Roasted, with Olives (M), 214, *215*

Caramelized Onions (P), 234

Carrot and Tomato Soup (M), 67

Carrot Salad (P), 102

Carrot-Ginger Soup (P), 68

Carrots, Spiced (P), 115

Cauliflower, Roasted (P), 120

Cauliflower Sauce for Penne (P), 145

Cauliflower with Capers (P), 44

Celery Root and Porcini Soup (P), 78

Celery Root Soup (D), 58

Ceviche (P), 33

Challah (P), 189

Cheese Filling for Blintzes (D), 305

Cheese, storing, 338
Chestnut and Mushroom Soup (P), 82
Chicken Broth (M), 60; uses, 339
Chicken Glaze (M), 205
Chicken Dishes
   Chicken, Black Bean, and Corn Salad (M), 96
   Chicken Liver, Chopped (M), 15
   Chicken Livers with Vinegar (M), 234
   Chicken Puttanesca (M), 207
   Chicken Rolls with Mushrooms (M), 196
   Chicken Rolls with Orange Sauce (M), *191*,
     198, *199*
   Chicken Salad with Radicchio and Pine Nuts
     (M), 94, *95*
   Chicken Salad with Thyme (M), 93
   Chicken Shish Kebabs with Two Marinades
     (M), 202
   Chicken Soup with Matzoh Balls (M), 60
   Chicken with Chestnuts (M), 193
   Chicken with Citrus and Tarragon (M), 195
   Chicken with Honey and Mustard (M), 194
   Chicken with Potatoes and Olives (M), 201
   Chicken with Rosemary (M), 210
   Curried Chicken (M), 211
   Glazed Chicken with Glazed Mushrooms
     (M), *204*, 205
   Sake-Steamed Chicken (M), 208, *209*
   Stir-Fried Chicken with Snow Peas (M),
     212, 213
Chicken, Black Bean, and Corn Salad (M), 96
Chicken Liver, Chopped (M), 15
Chicken Livers with Vinegar (M), 234
Chicken Salad with Radicchio and Pine Nuts
   (M), 94, *95*
Chicken Salad with Thyme (M), 93
Chicken Soup with Matzoh Balls (M), 60
Chickpea and Bulgur Salad (P), 97
Chickpea and Feta Salad (D), *90*, 91
Chili, Black Bean (P), 276
Chili, Bulgur (P), 274
Chili, Meat (M), 245
Chili, White Bean (P), 275
Chive Oil, for Salmon with Mustard Sauce (P),
   180, *181*; uses, 342
Chives, uses, 340
Chocolate, cooking with, 339

Chocolate Desserts
   Chocolate Almond Cake with Orange (P), 313
   Chocolate Almond Truffles (P), 308, *322*
   Chocolate Hazelnut Torte with Raspberry
     Sauce (P), 311
   Chocolate Meringue Squares (P), 321
   Chocolate, Prune, and Walnut Torte (P), 315
   Chocolate Roll (D), 284
   Chocolate Soufflé (P), *277*, 318, *319*
   Chocolate Velvet Cake (D), 279
   Easy Brownies (P), 320
   Flourless Chocolate Nut Torte (P), 309
   Warm Chocolate Surprises (D), *280*, 281
   Warm Chocolate-Coconut Surprises (P), 317
Chocolate Almond Cake with Orange (P), 313
Chocolate Almond Truffles (P), 308, *322*
Chocolate Hazelnut Torte with Raspberry
   Sauce (P), 311
Chocolate Meringue Squares (P), 321
Chocolate, Prune, and Walnut Torte (P), 315
Chocolate Roll (D), 284
Chocolate Soufflé (P), *277*, 318, *319*
Chocolate Velvet Cake (D), 279
Cholent (M), 244
Chopped Broccoli (P), 118
Chopped Chicken Liver (M), 15
Cilantro, handling, 337, 340
Citrus Pound Cake (D), 294
Citrus-Tarragon Marinade for Chicken Breasts
   (P), 195
Cocoa Powder, what to buy, 339
Coconut Rice, Creamy (P), 157
Coconut-Milk Sauce for Red Snapper (P), 179
Coffee, Ground, storing, 338
Coleslaw, Anna's (P), 98
Cookie Sheets, what to buy, 345
Corn, Chicken, and Black Bean Salad (M), 96
Corn Soup, Summer (P), 69
Couscous and Lentil Salad, Mediterranean
   (D), 92
Cream, whipping, 338
Creamy Coconut Rice (P), 157
Crêpes for Blintzes (D), 305
Cucumbers, seeding, 338
Curried Chicken (M), 211
Curried Veal Roast (M), 227
Curried Wontons (M), 16
Curry Coating (P), 211

D

Daikon, uses, 339
Desserts
  Apricot or Prune Clafouti (D), 303
  Apricot Soufflé (P), *328*, 329
  Blintzes (D), 305
  Cheese Filling for Blintzes (D), 305
  Chocolate Almond Cake with Orange (P), 313
  Chocolate Almond Truffles (P), 308, *322*
  Chocolate Hazelnut Torte with Raspberry
    Sauce (P), 311
  Chocolate Meringue Squares (P), 321
  Chocolate, Prune, and Walnut Torte (P), 315
  Chocolate Roll (D), 284
  Chocolate Soufflé (P), *277*, 318, *319*
  Chocolate Velvet Cake (D), 279
  Citrus Pound Cake (D), 294
  Crêpes for Blintzes (D), 305
  Easy Brownies (P), 320
  Farmer Cheese Squares (D), 290
  Flourless Chocolate Nut Torte (P), 309
  Fruit Crumble (P), 331
  Fruit Loaf (D), 299
  Hamentashen (D), 292
  Hamentashen (P), 326
  Hazelnut Balls (D), 282, *283*
  Honey Cake (P), 334
  Mandelbrot (P), *322*, 325
  Mini Fruit Truffles (P), *322*, 333
  Mocha Pecan Balls (P), *322*, 324
  Peach Almond Cake (D), 298
  Pear Clafouti (D), 304
  Pear Tart (P), 332
  Pine Nut Balls (P), *322*, 323
  Prune or Apricot Clafouti (D), 303
  Raspberry Sauce (P), 301
  Ricotta Cake (D), 302
  Ricotta Flan with Raspberry Sauce (D),
    300, 301
  Rugelach (D), 307
  Shortbread Biscuits (D), *283*, 289
  Tuscan Cake (D), 296, *297*
  Walnut Roll (D), *286*, 287
  Warm Chocolate Surprises (D), *280*, 281
  Warm Chocolate-Coconut Surprises (P), 317
  Zucchini Cake (P), 335
Dice, how to, 352
Dill, handling, 337, 340
Dill Marinade for Salmon (P), 185
Double Boiler, 345
Dough for Rugelach (D), 307
Dressings
  Balsamic Vinaigrette (P), 111
  Dressing for Spinach (P), 182
  Lemon–Olive Oil Dressing for Chickpea and
    Feta Salad (P), 91
  Mayonnaise (P), 112
  Miso Dressing for Rice Salad (P), 108
  Mustard Dressing for Haricots Verts (P), 39
  Oriental Dressing for Roasted Eggplant (P), 51
  Rice-Vinegar Dressing for Napa Cabbage
    Salad (P), 99
  Sesame-Ginger Dressing (P), 111
  Sweet and Sour Dressing for Chicken Salad
    (P), 94
  Tahini Dressing for Eggplant (P), 48
Dried Beans, where to buy, 339
Duck, Braised (M), 222
Duck Breasts, Broiled, with Ginger Sauce (M),
221

E

Easy Brownies (P), 320
Edamame (Soy Beans), 170, 208, *209*
Egg Whites, beating, stiffening, 338, 339
Eggplant Caviar (P), 26
Eggplant, Oriental (P), 51
Eggplant Parmigiana (D), 258
Eggplant Relish (P), 50
Eggplant, Smoky (P), 28
Eggplant Tart (D), 256, *257*
Eggplant with Ground Meat, Tomatoes, and Pine
  Nuts (M), *240*, 241
Eggplant with Mushrooms (P), 52
Eggplant with Tahini Dressing (P), 48, *49*
Eggs, separating; beating whites, stiffening
  whites, 338, 339
Electric Knife, uses, 345
Electric Mixer, about, 345
Equipment, Notes on, 345-350
  Blender, 345
  Broiler Pan, 347
  Broiler-Pan Rack Insert, 347
  Cake Tester, 345
  Cookie Sheets, 345
  Double Boiler, 345

Electric Mixer, 345
Electric Knife, 345
Flour Sifter, 345
Food Mill, 345
Food Processor, 345
Knives, 345
Mandoline, 345
Measuring Cups, 347
Measuring Spoons, 347
Meat Thermometer, 347
Mouli Grater, 347
Oven, Electric vs Gas, 347
Oven Thermometer, 347
Pastry Brushes, 347
Poultry Shears, 347
Salad Spin-Dryer, 347
Saucepans, 348
Scissors, 348
Sieves and Strainers, 348
Skillets, 348
Spatulas, Rubber, Metal, and Wire, 348
Spoons, Wooden, 350
Steamers, 348
Strainers and Sieves, 348
Thermometers, Meat, Oven, 347
Tongs, 350
Whisks, 350
Wire Racks, 350
Wok, 350
Wooden Spoons, 350

F

Farfalle with Peppers and Basil (P), 148, *149*
Farmer Cheese Squares (D), 290
Feta and Chickpea Salad (D), *90*, 91
Feta Cheese, about, 339
Fish Dishes
    Arctic Char with Honey and Wasabi (P), 166
    Black Cod with Honey and Soy Sauce (P), 172
    Black Cod with Miso (P), 173
    Black Sea Bass with Ginger and Scallions (P), 175
    Black Sea Bass with Potatoes and Tomatoes (P), 174
    Ceviche (P), 33
    Fish Soup with Vegetables (P), 84
    Gefilte Fish with Challah (P), 187
    Glazed Arctic Char (P), 167
    Grey Sole with Cilantro (D), 163
    Halibut Nuggets with Yukon Gold Potatoes (P), 177
    Halibut with Butternut Squash (D), *161*, *164*, 165
    Halibut with Caper Sauce (P), 176
    Herring Salad (P), 38
    Marinated Salmon (P), 185
    Marinated Salmon with Mango-Kiwi Relish (P), 186
    Red Snapper with Coconut Milk (P), *178*, 179
    Salmon Burgers with Spinach (P), 182
    Salmon Tartare (P), 34
    Salmon Teriyaki (P), 184
    Salmon with Mustard Sauce and Chive Oil (P), 180, *181*
    Salmon with Orange (P), 183
    Seared Tuna with Two Dressings (P), 168, *169*
    Smoked Whitefish Pâté (P), 24
    Sole and Parmesan Soufflé (D), 260
    Tuna Burgers (P), 171
    Tuna Sauce for Spaghetti (P), 154
    Tuna Tartare (P), 35
    Tuna Tartare with Avocado (P), 36, *37*
Fish Soup with Vegetables (P), 84
Fish Stock for Fish Soup with Vegetables (P), 84
Fish Stock for Gefilte Fish with Challah (P), 187
Flan, Ricotta, with Raspberry Sauce (D), 301
Flour, measuring, 338
Flour Sifter, 345
Flourless Chocolate Nut Torte (P), 309
Food Mill, 345
Food Processor, 345
Frisée, uses, 340
Frittatas
    Bean and Rice Frittata with Guacamole (P), 268
    Bell Pepper and Potato Frittata (P), *247*, 266, *267*
    Mushroom Frittata, (P), 265
    Zucchini Frittata (D), 255
Fruit Crumble (P), 331
Fruit Loaf (D), 299
Fruit Truffles, Mini (P), *322*, 333

G

Gefilte Fish with Challah (P), 187
Ginger Root, how to store, 340
Ginger Sauce for Duck (P), 221
Ginger Sauce for Tuna (P), 170
Ginger-Sesame Sauce for Chicken (P), 196
Glazed Arctic Char (P), 167
Glazed Chicken with Glazed Mushrooms (M), *204*, 205
Grated Potato Pancake (P), 127
Grater, Mouli, 347
Gravlax with Mustard-Dill Sauce and Potato Bread (P), *20*, 21
Green Bean and Almond Soup (P), 83
Green Pea and Zucchini Soup (D), 56
Greens, Salad, handling and storing, 337, 340, 343
Grey Sole with Cilantro (D), 163
Guacamole (P), 269

H

Halibut Nuggets with Yukon Gold Potatoes (P), 177
Halibut with Butternut Squash (D), *161*, *164*, 165
Halibut with Caper Sauce (P), 176
Hamentashen (D), 292
Hamentashen (P), 326
Hanukkah, Recipes for, *see* Holiday Recipes
Haricots Verts with Mustard Dressing (P), 38, *39*
Hazelnut Balls (D), 282, *283*
Hazelnuts, storing, 338; grating 338, 342; blanching, 351
Hearty Beef Stew (M), 238
Helpful Tips, 337-338
  Basil leaves, handling, 337
  Beets, working with, 338
  Brown Sugar, Dark, storing, 338
  Cheese, storing, 338
  Cilantro, handling, 337
  Coffee, ground, storing, 338
  Cream, whipping, 338
  Cucumbers, seeding, 338
  Dill, handling, 337
  Eggs, separating; beating whites, stiffening whites, 338
  Flour, measuring, 338
  Greens, handling and storing, 337
  Jalapeño Peppers, seeding, 338
  Kitchen Timer, using, 337
  Mushrooms, buying, handling, 337
  Nuts (hazelnuts, walnuts, pine nuts), storing, grating, 338
  Parmesan Cheese, grating, 338
  Oven Thermometer, checking oven accuracy, 337, 347
  Raspberries, handling, 337
  Salad Greens, handling and storing, 337
  Salt, saving too-salty soups and stews, 337
  Strawberries, handling, 337
  Tomatoes, ripening, 337
Herbs, cooking with, 340
Herring Salad (P), 38
Holiday Recipes
  Hanukkah
    Potato Latkes (P), 27
  Passover
    Boneless Rack of Veal (M), 229
    Chicken with Citrus and Tarragon (M), 195
    Chicken with Potatoes and Olives (M), 201
    Chocolate Almond Cake with Orange (P), 313
    Chocolate Almond Truffles (P), 308, *322*
    Chocolate Hazelnut Torte with Raspberry Sauce (P), 311
    Chocolate Meringue Squares (P), 321
    Chocolate, Prune, and Walnut Torte (P), 315
    Flourless Chocolate Nut Torte (P), 309
    Gefilte Fish with Challah (P), 187
    Mini Fruit Truffles (P), *322*, 333
    Pine Nut Balls (P), *322*, 323
    Potatoes with Garlic and Tarragon (P), 130
    Roast Capon with Olives (M), 214, *215*
    Salmon with Orange (P), 183
  Purim
    Hamentashen (D), 292
    Hamentashen (P), 326
  Rosh Hashana
    Honey Cake (P), 334
  Sabbath
    Cholent (M), 242
    Gefilte Fish with Challah (P), 187
    Marinated Salmon (P), 185
    Potatoes with Garlic and Tarragon (P), 130
  Shavout
    Blintzes (D), 305
    Farmer Cheese Squares (D), 290

Sukkoth
    Cabbage Rolls Stuffed with Barley (P), 272
    Cabbage Rolls Stuffed with Meat (M), 243
Honey and Mustard Marinade for Chicken (P), 194
Honey and Soy Sauce Marinade for Black Cod (P), 172
Honey and Wasabi Marinade for Arctic Char (P), 166
Honey Cake (P), 334
Honey-Lemon Marinade for Chicken (P), 203
Honey-Soy Marinade for Salmon (P), 186
Hors d'Oeuvres
    Chopped Chicken Liver (M), 15
    Curried Wontons (M), 16
    Eggplant Caviar (P), 26
    Gravlax with Mustard-Dill Sauce and Potato Bread (P), *20*, 21
    Hummus (P), 29
    Parmesan Crisps (D), 14
    Parmesan Puffs (D), *11*, 13
    Pearl Tidbits (M), 18, *19*
    Potato Bread (P), 22
    Potato Latkes (P), 27
    Smoked Whitefish Pâté (P), 24
    Smoky Eggplant (P), 28
    Wonton Shells with Mushrooms (P), 25
Horseradish (P), 188
Hummus (P), 29

I

Ingredients, Notes on, 339-344
    Balsamic Vinegar, 344
    Basil, 340
    Beans, Dried, 339
    Broth, Chicken, 339
    Broth, Vegetable, 339
    Bulgur, 339
    Butter, 339
    Capers, 339
    Chives, 340
    Chocolate, 339
    Cilantro, 340
    Cocoa Powder, 339
    Daikon, 339
    Dill, 340
    Dried Beans, 339
    Dried Lentils, 339

Eggs, 339
Feta Cheese, 339
Frisée, 340
Ginger Root, 340
Greens, 343
Herbs, 340
Kosher Salt, 342
Lentils, Dried, 339
Margarine, 342
Mint, 340
Mirin, 342
Miso, 342
Mushrooms, fresh and dried, 342
Mushrooms, Polish, 342
Mushrooms, Porcini, 342
Mushrooms, Shiitake, 342
Nuts, 342
Oils, 342
Olive Oil, 342
Parsley, 340
Pasta, 343
Polish Mushrooms, 342
Porcini Mushrooms, 342
Rice Vinegar, 343
Salad Greens, 343
Salt, Kosher, 342
Seasoned Rice Vinegar, 343
Sesame Oil, 343
Sesame Seeds, 343
Shallots, 343
Shiitake Mushrooms, 342
Soy Sauce, 343
Star Anise, 343
Sun-Dried Tomatoes, 343
Tarragon, 342
Thyme, 342
Tomatoes, fresh and canned, 343
Tomatoes, Sun-Dried, 343
Truffle Oil, 343
Vegetable Oil, 343
Vinegar, 343
Wasabi, 344
Wonton Wrappers, 344

J

Jalapeño Peppers, seeding, 338
Julienne, how to, 352

K

Kiwi-Mango Relish (P), 186
Kitchen Timer, setting, 337
Knives, about, 345
Kosher Salt, uses, 342

L

Latkes, Potato (P), 27
Lemon Syrup for Citrus Pound Cake (P), 294
Lemon–Olive Oil Dressing (P), 91
Lentil and Couscous Salad, Mediterranean (D), 92
Lentil (Red), Soup (P), 70
Lentil Salad (P), 107
Lentils, Dried, where to buy, 339
Lentils with Balsamic Vinegar (P), 132
Lime Cilantro Sauce (P), 33
Linguini in Olive Sauce (P), 155
Linguini with Pesto and Zucchini (D), 135
London Broil (Split Fillet) with Port Wine Glaze (M), *232, 233*
London Broil (Split Fillet) with Two Marinades (M), 230
Luncheon Dishes and Salads
    Acorn Squash Soufflé (D), 249
    Barley-Stuffed Cabbage Rolls (P), 272
    Bean and Rice Frittata with Guacamole (P), 268
    Bell Pepper and Potato Frittata (P), *247*, 266, *267*
    Black Bean Chili (P), 276
    Black Bean Salad (P), 104
    Bulgur Chili (P), 274
    Cabbage Rolls Stuffed with Barley (P), 272
    Cannellini Bean Salad (D), 89
    Chicken, Black Bean, and Corn Salad (M), 96
    Chicken Salad with Radicchio and Pine Nuts (M), 94, *95*
    Chicken Salad with Thyme (M), 93
    Chickpea and Feta Salad (D), *90*, 91
    Eggplant Parmigiana (D), 258
    Eggplant Tart (D), 256, *257*
    Mediterranean Couscous and Lentil Salad (D), 92
    Mushroom Frittata (P), 265
    Mushroom Ragoût (P), 264
    Rice Salad (P), *87*, 108, *109*
    Sole and Parmesan Soufflé (D), 260
    Southwestern Ratatouille (P), 262
    Spinach Pie (D), 250
    Stuffed Portobello Mushrooms (D), *252*, 253
    Tofu with Mushrooms (P), 263
    Vegetarian Burgers (P), 270, *271*
    White Bean Chili (P), 275
    Zucchini Frittata (D), 255

M

Mandelbrot (P), *322*, 325
Mandoline, 345
Mango-Kiwi Relish (P), 186
Margarine, what to buy, 342
Marinated Salmon (P), 185
Marinated Salmon with Mango-Kiwi Relish (P), 186
Matzoh Ball Soup (M), 60
Matzoh Balls for Chicken Soup (M), 60
Mayonnaise (P), 112
Measuring Cups, 347
Measuring Spoons, 347
Meat Dishes
    Baked Eggplant with Ground Meat, Tomatoes, and Pine Nuts (M), *240*, 241
    Barbecued Split Fillet (London Broil) with Two Marinades (M), 230
    Beef Stew with Thyme (M), 239
    Boneless Rack of Veal (M), 229
    Braised Short Ribs of Beef (M), *223*, 236, *237*
    Braised Veal Shanks (Osso Buco) (M), 225
    Chicken Livers with Vinegar (M), 234
    Cholent (M), 244
    Chopped Chicken Liver (M), 15
    Curried Veal Roast (M), 227
    Hearty Beef Stew (M), 238
    Meat Chili (M), 245
    Meat Sauce for Spaghetti (M), 142
    Meatloaf (M), 246
    Osso Buco (Braised Veal Shanks) (M), 225
    Pot Roast (M), 235
    Split Fillet (London Broil) with Port Wine Glaze (M), *232, 233*
    Stuffed Cabbage Rolls (M), 242
    Veal Stew (M), 228
Meat Thermometer, 347
Mediterranean Couscous and Lentil Salad (D), 92
Midseason Tomato Sauce (P), 159
Mince, how to, 352
Mini Fruit Truffles (P), *322*, 333

Mint, about, 340
Mirin, about, 342
Miso Dressing for Rice Salad (P), 108
Miso Marinade for Black Cod (P), 173
Miso, uses, 342
Mocha Pecan Balls (P), *322*, 324
Mouli Grater, 347
Mushroom and Cabbage Soup (M), 66
Mushroom and Chestnut Soup (P), 82
Mushroom and Radicchio Sauce for Orecchiette (P), 152
Mushroom Filling for Chicken Rolls (P), 196
Mushroom Filling for Lasagna (D), 138
Mushroom Filling for Wonton Shells (P), 25
Mushroom Frittata (P), 265
Mushroom Glaze for Glazed Chicken (P), *204*, 205
Mushroom Lasagna (D), 138
Mushroom Ragoût (P), 264
Mushroom Soup (D), 55
Mushroom Soup with Soy Milk (P), 79
Mushroom Tarts (P), 46
Mushrooms, dried, reconstituting, 342; types, 342
Mushrooms, fresh, buying, handling, 337, 342
Mushrooms, Glazed, for Glazed Chicken (M), *204*, 205
Mushrooms, Polish, using, 342
Mushrooms, Porcini, using, 342
Mushrooms, Portobello, *252*, 253
Mushrooms, Shiitake, using, 342
Mushrooms, Stuffed Portobello (D), *252*, 253
Mushrooms with Tofu (P), 263
Mushrooms, White, buying, 337
Mustard Dressing for Haricots Verts (P), 39
Mustard Sauce for Salmon (P), 180
Mustard-Dill Sauce for Gravlax (P), 21

N

Napa Cabbage Salad (P), 99
Notes on Equipment (*see* Equipment)
Notes on Ingredients (*see* Ingredients)
Notes on Techniques (*see* Techniques)
Nuts, storing, grating, 338, 342

O

Oils, types and uses, 342
Olive Oil, uses, 342
Onions, Caramelized (P), 234

Orange Glaze for Arctic Char (P), 167
Orange Sauce for Chicken Rolls (P), 198
Orecchiette with Broccoli Pesto (P), *150*, 151
Orecchiette with Mushrooms and Radicchio (P), 152
Oriental Dressing for Roasted Eggplant (P), 51
Oriental Eggplant (P), 51
Osso Buco (Braised Veal Shanks) (M), 225
Oven, Electric vs Gas, 347
Oven Thermometer, checking oven accuracy, 337, 347

P

Parmesan and Sole Soufflé (D), 260
Parmesan Cheese, grating, 338
Parmesan Crisps (D), 14
Parmesan Puffs (D), *11*, 13
Parsley, about, 340
Parsnip and Potato Purée (P), 126
Passover, Recipes for, *see* Holiday Recipes
Pasta and Risotto
   Farfalle with Peppers and Basil (P), 148, *149*
   Linguini in Olive Sauce (P), 155
   Linguini with Pesto and Zucchini (D), 135
   Mushroom Lasagna (D), 138
   Orecchiette with Broccoli Pesto (P), *150*, 151
   Orecchiette with Mushrooms and Radicchio (P), 152
   Penne with Cauliflower (P), 145
   Penne with Mushroom Sauce (P), 146
   Penne with Uncooked Tomato Sauce (P), 147
   Rigatoni with Bell Pepper–Tomato Sauce (P), 143
   Rigatoni with Olives, Herbs, and Arugula (P), 144
   Risotto (D), *133*, *140*, 141
   Spaghetti with Meat Sauce (M), 142
   Spaghetti with Tuna (P), 154
   Ziti with Herbs and Mozzarella (D), 136, *137*
   Ziti with Roasted Vegetables (P), 153
Pasta, buying, 343
Pastry Brushes, 347
Pâté, Smoked Whitefish (P), 24
Peach Almond Cake (D), 298
Pear Clafouti (D), 304
Pear Tart (P), 332
Pearl Tidbits (M), 18, *19*
Pecan Mocha Balls (P), *322*, 324

Penne with Cauliflower (P), 145
Penne with Mushroom Sauce (P), 146
Penne with Uncooked Tomato Sauce (P), 147
Pepper and Basil sauce for Farfalle (P), 148, *149*
Pepper, Roasted, and Zucchini Soup (M), 63
Peppers, Bell, skinning, 352
Peppers, Jalapeño, seeding, 338
Peppers, Roasted Bell (P), 45
Pine Nut Balls (P), *322*, 323
Pine Nuts, storing, grating, 338, 342
Piquant Asian Sauce for Seared Tuna (P), 170
Polish Mushrooms, using, 342
Porcini and Cannellini Bean Soup (M), 62
Porcini and Celery Root Soup (P), 78
Porcini Mushrooms, using, 342
Port Wine Glaze for Split Fillet (M), 233
Portobello Mushrooms, Stuffed (D), *252*, 253
Pot Roast (M), 235
Potato and Bell Pepper Frittata (P), *247*, 266, *267*
Potato and Parsnip Purée (P), 126
Potato and White Bean Purée (P), 131
Potato Bread (P), 22
Potato Latkes (P), 27
Potato Pancake (P), 127
Potato Tart, Thin (P), *128*, 129
Potatoes with Garlic and Tarragon (P), 130
Potaoes, Yukon Gold, with Halibut Nuggets (P), 177
Poultry Shears, 347
Prune or Apricot Clafouti (D), 303
Puff Pastry Squares (P), frozen, 47
Purée, how to, 32
Puréed Vegetable Soup (D), 59
Purim, Recipes for, *see* Holiday Recipes

Q

Quinoa (P), 105, 158
Quinoa and Black Bean Salad (P), 105

R

Rack of Veal, Boneless (M), 229
Racks, Wire 350
Raspberry Sauce (P), 301
Raspberries, handling, 337
Ratatouille, Simple (P), 122
Ratatouille, Southwestern (P), 262
Raw Beet Salad (P), 103
Red Cabbage with Capers (P), 119

Red Lentil Soup (P), 70
Red Snapper with Coconut Milk (P), *178*, 179
Relish, Eggplant (P), 50
Relish, Mango-Kiwi (P), 186
Rice, Arborio, 141
Rice, Basmati, 157
Rice, Carnaroli, 141
Rice, Creamy, with Coconut Milk (P), 157
Rice Filling for Chicken Rolls (P), 198
Rice Salad (P), *87*, 108, *109*
Rice, Sushi (P), 158
Rice Vinegar, about, 343
Ricotta Cake (D), 301
Ricotta Flan with Raspberry Sauce (D), *300*, 301
Rigatoni with Bell Pepper-Tomato Sauce (P), 143
Rigatoni with Olives, Herbs, and Arugula (P), 144
Risotto (D), *133*, *140*, 141
Roast Capon with Olives (M), 214, *215*
Roast Turkey (M), 219
Roasted Bell Peppers (P), 45
Roasted Brussels Sprouts (P), 115
Roasted Butternut Squash (P), 124
Roasted Cauliflower (P), 120
Roasted Pepper and Zucchini Soup (M), 63
Roasted Tomato Soup (P), 71
Roasted Turkey Breast (M), 218
Roasted Vegetables for Ziti (P), 153
Rosemary Marinade for Chicken (P), 210
Rosh Hashana, Recipes for, *see* Holiday Recipes
Rugelach (D), 307

S

Sabbath, Recipes for, *see* Holiday Recipes
Sake Marinade for Steamed Chicken, 208
Sake-Steamed Chicken (M), 208, *209*
Salad Dressings, 91, 94, 99, 108, 111, 112, 182
Salad Greens, handling and storing, 337, 340, 343
Salad Spin-Dryer, 347
Salads
    Anna's Coleslaw (P), 98
    Asian Cabbage Salad (P), *100*, 101
    Barley Salad (P), 106
    Black Bean and Quinoa Salad (P), 105
    Black Bean Salad (P), 104
    Cannellini Bean Salad (D), 89
    Carrot Salad (P), 102

Chicken, Black Bean, and Corn Salad (M), 96

Chicken Salad with Radicchio and Pine Nuts (M), 94, *95*

Chicken Salad with Thyme (M), 93

Chickpea and Bulgur Salad (P), 97

Chickpea and Feta Salad (D), *90*, 91

Lentil Salad (P), 107

Mediterranean Couscous and Lentil Salad (D), 92

Napa Cabbage Salad (P), 99

Raw Beet Salad (P), 103

Rice Salad (P), *87*, 108, *109*

Savoy Cabbage Salad (P), 98

Salmon Burgers with Spinach (P), 182

Salmon, Marinated in Dill (P), 185

Salmon, Marinated, with Mango-Kiwi Relish (P), 186

Salmon Tartare (P), 34

Salmon Teriyaki (P), 184

Salmon with Mustard Sauce and Chive Oil (P), 180, *181*

Salmon with Orange (P), 183

Salt, Kosher, using, 342

Salt, rescuing over-salted soups and stews, 337

Saucepans, buying, 348

Sauces

Apricot Sauce for Turkey Scaloppini (P), 216

Bell Pepper and Tomato Sauce for Rigatoni (P), 143

Broccoli Pesto Sauce for Orecchiette (P), *150*, 151

Caper Sauce for Halibut (P), 176

Caper Sauce for Turkey Scaloppini (P), 217

Coconut-Milk Sauce for Red Snapper (P), 179

Ginger Sauce for Broiled Duck Breasts (P), 221

Ginger Sauce for Seared Tuna (P), 170

Ginger-Sesame Sauce for Chicken Rolls with Mushrooms (P), 196

Lemon Syrup for Citrus Pound Cake (P), 294

Lime Cilantro Sauce for Ceviche (P), 33

Meat Sauce for Spaghetti (M), 142

Midseason Tomato Sauce (P), 159

Mushroom and Radicchio Sauce for Orecchiette (P), 152

Mushroom Sauce for Penne (P), 146

Mustard Sauce for Salmon (P), 180, *181*

Mustard-Dill Sauce for Gravlax (P), 21

Olive Sauce for Linguini (P), 155

Orange Sauce for Chicken Rolls (P), 198

Piquant Asian Sauce for Seared Tuna (P), 170

Pesto and Zucchini Sauce for Linguini (D), 135

Raspberry Sauce (P), 301, 311

Sweet-and-Sour Sauce for Barley-Stuffed Cabbage Rolls (P), 272

Sweet-and-Sour Sauce for Meat-Stuffed Cabbage Rolls (M), 243

Summer Tomato Sauce (P), 160

Tomato Sauce for Eggplant Parmigiana (P), 258

Tomato Sauce for Mushroom Lasagna (P), 138

Uncooked Tomato Sauce for Penne (P), 147

Winter Tomato Sauce (P), 159

Zucchini and Pesto Sauce for Linguini (D), 135

Sauté, how to, 352

Sautéed Baby Artichokes (P), 43

Savoy Cabbage Salad (P), 98

Scissors, 348; poultry shears, 347

Seared Tuna with Two Sauces (P), 168, *169*

Seasoned Rice Vinegar, about, 341

Seeding Tomatoes, 352; Jalapeño Peppers, 338

Sesame Oil, using, 343

Sesame Seeds, about, 343

Sesame-Ginger Dressing for Salad (P), 111

Sesame-Thyme Marinade for Chicken Shish Kebabs (P), 202

Shallots, about, 343

Shavout, Recipes for, *see* Holiday Recipes

Shears, poultry, 347; scissors, 348

Shiitake Mushrooms, *see* Mushrooms, Shiitake

Short Ribs of Beef (M), *223*, 236, *237*

Shortbread Biscuits (D), *283*, 289

Shredded Sweet Potatoes with Cumin and Scallions (P), 123

Sieves and Strainers, using, 348

Sift, how to, 352

Simple Ratatouille (P), 122

Skillets, 348

Skinning Peppers, how to, 352

Smoked Whitefish Pâté (P), 24

Smoky Eggplant (P), 28

Sole and Parmesan Soufflé (D), 260

Souffles

Acorn Squash Soufflé (D), 249

Apricot Soufflé (P), *328*, 329

Chocolate Soufflé, (P), *277*, 318, *319*

Sole and Parmesan Soufflé (D), 260

Soups
  Asparagus Soup (M), *53*, *64*, 65
  Barley Soup with Miso (P), 80, *81*
  Beet Soup (P), *76*, 77
  Cabbage and Mushroom Soup (M), 66
  Cannellini Bean and Porcini Soup (M), 62
  Carrot and Tomato Soup (M), 67
  Carrot-Ginger Soup (P), 68
  Celery Root and Porcini Soup (P), 78
  Celery Root Soup (D), 58
  Chestnut and Mushroom Soup (P), 82
  Chicken Soup with Matzoh Balls (M), 60
  Corn Soup, Summer (P), 69
  Fish Soup with Vegetables (P), 84
  Green Bean and Almond Soup (P), 83
  Green Pea and Zucchini Soup (D), 56
  Matzoh Ball and Chicken Soup (M), 60
  Mushroom Soup (D), 55
  Mushroom Soup with Soy Milk (P), 79
  Puréed Vegetable Soup (D), 59
  Red Lentil Soup (P), 70
  Roasted Tomato Soup (P), 71
  Summer Corn Soup (P), 69
  Summer Tomato Soup (P), 72
  Sun-Dried Tomato Soup (P), 73
  Sweet Potato Soup (D), 57
  Tomato and Bell Pepper Soup (P), 74, 75
  Zucchini and Roasted Pepper Soup (M), 63
Southwestern Ratatouille (P), 262
Soy Beans, *see* Edamame
Soy Sauce, about, 343
Spaghetti with Meat Sauce (M), 142
Spaghetti with Tuna (P), 154
Spatulas, 348
Spiced Carrots (P), 115
Spicy Marinade for Split Fillet (P), 231
Spinach for Salmon Burgers (P), 182
Spinach Pie (D), 250, *251*
Spin-Dryer for Salad, 347
Split Fillet (London Broil) with Port Wine Glaze (M), *232*, 233
Spoons, Wooden, 350
Squash, Acorn, Soufflé (D), 249
Squash, Acorn, Sweet-and-Sour (P), *113*, 124, *125*
Squash, Butternut, Roasted (P), 124
Squash, Butternut, with Halibut (D), *161*, *164*, 165
Star Anise, about, 343
Steam, how to, 352

Steamers, 348
Stir-Fried Chicken with Snow Peas (M), *212*, 213
Stir-Fried Spinach (P), 120
Stir-Fry, how to, 352
Stock, Chicken, *see* Broth, Chicken
Stock, Fish, for Fish Soup with Vegetables (P), 84
Stock, Fish, for Gefilte Fish with Challah (P), 187
Strain, how to, 352
Strainers and Sieves, 348
Strawberries, handling, 337
Stuffed Cabbage Rolls, Barley (P), 272
Stuffed Cabbage Rolls, Meat (M), 242
Stuffed Portobello Mushrooms (D), *252*, 253
Sukkoth, Recipes for, *see* Holiday Recipes
Summer Corn Soup (P), 69
Summer Tomato Sauce (P), 160
Summer Tomato Soup (P), 72
Sun-Dried Tomato Soup (P), 73
Sun-Dried Tomatoes, about, 343
Sushi Rice (P), 158
Sweet Potato Fries (P), 126
Sweet Potato Soup (D), 57
Sweet Potatoes with Cumin and Scallions (P), 123
Sweet-and-Sour Acorn Squash (P), *113*, 124, *125*
Sweet-and-Sour Dressing for Chicken Salad (P), 94
Sweet-and-Sour Sauce for Cabbage Rolls Stuffed with Barley (P), 272
Sweet-and-Sour Sauce for Cabbage Rolls Stuffed with Meat (M), 243

T
Tahini, 28, 29, 48
Tahini Dressing for Eggplant (P), 48
Tarragon, using, 342
Tart, Thin Potato (P), *128*, 129
Tarts, Mushroom (P), 46
Techniques, Notes on, 351-352
  Blanching Almonds, Hazelnuts, Tomatoes, 351
  Braise, 351
  Broil, 351
  Dice, 352
  Julienne, 352
  Mince, 352
  Purée, 352
  Sauté, 352
  Seeding Tomatoes, 352
  Sift, 352

Skinning Peppers, 352
Steaming, 352
Stir-Fry, 352
Strain, 352
Teriyaki Marinade for Salmon (P), 184
Thermometers, Meat, 347
Thermometers, Oven, 337, 347
Thin Potato Tart (P), *128*, 129
Thyme, about, 342
Timer, Kitchen, setting, 337
Tips, Helpful, *see* Helpful Tips, 337
Tofu with Mushrooms (P), 263
Tomato and Bell Pepper Sauce for Rigatoni (P), 143
Tomato and Bell Pepper Soup with Basil Garnish (P), 74, *75*
Tomato and Carrot Soup (M), 67
Tomato Sauce for Eggplant Parmigiana (P), 258
Tomato Sauce for Mushroom Lasagna (P), 138
Tomato Sauce, Midseason (P), 159
Tomato Sauce, Summer (P), 160
Tomato Sauce, Uncooked, for Penne (P), 147
Tomato Sauce, Winter (P), 159
Tomato Soup, Roasted (P), 71
Tomato Soup, Summer (P), 72
Tomato Soup, Sun-Dried (P), 73
Tomatoes, blanching, 351; canned, 343; ripening, 337; seeding, 352; skinning, 351; sun-dried, 343
Tongs, 350
Truffle Oil, using, 343
Tuna Burgers (P), 171
Tuna, Seared, with Two Dressings (P), 168, *169*
Tuna Tartare (P), 35
Tuna Tartare with Avocado (P), 36
Turkey
    Roast Turkey (M), 219
    Roasted Turkey Breast (M), 218
    Turkey Burgers (M), 220
    Turkey Scaloppini with Two Sauces (M), 216
Tuscan Cake (D), 296, *297*

V

Veal Dishes
    Baked Eggplant with Ground Meat, Tomatoes, and Pine Nuts (M), *240*, 241
    Boneless Rack of Veal (M), 229
    Curried Veal Roast (M), 227
    Meatloaf (M), 246
    Osso Buco (Braised Veal Shanks) (M), 225
    Stuffed Cabbage Rolls (M), 243
    Veal Stew (M), 228
Vegetable Broth, uses, 339
Vegetable Medley, Asian Style (P), 121
Vegetable Oil, using, 343
Vegetable Soup, Puréed (D), 59
Vegetables, Roasted, for Ziti (P), 153
Vegetarian Burgers (P), 270, *271*
Vinegar, varieties, 343

W

Walnut Roll (D), *286*, 287
Walnuts, storing, 338, 342; grating, 342; blanching, 351
Warm Chocolate Surprises (D), *280*, 281
Warm Chocolate-Coconut Surprises (P), 317
Wasabi, about, 344
Whisks, 350
White Bean and Potato Purée (P), 131
White Bean Chili (P), 275
Whitefish Pâté, Smoked (P), 24
Winter Tomato Sauce (P), 159
Wire Racks, 350
Wok, using, 350
Wonton Shells with Mushrooms (P), 25
Wonton Wrappers, using, 344
Wontons, Curried (M), 16
Wooden Spoons, 350

Z

Ziti with Herbs and Mozzarella (D), 136, *137*
Ziti with Roasted Vegetables (P), 153
Zucchini and Green Pea Soup (D), 56
Zucchini and Roasted Pepper Soup (M), 63
Zucchini Cake (P), 335
Zucchini Frittata (D), 255